"This clear and courageous book starts from a simple but often ignored question: what changes when mental suffering is no longer broken down into symptoms, diagnoses, and protocols, but taken seriously as a human, relational, and contextual experience? Tomi Bergström shows why reductionist psychiatry has reached its limits and weaves philosophy, clinical practice, and systems thinking into a coherent alternative that is neither vague nor idealistic, but precise and workable. Written for professionals and policymakers who sense that the current system no longer fits, the book offers language, direction, and practical grounding for a mental health care system that takes complexity seriously without losing sight of the person."

Jim van Os, PhD, *Professor of Psychiatry and Neuroscience Division Leader at Utrecht University Medical Center, the Netherlands*

"This book presents an exceptionally clear, accurate, and well-argued diagnosis of the conceptual issues at the heart of modern-day mental health work. Bergström does not dismiss the currently dominant reductionist approach but makes a compelling case for its limitations when confronted with the messy complexity of this work. Progress in mental health care will depend on our ability to move towards the sort of holistic framework that he describes. This book should be essential reading for mental health professionals everywhere!"

Pat Bracken, PhD, *Independent Consultant Psychiatrist*

"Having a background in the Open Dialogue approach, Tomi Bergström provides an extraordinary analysis of the problems of reductionistic thinking in the development of mental health practices. This topic has not been analyzed sufficiently to understand why, within the mainstream tradition of psychiatry, inadequate conclusions are often drawn both about the nature of mental health problems and about the interventions needed. The problem lies in focusing too much on psychopathological aspects of mental suffering, without recognizing mental health crises as responses of individuals under severe stress. From this perspective, Bergström introduces a holistic view in which human resources are recognized as central to surviving stressful situations in life. Recommended reading for professionals, service users, family members, and all who are interested in finding alternatives to over-medicalization."

Jaakko Seikkula, PhD, *Professor of Psychotherapy (emeritus) at the University of Jyväskylä, Finland*

Holistic Psychiatry

Holistic Psychiatry offers a timely rethinking of psychiatry by showing why today's symptom-based, reductionist models are no longer enough—and what can replace them.

Drawing together philosophy, research, clinical practice, and service system design, this book presents a coherent, holistic framework that understands phenomena labeled as mental disorders not as internal defects, but as evolving, context-dependent situations shaped by biology, experience, relationships, and society. It provides a rigorous theoretical foundation, a realistic model of dialogical care, and concrete guidance for reorganizing services, research, and professional roles, including how to implement the World Health Organization's guidance on community mental health services. Grounded in human rights, empirical evidence, and real-world practice, this book shows how mental health care can become more humane, effective, and sustainable without abandoning scientific responsibility.

This book is essential reading for clinicians, researchers, policymakers, students of psychiatry, psychology, and mental health, and anyone concerned with the future of mental health care.

Tomi Bergström, PhD, is a psychologist and Adjunct Professor of Clinical Psychology with extensive clinical experience in Open Dialogue at Keropudas Psychiatric Hospital and a research focus on holistic approaches at the University of Jyväskylä, Finland.

Holistic Psychiatry

From Theory to Practice in Mental Health Care

Tomi Bergström

Routledge
Taylor & Francis Group
NEW YORK AND LONDON

Designed cover image: Getty Images

First published 2027
by Routledge
605 Third Avenue, New York, NY 10158

and by Routledge
4 Park Square, Milton Park, Abingdon, Oxon, OX14 4RN

Routledge is an imprint of the Taylor & Francis Group, an informa business

ISBN: 9781041311867 (hbk)
ISBN: 9781041300977 (pbk)
ISBN: 9781003777939 (ebk)

DOI: 10.4324/9781003777939

Typeset in Sabon
by codeMantra

Access the Support Material: www.routledge.com/9781041300977

Contents

Author Bio

Tomi Bergström, PhD, is Adjunct Professor in Clinical Psychology and a psychologist working in psychiatric services in the City of Helsinki, Finland. He is also a researcher in the Department of Psychology at the University of Jyväskylä, where his work focuses on holistic and dialogical approaches to mental health care, integrating clinical practice and research.

Previously, Bergström worked for many years as a clinical and head psychologist at Keropudas Psychiatric Hospital, where the holistic Open Dialogue approach to mental health care was developed. During this time, he played a central role in both the clinical development and research of Open Dialogue and is internationally recognized for his long-term outcome studies conducted in real-world mental healthcare settings.

In addition to his clinical and academic work, Bergström has contributed as a member of an expert writing and review group to recent World Health Organization guidance on community mental health services. This guidance highlights Open Dialogue, alongside other holistic and rights-based approaches, as a key direction for the future development of mental health systems worldwide.

Introduction

The term *holistic psychiatry* can evoke a wide range of associations. Some link it to alternative or complementary treatments; others regard it as a positive aspiration to understand and treat mental disorders in a more comprehensive manner. Many clinicians feel that they already think and work holistically, for instance, by acknowledging the biopsychosocial nature of mental disorders and recognizing that no single form of treatment suits everyone. For some, the concept means very little, or it is interpreted as an "anything goes" approach without practical value.

As a mode of thinking, however, holism has a clear and well-defined meaning. It refers to the view that a whole cannot be fully understood by examining its constituent parts alone; one must also consider how the parts interact. Wholes are thus seen as involving so-called *emergent phenomena*—features that cannot be identified in the parts taken in isolation, even though those parts are necessary for the whole to exist. Hydrogen and oxygen atoms, for example, are not wet in themselves, but together they form water, which is experienced as wet. A single neuron is not conscious, yet the interaction of neural networks can give rise to conscious experience. Likewise, culture arises through interactions among individuals, but it is no longer dependent on any single member of the group.

The opposite of holism is reductionism, which seeks to understand wholes by breaking them down into simpler and more manageable elements. A computer malfunction, for example, can often be diagnosed by examining its individual components separately and repairing the faulty part. In medicine, a reductionist approach may involve tracing symptoms to a specific pathogen and treating it directly, as in the use of antibiotics for a bacterial infection. By isolating a phenomenon to a single component, researchers can measure and model it with greater precision.

Reductionism is currently the dominant approach in both science and culture. It has enabled major technological advances and is intuitively easy to grasp: humans have a natural tendency to divide reality into parts, for example, by categorizing. Yet this approach is not always the

DOI: 10.4324/9781003777939-1

most effective. Many complex problems arise from intricate interactions among biological, psychological, and social factors, and the meanings assigned to them are interpretive and context-dependent. Such phenomena cannot be adequately understood or treated by focusing on their components alone.

Psychiatry is a field in which such complexity is particularly pronounced, as both treatment and research engage with subjective and interpretive experiences for which no unambiguous etiology has been established; if such etiologies were known, these conditions would fall under other branches of medicine or the human sciences. Nevertheless, psychiatric practice remains largely reductionist, and the discipline's commitment to theoretical neutrality—most clearly reflected in diagnostic systems of mental disorders—has led to situations in which even ostensibly holistic approaches are implemented and interpreted through a reductionist lens.

In 2021, the World Health Organization (WHO) issued guidance calling for the development of more holistic approaches to mental health care. These international calls highlight the need not only for new practices but also for a clearer conceptual reorientation of existing mental health systems. Without such reorientation, calls for holism risk remaining rhetorical, while underlying reductionist assumptions continue to shape diagnosis, service structures, and everyday clinical work. This is seen in many countries, as these calls have thus far received relatively little attention, partly because many believe that existing systems already operate in a sufficiently comprehensive manner. A key challenge is that the concept of holism is often only partially understood.

This book aims to provide a foundation for holistic psychiatry and broader, more comprehensive approaches to supporting people facing complex life challenges currently framed as mental disorders or problems. It is divided into three sections: theory, practice, and research. The first section describes both the benefits and the limitations of the dominant reductionist framework. It also examines how phenomena defined as mental disorders can be understood from the perspective of a holistic ontology—that is, a holistic conception of reality—and how this framework can account for many phenomena that remain inadequately explained within a reductionist framework.

For some readers, the philosophical questions addressed in this book will be familiar, while for others, they may initially feel unfamiliar. Nonetheless, the core ideas of holistic thinking are often intuitive and resonate with everyday experience. The complexity of the framework does not arise from abstract theory but from the need to consider three interconnected levels simultaneously:

1 Ontological level: how psychological and social phenomena are constituted.
2 Epistemological level: how such phenomena can be studied, explained, and understood.
3 Practical level: how these foundations inform treatment practices and the organization of services.

Distinguishing these levels is a practical consideration. When the reductionist limitations of psychiatry are taken into account, it is useful to consider alternative ontological frameworks. A holistic ontology can, in practice, support a pluralistic epistemology by encouraging the use of multiple, complementary methods for understanding and explaining psychiatric phenomena. Likewise, if psychiatric problems are not well captured by simple mechanical chains of cause and effect, it is sensible to question whether treatments based solely on such models are sufficient. From a practical standpoint, it follows that the organization of the service system may benefit from being aligned with the multilevel nature of the phenomena it is designed to address.

Although the theoretical section strives for philosophical precision, the practical sections are intended to be accessible and useful even to readers who do not fully master the underlying theory. These chapters describe what a holistic mental healthcare system might look like in practice and outline concrete guidelines for its implementation. Particular attention is given to interaction strategies that can enhance the quality of encounters and strengthen the collaborative relationship among the various parties involved.

The framework is illustrated with case examples based on the author's long clinical experience and work as a chief psychologist at Keropudas Psychiatric Hospital, where the Open Dialogue treatment approach—referenced by WHO as an exemplar of holistic mental healthcare system—was developed. These cases have been modified and combined so that they do not refer to real individuals.

Later chapters explore questions and challenges related to adopting and researching holistic approaches, many of which stem from tensions between reductionist and holistic modes of understanding. Implementing a holistic system is not without risks, but advancing and studying such approaches is essential if mental health services are to respond more effectively to the nature of complex problems than current frameworks allow.

In this book, holism is examined within the framework of psychiatry as a response to the reductionist models that currently dominate the field. Due to diagnostic inflation, a wide range of human experiences, life situations, and social difficulties are increasingly operationalized as psychiatric concerns and addressed within psychiatry and the broader mental health service system. Because psychiatry holds a powerful position in defining what counts as a mental health–related issue, this has resulted in situations where a single field exercises disproportionate influence over both the conceptualization of human suffering and the ways it is responded to.

While this book aims to contribute to the development of holistic psychiatry, holism alone does not resolve the institutional power relations shaping mental health services, and there is a risk that holistic psychiatry may be understood as an expansion of psychiatry rather than a challenge to disciplinary hierarchies. Holistic psychiatry is therefore treated here as a transitional concept—one that dismantles psychiatry's reductionist ontology while opening space for more pluralistic, phenomenon-oriented, and multidisciplinary forms of support. Such an ontological shift enables broader participation by diverse professional, experiential, and community-based actors and supports approaches that extend beyond specialized services into everyday contexts and communities, with helping practices grounded not in any single discipline but in people's lived experiences, life situations, and dialogical processes.

Although systemic change may be challenging, individual professionals and citizens can already begin to adopt more holistic ways of responding to the human challenges that become labeled as mental health disorders or problems. Holism also has relevance for other areas of medicine, particularly where etiology is unclear and the need for services is high. What is required above all is curiosity, openness, and a willingness to approach complex phenomena as they are.

The final chapters draw together existing research suggesting that a holistic, dialogical, and contextually sensitive approach to care may offer advantages over reductionist models. Although these studies are constrained by methodological limitations, they point toward promising directions for future inquiry. My hope is that this book will spark curiosity and motivation to further explore, refine, and develop more holistic approaches to helping and care.

This book is intended primarily for mental health and psychiatric professionals as well as policymakers. It offers a perspective on holistic and dialogical mental health care grounded in both research and practical experience and aims to support clinical work as well as the structural development of service systems. It is also suitable for service users, their families, and anyone interested in guiding mental health care toward a more comprehensive and human-centered model.

Part I

Theory

The first part establishes the conceptual and philosophical foundations of the holistic framework developed throughout this book. Its primary aim is to clarify what is meant by holism in psychiatry and to distinguish this framework from prevailing reductionist approaches. Rather than proposing a new treatment method or theoretical school, the part develops an ontological and epistemological reorientation: it asks what psychiatric phenomena fundamentally are, how they emerge, and how they can be meaningfully understood.

The part in this section moves from philosophical considerations to clinically relevant concepts. They examine the limitations of reductionist explanations, introduce the idea of unfavorable situations as the basic unit of analysis, and elaborate the notion of dialogical space as a core event of care through which change becomes possible. Together, these chapters provide the conceptual scaffolding required for the later sections. Without this theoretical groundwork, the practical and research-oriented arguments of this book would risk appearing as isolated innovations rather than as consequences of a holistic framework.

DOI: 10.4324/9781003777939-2

Chapter 1

The Nature of Mind and Mental Disorder

1.1 What Is the Mind?

What do we mean when we talk about the mind? Although we use the word constantly, there is no single correct or universally accepted definition. In scientific contexts as well, its meaning depends on the disciplinary framework. Typically, it refers to a person's internal experiences such as emotions, thoughts, and consciousness. What is called "the mind" is also often seen as qualitatively different from things that can be observed directly with the senses or physically touched.

If a human head is opened, we can confirm through sight and touch that the brain exists. With brain imaging and other research methods, we can also observe its activity. The brain, a brain scan, or an EEG trace looks essentially the same regardless of who is examining it.

The experiences evoked by a brain image, however, are far more difficult to observe and therefore harder to verify. A neuroscientist interprets the image through prior knowledge and may experience curiosity or interest, whereas a layperson might feel confusion or frustration if they do not understand what they are looking at. The researcher may begin analyzing the image and considering what can be inferred from it, while the layperson simply notes that it depicts a brain and moves on.

Although the observed object is the same, it gives rise to different thoughts and feelings in different individuals. These subjective experiences cannot be observed in the same way as the brain or the measurements depicting its activity. Yet they undeniably exist and can be communicated to others through language or behavior. Still, we cannot directly perceive what another person truly experiences or what that experience feels like from "the inside."

For instance, a person who feels confused by a brain image may say they do not understand what they are supposed to conclude from it and that thinking about it feels anxiety-provoking. "Anxiety" is a word that the person has learned to associate with a certain kind of unpleasant internal sensation. We cannot know whether their anxiety feels the same as

DOI: 10.4324/9781003777939-3

someone else's, as the interpretation of such an experience depends on one's developmental history and cultural background.

Although we can observe in various ways that the person's state has changed, we cannot directly feel it ourselves. For this reason, the mind cannot be verified in the same way as, say, the brain, a brain scan, a dog, a cat, or a car. Yet our inner experiential world is something we know with certainty to exist. In fact, it is the only thing we can verify beyond doubt, because all of our perceptions and interpretations of reality are mediated through the mind. However, we have direct access only to our own experiences; those of others we can only imagine.

Nor can we be completely certain that our perceptions of the world correspond to some "real" external reality that exists independently of the mind. The seventeenth-century philosopher René Descartes (1641/2008) arrived at his famous conclusion *cogito, ergo sum*—"I think, therefore I am"—through such reflection. For Descartes, the most certain fact is the existence of the thinking subject itself: without consciousness and thought, the very act of philosophical doubt would be impossible.

Even though the mind may be the only thing we can verify with certainty, it does not always feel as real as the external world. It appears more ambiguous than a dining table, a bicycle, a family member, a workplace, or a pet. The mind seems immaterial—something that cannot be touched and perhaps cannot be fully trusted.

How can a physical body give rise to something that feels immaterial—what we call "the mind"—and how are the two related? René Descartes' work played a central role in shaping dualism, the view that mind and body are qualitatively distinct (Robinson, 2020). The resulting mind–body problem has remained a central concern in philosophy and psychology and is particularly salient for medical disciplines—such as psychiatry—that aim to understand and influence mental phenomena.

1.2 What Is a Mental Disorder?

The nature of the mind and its relation to the material world remains an unresolved mystery. We do know, however, that the concept of mind typically refers to a person's internal experiences. But how can such phenomena be considered either healthy or disordered? In other words: *what do we mean when we say that someone suffers from a mental disorder?*

The World Health Organization (WHO, 2004) defines mental health as a state of well-being in which the individual realizes his or her own abilities, can cope with the normal stresses of life, can work productively and fruitfully, and is able to make a contribution to his or her community. Yet who can reliably claim to know their own abilities and limits? And what does "normal" mean, when its interpretation depends on the situation, culture, historical period, method of measurement, and many other factors?

The perceived problematic nature of a psychological or social phenomenon is always determined by its context—that is, by the culture and historical moment in which a person lives. For this reason, the concept of *mental disorder* does not refer solely to an individual's inner experiences, behavior, or traits; it cannot be fully reduced to an internal dysfunction or disease of the person.

In practice, the term mental disorder refers to emotions, thoughts, and behaviors that, in a particular context, are experienced as problematic from someone's perspective. Characteristics and behaviors that deviate from prevailing social norms and ideals have been managed, controlled, or treated in different ways throughout history, depending on what has been considered problematic in the first place.

For a long time, certain psychological and social difficulties were viewed primarily as spiritual, moral, or legal issues. During the eighteenth and nineteenth centuries, however, the rise of a scientific worldview gradually shifted responsibility from the Church and other institutions to the emerging field of medicine and its developing specialty, represented by the so-called *alienists* (Pietikäinen, 2019). The word *alienist* derives from the Latin *alienare* ("to estrange") and referred to physicians whose task was to treat individuals thought to be alienated from themselves, from their community, or from reality.

By the late nineteenth century, medicine was becoming increasingly specialized, and alienism acquired a new name. The term *psychiatry* was adopted to describe the medical branch concerned with the study and treatment of the mind and its disorders (*psyche* = mind, *iatreia* = healing/treatment) (Porter, 2002). By the early twentieth century, psychiatry had replaced alienism as the professional designation and had become an established medical specialty in most countries.

During the twentieth century, psychiatry's internal diversity and the multitude of competing theories fit poorly with the prevailing positivist orientation of modern science and medicine. Positivism is a philosophy of science that maintains that genuine knowledge is derived from observable and empirically verifiable phenomena (e.g., Park et al., 2020). Because positivism holds that knowledge is valid only when it can be observed and measured in specific ways, explanatory models based on subjective experiences or personal interpretations are often deemed non-scientific (Raatikainen, 2004).

Positivism is closely linked to reductionism—the idea that complex phenomena can be understood by breaking them down into simpler components, which can then be measured, classified, and studied more easily (Rosenberg, 2005). A key aim is to identify cause-and-effect relationships. When the influence of one component on another is known, the entire phenomenon can be explained through its constituent parts and their causal interactions. Reductionism thus provides a means of *operationalizing* complex phenomena—converting them into measurable variables that can be studied within a positivist framework.

In psychiatry, too, there were attempts to reduce mental difficulties to clearly defined psychological, social, or biological mechanisms through various theories. However, these theories could not be empirically confirmed. For example, psychoanalytic theory relied largely on interpretations of non-observable internal experiences, which cannot be directly perceived or measured and therefore cannot be tested in accordance with positivist assumptions.

For similar reasons, psychiatric diagnoses and theoretical models could not reliably determine the causes of a person's difficulties or identify the best possible treatment. In practice, different clinicians might assign different diagnoses to the same patient, depending on their individual interpretive frameworks. In other words, the reliability of psychiatric theories and definitions was weak.

During the 1980s, psychiatry attempted to resolve the problem of interpretive variability and low reliability by shifting toward diagnostic approaches based primarily on observable symptoms, thereby avoiding assumptions about causes or theoretical explanations (Frances, 1981). By focusing on observable signs rather than on theoretical interpretations, it appeared more likely that two clinicians would arrive at the same diagnosis. Although this approach was presented as theory-neutral, it still rested on a positivist and reductionist assumption: that by reducing complex psychological and social phenomena to more objectively observable symptoms, we eventually could better understand the causal mechanisms of mental disorders and more accurately target treatments (e.g., Patil & Giordano, 2010).

References

Descartes, R. (2008). *Meditations on first philosophy: With selections from the objections and replies* (M. Moriarty, Trans.; Oxford World's Classics ed.). Oxford University Press.

Frances, A. (1981). Descriptive and dynamic psychiatry: A perspective on DSM-III. *American Journal of Psychiatry, 138*(9), 1198–1202. https://doi.org/10.1176/ajp.138.9.1198

Park, Y. S., Konge, L., & Artino, A. R., Jr (2020). The positivism paradigm of research. *Academic Medicine : Journal of the Association of American Medical Colleges, 95*(5), 690–694. https://doi.org/10.1097/ACM.0000000000003093

Patil, T., & Giordano, J. (2010). On the ontological assumptions of the medical model of psychiatry: Philosophical considerations and pragmatic tasks. *Philosophy, Ethics, and Humanities in Medicine, 5*(1), 3. https://doi.org/10.1186/1747-5341-5-3

Pietikäinen, P. (2019). *Hulluuden historia*. Gaudeamus.
Porter, R. (2002). *Madness: A brief history*. Oxford University Press.
Raatikainen, P. (2004). *Ihmistieteet ja filosofia*. Gaudeamus.
Robinson, H. (2020). "Dualism." In E. N. Zalta (Ed.), *The Stanford encyclopedia of philosophy* (Fall 2020 Edition). Stanford University. https://plato.stanford.edu/entries/dualism/
Rosenberg, A. (2005). *Philosophy of science: A contemporary introduction* (2nd ed.). Routledge.
World Health Organization. (2004). *Promoting mental health: Concepts, emerging evidence, practice (summary report)*. World Health Organization.

Chapter 2

Reductionist Psychiatry

2.1 The Reductionist Understanding of Mental Disorders

Reductionism is generally understood as the doctrine that a given theory or phenomenon can be reduced to another, more fundamental one (Rosenberg, 2005). Within this view, scientific disciplines are seen as hierarchically ordered: the objects of study in specialized sciences such as psychology and sociology are to be reduced to more basic sciences, such as biology and ultimately physics (Raatikainen, 2004).

As noted above, reductionism is rooted in a positivist conception of science and causality, which holds that genuine knowledge is based on observable and measurable phenomena and on their repeatable correspondences: if A is observed, B is also observed. The aim of research therefore becomes the identification of such linear cause–effect relationships, approached through empirical methods that rely on direct observation.

Because positivism counts as scientific knowledge only those phenomena that can be systematically and reliably tested through specific experimental designs, it easily leads to methodological monism—the assumption that the same scientific method can be applied regardless of the nature of the object under investigation (Gonzalez, 2020). In psychology, this was seen most clearly in the behaviorist movement, which focused exclusively on externally observable behavior.

Reductionism has been particularly influential in the natural sciences and in technology. For example, an electrical device can be taken apart and its functioning understood by examining its individual components. Oxygen can be traced back to photosynthesis, which, in turn, can be traced to biochemical reactions in plant cells. The experience of excruciating pain can be traced to irritation of nerve endings in the periosteum, which can be traced to a bone fracture, which, in turn, can be traced to the impact of falling off a bicycle. According to the reductionist logic, influencing specific points along such chains of causation allows us to achieve desired

DOI: 10.4324/9781003777939-4

outcomes—for instance, building an electrical device step by step for a specific purpose, or treating a bone fracture by aligning and supporting it, and preventing further injury by riding more carefully.

In the study and treatment of mental disorders, reductionism can be seen, for example, in the widely used biopsychosocial model, in which complex psychosocial problems are reduced to three main components: biological, psychological, and social. This makes phenomena that are inherently complex and interpretive easier to conceptualize and manage.

For instance, low mood leading to impaired functioning may be diagnosed as a depressive disorder and traced back to psychological and social factors that cause or maintain depression. These may include relational patterns of interpreting social situations in ways that reinforce negative self-conceptions and sustain depressive symptoms (e.g., Beck, 1967). Such psychological processes can then be further reduced to biological mechanisms, such as changes in neurotransmitter systems to which an individual may have a genetic predisposition, activated by stressful life events (e.g., Caspi et al., 2003).

The same logic can be applied to other psychiatric diagnoses. If a person has thoughts interpreted as hallucinations or delusions that cannot be explained by intoxication or a neurological condition, these can be diagnosed as symptoms of psychotic illness. Psychosis can then be understood within the vulnerability–stress model: a person may have a genetic predisposition linked to structural changes in the brain that increase the risk of psychotic symptoms, but the symptoms emerge only under significant life stress (e.g., Walker & Diforio, 1997).

Similarly, the risk of anxiety disorders is often considered higher in individuals with a hereditary tendency toward a strong "fight or flight" reaction. If a person repeatedly experiences anxiety in certain situations, they may learn to anticipate and experience it again in similar contexts. This can lead to avoidance or compulsive behaviors intended to manage anxiety, but which ultimately maintain it over time (e.g., Barlow, 2002).

Attention-deficit/hyperactivity disorder (ADHD) is often reduced to developmental delay in the prefrontal cortex, as these brain regions regulate executive functioning (e.g., Shaw et al., 2007). Post-traumatic stress disorder is reduced to exposure to a traumatic event, which gives rise to intrusive recollections and avoidance of associated stimuli (e.g., Yehuda & LeDoux, 2007). Personality disorders are frequently linked to early relational experiences and their influence on psychological development. For example, insecure, inconsistent, or traumatic early attachments may impair emotion regulation and the ability to maintain stable relationships (e.g., Fonagy et al., 2002).

In practice, the reductionist approach breaks down complex psychosocial problems into more manageable components using prevailing theoretical models and hypotheses derived from them and attempts to direct treatment and prevention efforts at these components. Psychotherapy and its exercises may target perceptual, interpretive, and behavioral patterns that sustain depressive or anxious states. Psychoeducation may teach individuals to identify early warning signs of psychosis or mania, enabling them to prevent exacerbations and avoid triggers. Psychotropic medications target neurotransmitter systems associated with symptoms. Preventive work may include public education about risk factors and screening programs to identify high-risk groups before symptoms escalate.

A central aim of reductionism in psychiatry, as in many other branches of medicine, is to intervene as early as possible in the causal chain in order to prevent or reduce unwanted downstream effects. For example, if individuals with a genetic predisposition to psychotic disorders could be reliably identified, it might be possible to develop medications to prevent "illness onset." This logic is reflected in the areas to which psychiatric research has devoted the most resources (e.g., Cuthbert & Insel, 2013; Lewis-Fernández et al., 2016): developing more precise diagnostic systems to identify mechanisms that could eventually reduce diagnoses to basic biological components, such as brain function and genetics, and developing more refined treatments and assessment methods that allow interventions to be targeted as accurately as possible to these component causes.

Thus far, however, the precise identification of causal chains in mental disorders has not succeeded. We lack laboratory tests or imaging methods that can independently verify the presence of a mental disorder, as well as tests that would enable treatments to be targeted to early-stage causes in ways that reliably prevent the emergence of later difficulties.

In practice, the treatment of mental disorders is largely symptom-relieving rather than cause-correcting or preventive. When predefined symptom criteria are met, a diagnosis can be assigned, and treatment begins according to guidelines and recommendations developed for that specific disorder. Accordingly, service systems are organized along reductionist lines: different units and professionals specialize in treating particular symptom clusters—that is, diagnostic categories—even though psychiatric diagnoses do not reveal the causes of observed symptoms and therefore do not permit reliable conclusions about underlying causal mechanisms.

In other words, psychiatry remains in a situation where psychosocial problems are reduced to component parts through various theories, yet these components cannot be adequately measured or empirically tested. Although symptom-centered classification systems have improved diagnostic reliability, validity remains a challenge: using predefined symptom criteria, two clinicians are more likely to reach the same diagnosis, but it is not clear what the diagnosis actually signifies or how it can be reliably reduced to biopsychosocial components.

For these reasons, especially strong reductionism—which equates mental disorders directly with biological correlates—has been widely criticized, and its limitations are broadly acknowledged within psychiatry (e.g., Kendler, 2005; Parnas et al., 2013; van Os et al., 2019; Zachar et al., 2023). In fact, the prevailing descriptive psychiatric diagnostic approach—in which no stance is taken on etiology—can itself be seen as an attempt to avoid unwarranted assumptions about the causes of disorders.

One proposed solution to the problems of strong reductionism in psychiatry is a clearer distinction between *natural kinds* and *practical kinds* (Zachar, 2015). Natural kinds are entities that are non-artificial, clearly delineated, and composed of features that can be operationalized into measurable properties. Natural kinds are thought to possess *essential* features—that is, stable and defining properties that make a thing what it is (Gelman, 2004). Examples include chemical structures or genetic inheritance patterns that distinguish one biological species from another.

According to an essentialist perspective, psychiatric disorders would also have a single, common underlying cause—shared by all individuals with the disorder and in principle measurable. Taken to its extreme, this essentialism would lead back to a strong form of reductionism, for which empirical support is lacking. Essentialism in psychiatry can therefore be considered a kind of classification-induced illusion, since psychiatric diagnoses are fundamentally *constructed*, or *practical kinds*, grounded not in essence but in clinical, organizational, and convention-based aims (Zachar, 2015).

Some scholars have nevertheless suggested that certain psychiatric disorders may be closer to natural kinds than others, on the assumption that they correspond to discrete biological mechanisms (e.g., Tsou, 2016). Although such mechanisms have not yet been clearly identified—and current diagnostic categories are so heterogeneous in causes, manifestations, and outcomes that they cannot readily be considered natural kinds—this does not rule out the possibility that future research, aided by more fine-grained diagnostic models, might identify some natural kinds (Werkhoven, 2021). This reductionist logic is evident in contemporary efforts to reform psychiatric classification. The most prominent example is the *Research Domain Criteria* framework, which seeks to identify underlying biological, psychological, and social processes rather than relying on categorical symptom-based diagnoses (Cuthbert & Insel, 2013).

Although psychiatric research and the development of newer diagnostic systems have challenged strong biological reductionism and especially eliminative reductionism, which aims to replace mentalistic vocabulary altogether with biological terminology (Cuthbert, 2022)—reductionism remains deeply embedded in clinical practice and still continues to shape research as described above. One reason is the lack of alternative models that are both equally systematic and functional; another is pragmatism: equating diagnoses and symptoms with specific categories yields many practical benefits that help explain the persistence of reductionist thinking in the organization of services and in everyday clinical work.

2.2 The Benefits of the Reductionist Framework

There are many advantages associated with the reductionist framework, which help explain its popularity. First, it aligns closely with the assumptions of modern science—particularly medicine. In medicine, reductionism is often an effective way to structure and treat problems, because in many illnesses, causal chains can be at least partly identified.

For example, the causal sequence underlying cancer development is relatively well understood; it begins with exposure to risk factors that cause deoxyribonucleic acid (DNA) damage and genetic mutations within cells. These changes may lead to uncontrolled cell growth, forming a tumor and producing observable clinical symptoms. Because the symptoms can be traced directly to the causal factor—the tumor—treatment can target this cause by removing or destroying the tumor, for example, through surgery, radiation, or medication that kills cancer cells or stops their growth. Many cancer risk factors are also well defined, enabling preventive efforts through public policy and public health initiatives.

To ensure that treatment is directed at the correct point in the causal chain, research is needed to establish efficacy and effectiveness. In medicine, treatment effects are often investigated using randomized controlled trials (RCTs), in which patients are assigned to treatment or control groups at random. Randomization reduces the influence of confounding variables and increases confidence that observed changes are attributable to the treatment rather than to preexisting group differences.

The same logic is applied in psychiatry. When observable psychosocial problems and symptoms are classified as medical diagnoses, controlled study designs can be used to investigate treatment effects. When sufficient evidence accumulates, clinical guidelines can be developed to direct professional practice in accordance with research findings. Psychiatry can thus be viewed as part of standardized, evidence-based medical practice, which strengthens its legitimacy as a public or insurance-funded service: once a disorder is diagnosed, treatment proceeds according to agreed-upon evidence-based methods, largely independent of individual causal circumstances.

Because the causes of psychiatric disorders cannot be clearly identified and psychiatric diagnoses are therefore intentionally descriptive, the development of symptom-relieving treatments has often progressed through trial and error. Reductionism, however, offers the prospect—at least in principle—of developing more effective and better-targeted treatments, provided that causal mechanisms become better understood and interventions can be directed at them directly. As mentioned above, much of psychiatric research funding has therefore long been directed toward studying genetic and neurobiological mechanisms, which, in turn, reinforces and sustains reductionist thinking in research and training.

Beyond its alignment with prevailing medical paradigms, reductionism is also cognitively intuitive for humans. We have an innate tendency to categorize phenomena into simpler classes and to perceive causal relationships—an evolutionary prerequisite for survival. Categorization enables rapid judgments about environmental stimuli: we avoid a growling bear, stay away from fire, do not eat poisonous mushrooms, and seek the company of familiar and trusted individuals. Likewise, in daily life, we constantly evaluate the motives underlying others' actions and the potential consequences of our own.

This categorization-based decision-making occurs largely automatically. When we perceive a certain feature, we link it to a familiar category, which allows us to predict consequences and act quickly. The same mechanism operates in mental health care: psychiatric diagnoses transform complex and interpretive phenomena into simpler and more manageable forms, making it easier to draw inferences about potential causes, treatment options, and eligibility for certain forms of financial or insurance-based support.

Clear, predefined, and diagnosis-specific procedures enhance the sense of control in uncertain situations. They also make work faster and more straightforward. When health professionals are trained to identify and classify problems and to select predetermined treatments for each category, the need to analyze each situation from scratch is reduced. This predictability and the act of naming phenomena create a sense of safety: for example, when a person reports hearing accusatory voices leading to self-harm, the situation is often frightening also for staff. Linking such experiences to a diagnostic category provides a starting point for forming hypotheses and treatment plans, and the situation may feel less overwhelming or alarming.

In addition to offering a sense of control and safety, the reductionist approach provides literal protection within the system: by following predefined procedures and rules, a practitioner can justify decisions objectively and is typically protected both legally and in terms of liability.

Reductionism not only supports professional work and the organization of services but also often provides patients with a sense that their situation is understood and manageable. When symptoms are given a clear name, it becomes cognitively easier to process and discuss them. A single term simplifies communication with others, reducing the need to explain complex or difficult-to-articulate experiences in depth. Diagnosis can also relieve feelings of guilt—and reduce external blame. If psychological and social difficulties are seen as resulting from an objectively identifiable medical disorder, the individual is not necessarily viewed as "personally responsible" in the same way.

From a societal and organizational perspective, the reductionist framework makes systems more structured and manageable. Clear definitions of problems, designated treatment locations, and the work of specialized professionals following predetermined procedures facilitate resource allocation, ensure patient safety, and help resolve potential conflicts. This supports fair distribution of publicly funded treatments, reducing reliance on the subjective judgments or preferences of individual workers and officials. This orientation aligns closely with the utilitarian assumption (Chase & Mosse, 2025): that the ethical legitimacy of mental health interventions rests primarily on their demonstrable effects, and that moral responsibility in public health care is best discharged by selecting those interventions that can be shown, through standardized and comparable evidence, to produce the greatest aggregate benefit. Within this framework, reduction and standardization are not merely practical necessities but moral safeguards, ensuring that decisions about care are justified by measurable outcomes rather than by individual values, aspirations, or ethical intuitions.

For these reasons, the reductionist approach is often experienced not only as useful but, in many practical situations, also as the only feasible option.

2.3 Problems of Reductionism in Defining Mental Disorders

The central challenge of the reductionist approach in psychiatry is that psychosocial phenomena classified as mental disorders cannot be reduced to biological, psychological, or social components that would explain them consistently across situations and individuals. Because psychiatric concepts inevitably refer to psychological processes, they are always, to some extent, dependent on subjective experience (Kendler, 2005). Accordingly, the factors underlying symptom patterns that meet a given set of diagnostic criteria are, like other psychological and social phenomena, by default pluralistic and multicausal (Kendler, 2024).

In practice, symptom patterns that satisfy the criteria for the same diagnosis may arise from entirely different causes: for one person, they may follow from interactional patterns learned in relationships; for another, from current life stress; for a third, from an inherited sensitivity to intense emotions; for a fourth, from an unknown disturbance in brain functioning; and for a fifth, from some combination of these. Conversely, the same putative causes may lead to very different symptoms and diagnoses.

Psychiatric symptoms often overlap across diagnostic categories and vary substantially within a single diagnosis, limiting the validity of reductionist inferences (van Os et al., 2019). In practice, the same constellation of symptoms may satisfy different diagnostic criteria depending on how patients articulate their experiences and which features clinicians emphasize.

At the same time, individuals can meet the same diagnostic category with entirely different sets of symptoms, and symptom profiles within a single diagnosis may even be mutually contradictory. For example, a diagnosis of depression may be applied both to someone who sleeps and eats too little and to someone who sleeps and eats too much. This is because current diagnostic categories have been created through consensus-based committee processes rather than grounded in well-defined psychometrics or biological mechanisms, resulting in constructs that often lack clear boundaries and internal coherence.

A psychiatric diagnosis, then, is not the same as a causal factor targeted by treatment. It is a label for a cluster of symptoms interpreted as frequently co-occurring, and this is precisely how diagnostic categories were originally designed—to facilitate professional communication, statistical reporting, and service organization in a field where the object of treatment and research is too interpretive and context-dependent for reliable reductionist reasoning (Frances, 1981). This is reflected, for instance, in the American Psychiatric Association's DSM (2022) classification, which emphasizes in its opening sections that psychiatric categories are descriptive and consensus-based, and are not intended to provide etiological explanations.

Practice, however, often diverges from this principle. Psychiatric diagnoses are easily treated as if they were explanations of the problems they describe. This produces *reification* (Hyman, 2010)—the objectification of a descriptive classification, or in this case, its transformation into a seemingly real disease entity that is assumed to cause the symptoms—leading to circular reasoning: symptoms are explained by the diagnosis even though the diagnosis was originally defined on the basis of those very symptoms (Bergström, 2023).

An anxiety disorder, for example, does not *cause* the experience of anxiety; rather, it is a label for a situation in which experiences called anxiety are so intense that they impair everyday life. Similarly, a psychotic disorder does not *cause* hallucinations or delusions; it describes a state in which such experiences have occurred for a certain period. ADHD does not *cause* executive-function difficulties; it is a description that a person, at a particular age and in a particular context, has manifested such difficulties.

The conceptual confusion arising from reification is not merely an academic concern; it has practical consequences. When a psychiatric diagnosis is treated as a cause or an explanation, attention shifts away from the actual factors that generate or sustain a person's problems—whether these lie in life circumstances, relational contexts, patterns of thought, or biological disturbances. At the same time, diagnosis begins to shape how people understand themselves and others. A psychosis diagnosis may evoke fear and guardedness that, at worst, leads to othering and inappropriate encounters. A depression diagnosis may cause a person to doubt their own capacities and positive feelings, and to believe that their condition can be influenced only through medication, leaving other forms of help underused.

Although diagnosis may bring relief and reduce guilt, it does not in itself explain or change the underlying determinants of the problem. Using diagnosis as an explanation may therefore be ethically questionable if it sustains the misleading impression that a disorder is a disease entity causing symptoms. Moreover, people may begin interpreting their own and others' difficulties through the stereotypes associated with diagnostic categories.

As noted earlier, humans have a natural tendency to simplify complex reality into categories. People also often perceive and interpret their environment in ways that fit with prior expectations. If a person has been given a psychosis diagnosis, their behavior may be interpreted through common assumptions about psychosis. A need to withdraw from relationships or medication-induced fatigue, for example, may be construed as "negative symptoms." Disagreements about treatment decisions, relational conflicts, or confusion following rapid discontinuation of neuroleptic medication may be interpreted as "positive symptoms." If there are no problems, that too may be read as "remission."

In a similar way, if a person has an ADHD diagnosis, certain challenges in meeting the ideals of a modern information society may be interpreted as symptoms, rather than seeing those ideals themselves as narrow and discriminatory toward particular human characteristics. If a person has a personality disorder diagnosis, interactional problems arising in treatment may be attributed to the disorder rather than to clinicians' limitations in adapting to the situation. A depressed person's unemployment may be interpreted as the result of incapacity due to depression, even if the depressive state was originally an understandable response to lack of work or to working conditions that the person could not realistically meet at that time.

In practice, treating diagnoses as explanations easily results in a self-fulfilling dynamic: behavior is interpreted in line with stereotypes linked to the diagnosis (e.g., Timimi, 2014). According to the so-called *looping effect* (Hacking, 1995), a psychological concept such as a psychiatric diagnosis reshapes both a person's self-understanding and professionals' responses in ways that may make the individual appear increasingly "diagnosis-consistent"—not because the diagnosis originally captured them accurately, but because the social environment begins to treat them according to diagnostic expectations. People also tend to notice and reinforce information that aligns with their preexisting beliefs.

Using diagnoses as tools for explanation and interpretation can thus sustain self-reinforcing arrangements, weaken the targeting of care, and narrow the understanding of what counts as "normal" human variation. Because diagnoses often describe common human traits and experiences, they may feel highly relatable and can be readily internalized as part of identity. Some diagnoses have also become socially accepted ways of framing difficulties—through stigma-reduction campaigns and social media—so that they can provide relief and reduce feelings of blame (e.g., Sims et al., 2021). At the same time, this may encourage reductionist medical responses even in situations where the issue is not primarily an individual "disorder" or "defect" requiring medical "correction."

Beyond individual-level effects, reducing certain traits, experiences, and behaviors to mental disorders has wider societal consequences (Beeker et al., 2021). First, it increases demand for services and brings a growing number of people into the mental health system. This further narrows perceptions of normal human responses to life stress and reduces tolerance for difference and norm-deviating traits. Once people internalize the idea that medical problems require medical solutions, interpreting human reactions and characteristics as medical disorders promotes costly and potentially harmful overtreatment, while nonmedical forms of support are used less. In addition, diverse human traits, life challenges, and understandable contextual reactions may be misleadingly interpreted as symptoms of permanent illness (e.g., Horwitz & Wakefield, 2007), which can also affect social participation in multiple ways.

As stated above, research funding has likewise been directed toward supporting the reductionist hypothesis: the assumption that certain psychiatric diagnoses can be consistently reduced to biological components, which would eventually allow diagnoses to be confirmed through laboratory tests or brain-imaging methods (e.g., Cuthbert & Insel, 2013). However, this hypothesis is problematic in principle, since contemporary diagnostic categories are consensus-based classifications whose primary purpose was to improve reliability by focusing on reported or observable problems rather than on theoretical explanations. Although this approach is justified in many respects and has increased uniformity in assessment practice, individuals with the same diagnosis may present such diverse, interpretive, and context-bound symptom profiles that research cannot be expected to reveal clear, universal causal factors underlying current diagnoses—even as methods advance.

In line with reductionist logic, attempts to respond to diagnostic heterogeneity and validity problems have involved subdividing diagnostic categories into increasingly detailed entities and breaking symptom clusters into smaller, supposedly more homogeneous components (Paris & Phillips, 2013). As a consequence, diagnostic systems have expanded markedly over recent decades, both in the number of disorders and in the number of criteria.

Although this strategy has sharpened some distinctions between diagnoses and improved reliability (Regier et al., 2013), it does not resolve the interpretive nature of psychosocial difficulties. Instead, the simultaneous proliferation and broadening of diagnostic categories have contributed to *diagnostic inflation*, in which the boundaries of psychiatry have continuously expanded. Psychiatry then becomes less able to achieve its original aim of distinguishing "normal" psychological distress or challenging human experience from the "abnormal" (Frances, 2013).

At the same time that categories have been subdivided into ever-narrower components, comorbidity—the co-occurrence of multiple disorders—has increased: the majority of service users meeting criteria for one psychiatric diagnosis also meet criteria for two or more additional diagnoses (Nordgaard et al., 2023). The concept of comorbidity creates clinical and resource pressure to establish the "correct" diagnosis in situations where symptom profiles overlap and expression varies with life circumstances and environment. However, speaking of comorbidity is misleading in psychiatry, since apparent multi-disorder patterns often reflect artificial distinctions produced by classification rather than the true co-occurrence of categorically discrete diseases (Maj, 2005; Nordgaard et al., 2023; van Os et al., 2019).

As alternatives to categorical classification and its challenges, *transdiagnostic* and *dimensional* models have been proposed (e.g., Fusar-Poli et al., 2019; Kotov et al., 2017; Tomczyk et al., 2023). These approaches do not treat mental or social difficulties as qualitatively distinct from other psychosocial phenomena or reducible to diagnostic categories, but regard them as problems requiring care once they exceed a certain threshold of severity. Although such models capture the dimensional nature of psychosocial difficulties better than categorical systems, they still tend to locate problems within the individual and may thus fail to account for the fact that what counts as normal or abnormal is substantially dependent on culture and situation (Bassett & Baker, 2015; Bergström, 2023). Many of these approaches also lack the kind of clinical usability provided by categorical classification (Frances, 2013; Fusar-Poli et al., 2019).

In practice, resources devoted to reductionist psychiatric research and diagnostic-system development have been diverted away from other forms of research and service innovation. Moreover, the specialization required by reductionism can foster competitive dynamics and amplify economic interests. For example, from the perspective of the pharmaceutical industry, reductionism is particularly attractive because it seeks to translate complex—often partly societal—problems into individual-level neurochemical mechanisms, for which targeted drug treatments can be marketed. Reductionism has also encouraged competition among psychotherapies and other interventions, leading to the commodification of treatments and their presentation as distinct products, rather than fostering efforts to identify the common factors that account for effectiveness across helping practices. These forces help explain the dominance of the reductionistic framework in psychiatry.

2.4 Problems of Reductionism in the Treatment of Mental Disorders

In its most stringent form, the reductionist framework for defining mental health disorders rests on the assumption that psychological and social difficulties can be reduced to predefined diagnoses, and that diagnoses can, in turn, be reduced to clearly delineated social, psychological, or biological components—such as living conditions, traumatic events, psychological mechanisms, and specific bodily functions. From the perspective of treatment, such a premise would be ideal: if the root causes of a problem could be identified and specified with precision, one could develop targeted interventions that would be expected to alleviate symptoms linearly or remove their causal source. In practice, however, the effectiveness of mental health treatments does not follow this linear logic, not least because symptoms have not been reducible to unambiguous causal factors.

For example, the symptom-relieving or symptom-modifying effects of psychotropic medication have often been mistakenly interpreted as evidence that the symptoms must have originated in precisely the neurotransmitter system on which the medication primarily acts (e.g., Moncrieff et al., 2023; Schultz, 2015). This reverse causal inference is itself problematic (Schultz, 2015): the fact that a drug reduces symptoms through a particular neurochemical mechanism does not mean that the symptoms were caused by a disturbance in that mechanism. Intuitively, this is clear to most people when the effects of substances are considered in other contexts. Alcohol can reduce social inhibition, but this does not imply that a person has a biological deficit that alcohol "corrects." Opiates reduce the experience of fracture pain, even though they do not repair the fracture, nor is the pain caused by dysfunction of opioid receptors. Amphetamines and other stimulants help many people sustain interest in tasks that would not normally motivate them, even if they do not have developmentally delayed prefrontal cortices or other neurobiological abnormalities.

Interpreting the cause of symptoms through a medication's mechanism of action can lead to a situation where, once a diagnosis is assigned, medication is viewed as necessary to correct an assumed biological abnormality or dysfunction—even though no such abnormality has been demonstrated. Indeed, according to diagnostic logic, such abnormalities must typically be ruled out before the problem can be defined as a psychiatric disorder. As a consequence, pharmacological treatment may be initiated with a low threshold and continued long after diagnosis, even where there is no individual-level need for long-term medication.

Many psychotropic medications involve both immediate adverse effects and, especially with prolonged use, many common psychological and physical harms. Discontinuation of psychotropics can also produce withdrawal symptoms (Vinkers et al., 2024), which are sometimes misinterpreted as relapse of the "original disorder," even though they are more plausibly—and predictably—related to neurobiological adaptations to long-term drug exposure (Horowitz et al., 2021). When symptoms worsen during discontinuation, this can reinforce the diagnosis and the reductionist idea that a particular treatment is indispensable—despite the fact that many people would manage with lower doses or without medication if prescribing were more selective and discontinuation were gradual and systematically supported (Horowitz et al., 2021).

A further difficulty is that current diagnostic criteria do not reliably distinguish those who benefit from long-term pharmacotherapy from those who would do well without it (Maj et al., 2020; 2021). For reasons of resources and perceived safety, service systems often adopt a precautionary stance and favor maintenance medication in almost all situations—an approach that, over time, increases the risk of both adverse effects and withdrawal-related harms.

Reductionist thinking also shapes the use of psychosocial treatments. A given diagnosis is assumed to require a specific, clearly bounded method, even though it has long been known that differences in effectiveness between therapy modalities are small (e.g., Elkins, 2009; Leiman, 2004; Luborsky et al., 1975). More consequential are the so-called common factors, such as the therapist–client relationship, the person's experience of being heard, expectations, and the purposiveness of treatment (Wampold, 2015). Manualized methods may in some contexts provide helpful structure and clarity, but they do not guarantee effectiveness if individual and contextual needs are neglected (Elkins, 2009; Truijens et al., 2019).

Within reductionist logic, RCTs are treated as the "gold standard" for evaluating treatment effects, because randomization is assumed to reduce the effect of care to the specific method under investigation. This logic fits well for conditions and interventions with clearly defined boundaries. In psychiatry, however, it is problematic because diagnoses are not sharply delimited, diagnostic concepts refer to wide and heterogeneous phenomena, and outcomes are often based on self-reported change in subjective experience—experiences that are strongly shaped not only by the method used but also by expectations, the therapeutic relationship, and the broader context (van Os et al., 2019).

Moreover, RCTs require that the method under study differs from another method. This design constraint has meant that the interventions most readily accepted as evidence-based are precisely those that are tightly manualized and therefore suited to such research designs, even when they are not the most flexible, effective, or even usable in real-world practice. In reality, strict adherence to manuals can hinder the formation of a responsive therapeutic relationship and thereby weaken the common, nonspecific mechanisms through which much benefit occurs (e.g., Leiman, 2004; Thomas et al., 2012; Truijens et al., 2019). Trial results are then difficult to transfer to actual clinical environments, and treatments no longer meet the reductionist ideal of evidence-based practice in which effectiveness would be reducible to specific techniques or other method-specific factors (Alanen, 2009; Thomas et al., 2012; van Os et al., 2019).

At the level of service systems, the attempt to treat problems according to reductionist principles leads to increasing specialization both across units and among professionals, so that a precisely defined problem can be matched with the most appropriate evidence-based intervention (van Os et al., 2019). When care is organized around diagnoses and discrete methods, the service system tends to fragment, making it harder to manage. This fragmentation, in turn, produces a self-reinforcing pressure to specify problems and their "correct" treatments ever more precisely, requiring ever more specialized resources.

In practice, service users move from one unit and professional to another as their symptom profile changes. A considerable amount of resources is usually spent on assessment work in an attempt to determine the "right" evidence-based treatment method and service location. Once a diagnosis is assigned, symptoms are typically managed in a mechanistic manner using the methods judged most appropriate for treating that specific disorder, often leaving the individual's situation and life context insufficiently considered (e.g., Thomas et al., 2012; WHO, 2021).

Because symptom profiles often change over time regardless of the treatment provided, a person may no longer fit the original classification. This creates the need for repeated assessments and further transfers. Such a dynamic—combined with the expansion of diagnostic criteria (Frances, 2013)—helps explain what has been called the mental health service crisis in many Western countries (WHO, 2021): demand for services increases continually, while the long-term benefits for individual well-being remain limited and the mode of service provision consumes substantial resources.

The specialization of treatments and services described above also places demands on professionals, who are expected to master multiple evidence-based methods to be deployed according to the diagnosed disorder. This is cognitively burdensome, as both the practical implementation of methods and the problems being treated are complex and rarely categorical. Taking a hammer from a toolbox to drive a nail is far more straightforward than attempting to deliver, with methodological fidelity, interpersonal and relationship-focused therapy with one patient, cognitive behavioral therapy with the next, and systemic family therapy with a third.

Because no single practitioner can thoroughly master many psychosocial treatments or therapeutic orientations, a reductionist model of service provision requires extensive staffing and training resources so that each problem category can be matched with an evidence-based method. Advanced specialization leads professionals to focus on only a narrow segment of the service user's overall situation. As a result, the broader picture may be missed, and treatment begins to target secondary or irrelevant factors.

A psychotherapist may work on maladaptive emotional, cognitive, and behavioral patterns; a family therapist on family interaction; a social worker on financial circumstances; an occupational therapist on daily functioning; hospital staff on acute safety; physicians on medication plans; and nurses on monitoring conditions—and so on. If the symptom profile changes in ways that no longer match the remit of a specialized unit—either in nature or severity—the patient is redirected elsewhere, where new professionals again approach the situation from within their respective domains.

In such a system, professionals—who ought to be substantive experts in mental health—may gradually lose sight of the overall nature of a person's difficulties. At the same time, duplication of work increases, and competition between staff and units over roles, resources, and boundaries of responsibility may intensify, to the point where no party assumes overarching responsibility for treatment as a whole.

From the perspective of service users, specialization and stepped-care structures often manifest as difficulty accessing help, complexity of the system, and long waiting lists. When help is finally obtained, it may be experienced as mechanical or inattentive to the person's actual needs. Being passed from one professional to another also leads to the recurrent experience of having to repeat the same story, preventing the treatment process from properly beginning.

Diagnostic centrality creates further challenges. First, if diagnoses are treated as explanations for symptoms, the diagnostic label itself may predispose to conflict or shape professionals' attitudes. Some diagnoses carry substantial stigma, leading health professionals and others to approach a person with caution, even before genuinely getting to know them (Kamens, 2019). Conversely, some diagnoses are desired by individuals as explanations for their difficulties, which can create disappointment or conflict if the expected diagnosis is not given.

Second, many service users experience care as imposed or directive if, in accordance with reductionist thinking, certain treatments are deemed necessary whenever diagnostic criteria are met. This may contribute to poor treatment engagement, discontinuation of high-dose medication, and related harms that may then be misinterpreted as symptoms of the underlying disorder. Such patterns of dissatisfaction and disagreement are particularly problematic for treatment effectiveness, because mental health disorders and problems are inherently experiential: what matters most is the person's experience of being understood and helped.

Within a reductionist framework, however, treatment effectiveness is often evaluated using narrow, operationalized symptom measures, which are assumed to map onto diagnostic categories and thereby measure uniform reductions in symptoms. Short-term changes in questionnaire scores do not necessarily reflect outcomes such as social participation, long-term functioning, quality of close relationships, increased subjective well-being, or other factors that individuals themselves consider most important—and that often shape the situations defined as mental health disorders or problems (Bergström, 2023). When such outcomes are not regarded as indicators of treatment effectiveness, mental health services do not orient their efforts toward improving them (WHO, 2021).

2.5 Summary of the Benefits and Challenges of Reductionism in Psychiatry

In both the definition and treatment of mental disorders, a reductionist framework offers clarity, structure, and predictability. It supports the manageability of service systems, enables the allocation of resources, and provides clear and reproducible treatment protocols. At the same time, however, it introduces distortions: complex, individual, and context-bound phenomena are compressed into symptom-based diagnoses and standardized interventions that may not be well suited to addressing the highly individual, interpretive, and situational problems that come to be labeled as mental disorders.

Although neither academic psychiatry nor mainstream clinical practice explicitly endorses strict reductionism, more moderate forms of reductionist thinking continue to exert strong influence over diagnostic systems, service structures, and clinical routines. As a result, diverse human characteristics and life difficulties become construed within the system as individual "illnesses" or "disorders." Using descriptive symptom categories as explanations for those symptoms also fosters self-reinforcing circular reasoning, a narrowing of what counts as "normal," and increased demand for services. As demand grows, the perceived need to stratify services and more precisely define the nature of each problem—and the type of treatment to which a person is entitled—intensifies further.

At the level of care delivery, services risk fragmenting into specialized units. Because psychiatric disorders are not clearly bounded, diagnostic concepts refer to a wide array of phenomena, and symptom profiles change over time, this fragmentation easily results in unnecessary transfers between units and professionals.

Due to the constraints of reductionist research methodologies, the treatments that become recognized as evidence-based tend to be those that are readily operationalized and capable of alleviating discrete symptoms. Consequently, service systems often provide top-down, prespecified interventions that are delivered in the same manner regardless of context and that may be poorly connected to the person's actual life situation. The broader picture and the purposeful work of helping are easily compromised. This can lead to duplicated effort and a deepening cycle of resource scarcity—a situation in which the support system no longer responds effectively to people's real needs. From the perspective of service users, such dynamics amplify the risk of dissatisfaction and conflict, which, in turn, undermines the effectiveness of mental health care.

References

Alanen, Y. O. (2009). Towards a more humanistic psychiatry: Development of need-adapted treatment of schizophrenia group psychoses. *Psychosis, 1*(2), 156–166. https://doi.org/10.1080/17522430902795667

American Psychiatric Association. (2022). *DSM-5-TR: Diagnostic and statistical manual of mental disorders* (5th ed., text rev.). American Psychiatric Publishing.

Barlow, D. H. (2002). *Anxiety and its disorders: The nature and treatment of anxiety and panic* (2nd ed.). Guilford Press.

Bassett, A. M., & Baker, C. (2015). Normal or abnormal? 'Normative uncertainty' in psychiatric practice. *The Journal of Medical Humanities*, *36*(2), 89–111. https://doi.org/10.1007/s10912-014-9324-2

Beck, A. T. (1967). Depression: Clinical, experimental and theoretical aspects. Harper and Row.

Beeker, T., Mills, C., Bhugra, D., Te Meerman, S., Thoma, S., Heinze, M., & von Peter, S. (2021). Psychiatrization of Society: A Conceptual Framework and Call for Transdisciplinary Research. *Frontiers in Psychiatry*, *12*, 645556. https://doi.org/10.3389/fpsyt.2021.645556

Bergström, T. (2023). From treatment of mental disorders to the treatment of difficult life situations: A hypothesis and rationale. *Medical Hypotheses, 176,* 111099. https://doi.org/10.1016/j.mehy.2023.111099

Caspi, A., Sugden, K., Moffitt, T. E., Taylor, A., Craig, I. W., Harrington, H., McClay, J., Mill, J., Martin, J., Braithwaite, A., & Poulton, R. (2003). Influence of life stress on depression: Moderation by a polymorphism in the 5-HTT gene. *Science (New York, N.Y.), 301*(5631), 386–389. https://doi.org/10.1126/science.1083968

Chase, L., & Mosse, D. (2025). The Moral Blind Spots of Evidence-Based Psychiatry: Learning from Britain's Trial of "Peer-Supported Open Dialogue". *Medical Anthropology*, *44*(7), 636–649. https://doi.org/10.1080/01459740.2025.2563253

Cuthbert, B. N. (2022). Research Domain Criteria (RDoC): Progress and Potential. *Current Directions in Psychological Science*, *31*(2), 107–114. https://doi.org/10.1177/09637214211051363

Cuthbert, B. N., & Insel, T. R. (2013). Toward the future of psychiatric diagnosis: The seven pillars of RDoC. *BMC Medicine, 11,* Article 126. https://doi.org/10.1186/1741-7015-11-126

Elkins, D. N. (2009). The medical model in psychotherapy: Its limitations and failures. *Journal of Humanistic Psychology, 49*(1), 66–84. https://doi.org/10.1177/0022167807307901

Fonagy, P., Gergely, G., Jurist, E. L., & Target, M. (2002). *Affect regulation, mentalization, and the development of the self.* Other Press.

Frances, A. (1981). Descriptive and dynamic psychiatry: A perspective on DSM-III. *American Journal of Psychiatry, 138*(9), 1198–1202. https://doi.org/10.1176/ajp.138.9.1198

Frances, A. (2013). The past, present and future of psychiatric diagnosis. *World Psychiatry, 12*(2), 111–112. https://doi.org/10.1002/wps.20027

Fusar-Poli, P., Solmi, M., Brondino, N., Davies, C., Chae, C., Politi, P., Borgwardt, S., Lawrie, S. M., Parnas, J., & McGuire, P. (2019). Transdiagnostic psychiatry: A systematic review. *World Psychiatry: Official Journal of the World Psychiatric Association (WPA)*, *18*(2), 192–207. https://doi.org/10.1002/wps.20631

Gelman, S. A. (2004). Psychological essentialism in children. *Trends in Cognitive Sciences*, *8*(9), 404–409. https://doi.org/10.1016/j.tics.2004.07.001

Gonzalez, W. J. (2020). Pragmatism and pluralism as methodological alternatives to monism, reductionism and universalism. In W. J. Gonzalez (Ed.), *Methodological prospects for scientific research* (pp. 1–18). Springer.

Hacking, I. (1995). The looping effects of human kinds. In D. Sperber, D. Premack, & A. J. Premack (Eds.), *Causal cognition: A multidisciplinary debate* (pp. 351–394). Clarendon Press/Oxford University Press.

Horowitz, M. A., Jauhar, S., Natesan, S., Murray, R. M., & Taylor, D. (2021). A Method for Tapering Neuroleptic Treatment That May Minimize the Risk of Relapse. *Schizophrenia Bulletin*, *47*(4), 1116–1129. https://doi.org/10.1093/schbul/sbab017.

Horwitz, A. V., & Wakefield, J. C. (2007). *The loss of sadness: How psychiatry transformed normal sorrow into depressive disorder.* Oxford University Press.

Hyman, S. E. (2010). The diagnosis of mental disorders: The problem of reification. *Annual Review of Clinical Psychology*, *6*, 155–179. https://doi.org/10.1146/annurev.clinpsy.3.022806.091532

Kamens, S. (2019). De-othering "schizophrenia". *Theory & Psychology, 29*(2), 200–218. https://doi.org/10.1177/0959354319828531

Kendler, K. S. (2005). Toward a philosophical structure for psychiatry. *American Journal of Psychiatry*, 162(3), 433–440.

Kendler, K. S. (2024). Reflections on philosophy of psychiatry. *World Psychiatry: Official Journal of the World Psychiatric Association (WPA)*, *23*(2), 174–175. https://doi.org/10.1002/wps.21187

Kotov, R., Krueger, R. F., Watson, D., Achenbach, T. M., Althoff, R. R., Bagby, R. M., Brown, T. A., Carpenter, W. T., Caspi, A., Clark, L. A., Eaton, N. R., Forbes, M. K., Forbush, K. T., Goldberg, D., Hasin, D., Hyman, S. E., Ivanova, M. Y., Lynam, D. R., Markon, K., Miller, J. D., ... Zimmerman, M. (2017). The Hierarchical Taxonomy of Psychopathology (HiTOP): A dimensional alternative to traditional nosologies. *Journal of Abnormal Psychology, 126*(4), 454–477. https://doi.org/10.1037/abn0000258

Leiman, M. (2004). Vaikuttavuustutkimuksen pulmallisuus psykoterapiassa [Research of effectiveness is a challenge in psychotherapy]. *Duodecim; laaketieteellinen aikakauskirja, 120*(22), 2645–2653.

Lewis-Fernández, R., Rotheram-Borus, M. J., Betts, V. T., Greenman, L., Essock, S. M., Escobar, J. I., Barch, D., Hogan, M. F., Areán, P. A., Druss, B. G., DiClemente, R. J., McGlashan, T. H., Jeste, D. V., Proctor, E. K., Ruiz, P., Rush, A. J., Canino, G. J., Bell, C. C., Henry, R., & Iversen, P. (2016). Rethinking funding priorities in mental health research. *The British Journal of Psychiatry: The Journal of Mental Science, 208*(6), 507–509. https://doi.org/10.1192/bjp.bp.115.179895

Luborsky, L., Singer, B., & Luborsky, L. (1975). Comparative studies of psychotherapies: Is it true that "everyone has won and all must have prizes"? *Archives of General Psychiatry, 32*(8), 995–1008.

Maj, M. (2005). The aftermath of the concept of 'psychiatric comorbidity'. *Psychotherapy and Psychosomatics*, 74(2), 67–68. https://doi.org/10.1159/000083164

Maj, M., Stein, D. J., Parker, G., Zimmerman, M., Fava, G. A., De Hert, M., Demyttenaere, K., McIntyre, R. S., Widiger, T., & Wittchen, H. U. (2020). The clinical characterization of the adult patient with depression aimed at personalization of management. *World Psychiatry: Official Journal of the World Psychiatric Association (WPA), 19*(3), 269–293. https://doi.org/10.1002/wps.20771

Maj, M., van Os, J., De Hert, M., Gaebel, W., Galderisi, S., Green, M. F., Guloksuz, S., Harvey, P. D., Jones, P. B., Malaspina, D., McGorry, P., Miettunen, J., Murray, R. M., Nuechterlein, K. H., Peralta, V., Thornicroft, G., van Winkel, R., & Ventura, J. (2021). The clinical characterization of the patient with primary psychosis aimed at personalization of management. *World Psychiatry: Official Journal of the World Psychiatric Association (WPA), 20*(1), 4–33. https://doi.org/10.1002/wps.20809

Moncrieff, J., Cooper, R. E., Stockmann, T., Amendola, S., Hengartner, M. P., & Horowitz, M. A. (2023). The serotonin theory of depression: A systematic umbrella review of the evidence. *Molecular Psychiatry, 28*(8), 3243–3256. https://doi.org/10.1038/s41380-022-01661-0

Nordgaard, J., Nielsen, K. M., Rasmussen, A. R., & Henriksen, M. G. (2023). Psychiatric comorbidity: A concept in need of a theory. *Psychological Medicine, 53*(13), 5902–5908. https://doi.org/10.1017/S0033291723001605

Paris, J., & Phillips, J. (2013). *Making the DSM-5: Concepts and controversies.* Springer.

Parnas, J., Sass, L. A., & Zahavi, D. (2013). Rediscovering psychopathology: The epistemology and phenomenology of the psychiatric object. *Schizophrenia Bulletin, 39*(2), 270–277. https://doi.org/10.1093/schbul/sbs153

Raatikainen, P. (2004). *Ihmistieteet ja filosofia.* Helsinki: Gaudeamus.

Regier, D. A., Narrow, W. E., Clarke, D. E., Kraemer, H. C., Kuramoto, S. J., Kuhl, E. A., & Kupfer, D. J. (2013). DSM-5 field trials in the United States and Canada, Part II: Test-retest reliability of selected categorical diagnoses. *The American Journal of Psychiatry*, *170*(1), 59–70. https://doi.org/10.1176/appi.ajp.2012.12070999

Rosenberg, A. (2005). *Philosophy of science: A contemporary introduction* (2nd ed.). Routledge.

Schultz, W. (2015). The chemical imbalance hypothesis: An evaluation of the evidence. *Ethical Human Psychology and Psychiatry: An International Journal of Critical Inquiry, 17*(1), 60–75. https://doi.org/10.1891/1559-4343.17.1.60

Shaw, P., Eck strand, K., Sharp, W., Blumenthal, J., Lerch, J. P., Greenstein, D., Clasen, L., Evans, A., Giedd, J., & Rapoport, J. L. (2007). Attention-deficit/hyperactivity disorder is characterized by a delay in cortical maturation. *Proceedings of the National Academy of Sciences of the United States of America, 104*(49), 19649–19654. https://doi.org/10.1073/pnas.0707741104

Sims, R., Michaleff, Z. A., Glasziou, P., & Thomas, R. (2021). Consequences of a diagnostic label: A systematic scoping review and thematic framework. *Frontiers in Public Health*, *9*, Article 725877. https://doi.org/10.3389/fpubh.2021.725877

Thomas, P., Bracken, P., & Timini, S. (2012). The limits of evidence-based medicine in psychiatry. *Philosophy, Psychiatry, & Psychology, 19*(4), 295–308.

Timimi, S. (2014). No more psychiatric labels: Why formal psychiatric diagnostic systems should be abolished. *International Journal of Clinical and Health Psychology, 14*(3), 208–215. https://doi.org/10.1016/j.ijchp.2014.03.004

Tomczyk, S., Schlick, S., Gansler, T., McLaren, T., Muehlan, H., Peter, L. J., Schomerus, G., & Schmidt, S. (2023). Continuum beliefs of mental illness: A systematic review of measures. *Social Psychiatry and Psychiatric Epidemiology, 58*(1), 1–16. https://doi.org/10.1007/s00127-022-02345-4

Truijens, F., Zühlke-van Hulzen, L., & Vanheule, S. (2019). To manualize, or not to manualize: Is that still the question? A systematic review of empirical evidence for manual superiority in psychological treatment. *Journal of Clinical Psychology*, *75*(3), 329–343. https://doi.org/10.1002/jclp.22712

Tsou, J. Y. (2016). Natural kinds, psychiatric classification and the history of the DSM. *History of Psychiatry*, *27*(4), 406–424. https://doi.org/10.1177/0957154X16656580

van Os, J., Guloksuz, S., Vijn, T. W., Hafkenscheid, A., & Delespaul, P. (2019). The evidence-based group-level symptom-reduction model as the organizing principle for mental health care: Time for change? *World Psychiatry, 18*(1), 88–96. https://doi.org/10.1002/wps.20609

Vinkers, C. H., Kupka, R. W., Penninx, B. W., Ruhé, H. G., van Gaalen, J. M., van Haaren, P. C. F., Schellekens, A. F. A., Jauhar, S., Ramos-Quiroga, J. A., Vieta, E., Tiihonen, J., Veldman, S. E., Veling, W., Vis, R., de Wit, L. E., & Luykx, J. J. (2024). Discontinuation of psychotropic medication: A synthesis of evidence across medication classes. *Molecular Psychiatry*, *29*(8), 2575–2586. https://doi.org/10.1038/s41380-024-02445-4

Walker, E. F., & Diforio, D. (1997). Schizophrenia: A neural diathesis-stress model. *Psychological Review*, *104*(4), 667–685. https://doi.org/10.1037/0033-295x.104.4.667

Wampold, B. E. (2015). How important are the common factors in psychotherapy? An update. *World Psychiatry: Official Journal of the World Psychiatric Association (WPA)*, *14*(3), 270–277. https://doi.org/10.1002/wps.20238

Wampold, B. E., & Imel, Z. E. (2015). *The great psychotherapy debate: The evidence for what makes psychotherapy work* (2nd ed.). Routledge.

Werkhoven, S. (2021). Natural kinds of mental disorder. *Synthese*, *199*, 10135–10165. https://doi.org/10.1007/s11229-021-03239-9

World Health Organization. (2021). *Guidance on community mental health services: Promoting person-centred and rights-based approaches*. World Health Organization. https://creativecommons.org/licenses/by-nc-sa/3.0/igo/

Yehuda, R., & LeDoux, J. (2007). Response variation following trauma: A translational neuroscience approach to understanding PTSD. *Neuron*, *56*(1), 19–32. https://doi.org/10.1016/j.neuron.2007.09.006

Zachar, P. (2015). Psychiatric disorders: Natural kinds made by the world or practical kinds made by us?. *World Psychiatry: Official Journal of the World Psychiatric Association (WPA)*, *14*(3), 288–290. https://doi.org/10.1002/wps.20240

Zachar, P., Banicki, K., & Aftab, A. (2023). Historical and philosophical considerations in studying psychopathology. In P. H. Blaney, R. F. Krueger, & T. Millon (Eds.), *Oxford textbook of psychopathology* (2023 ed.). Oxford University Press.

Chapter 3

Holistic Framework

Next, the foundations for a more explicitly holistic alternative to reductionism are developed. The discussion begins by situating the current push toward holism in international policy and human rights discourse, focusing in particular on how the World Health Organization (WHO) and the United Nations (UN) have criticized the limitations of a predominantly biomedically reductionistic and symptom-focused mental health service model. It then traces the conceptual history of holism—from systems thinking and cybernetics to complexity theory, phenomenology, and embodied/embedded approaches to cognition—showing how these traditions converge on the idea that human distress is best understood as relational, context-dependent, and emergent. Building on this background, the analysis addresses common conceptual pitfalls of holism, including the risk of relativism and the confusion between weak and strong emergence.

The position adopted in this book—contextual emergence combined with critical realism—is then outlined as a way to integrate pluralistic explanations without collapsing into either mechanistic reduction or "anything goes" holism. Finally, the implications of this framework for understanding mental disorders are examined, including why, across modalities, treatment effects so often depend on nonspecific mechanisms related to meaning, relationship, and the quality of interaction.

3.1 The Position of the WHO and the UN

Over the past several decades, increasing international attention has been directed toward mental health and the development of mental health services. In many countries, mental health systems have been unable to meet rising demand, and treatment outcomes have remained unsatisfactory in numerous respects (WHO, 2021). National mental health strategies have been introduced in many regions in an effort to direct political and economic resources toward prevention and improvements in care (Guerrero et al., 2024). Despite these efforts, however, financial investment in mental

DOI: 10.4324/9781003777939-5

health services has remained relatively low—typically only a few percent of national health expenditures (WHO, 2017)—and many countries are now facing outright crises in their mental health systems (OECD, 2021; WHO, 2021), with widespread staff burnout (Ballout, 2025).

Although adequate resourcing and improved accessibility are essential conditions for functioning mental health services, the WHO emphasized in its 2021 guidance that simply increasing resources or expanding service provision will not, on their own, resolve systemic problems. One key reason, according to WHO, is that the majority of mental health spending still goes to institutional care—a model associated with numerous ethical and social concerns, including institutionalization, diminished social participation, and the use of various coercive practices.

At the same time, the dismantling of institutional care and investment in community-based services has not automatically improved access, quality, or outcomes. According to WHO (2021), one major reason is the dominance of a biologically reductionist model of mental health care, which tends to overlook the real and changing needs of individuals as well as many key determinants of mental well-being—such as experiences of violence, inequality, unemployment, homelessness, lack of social support networks, loneliness, and existential crises.

As outlined earlier, within a reductionist model, broader societal inequities or understandable reactions to difficult life circumstances become medicalized, often unintentionally, through psychiatric diagnoses. These diagnoses render such difficulties as individual problems. This, in turn, elevates individual-focused interventions, which require long-term commitment and carry risks, while simultaneously making it harder to address broader determinants of well-being—both in clinical practice and in political decision-making.

The medicalization of diverse traits and life challenges—and their reduction into individual problems—also maintains stigma and narrows conceptions of normality (e.g., Read et al., 2006). Although public campaigns have attempted to reduce stigma, their focus has largely been on dispelling prejudices associated with diagnostic labels. Consequently, certain life challenges and characteristics have become more socially acceptable only when described through specific diagnostic concepts. Yet, stigma has not decreased around the underlying experiences themselves; for instance, difficulties with social interaction or meeting societal expectations still evoke shame and blame, even if describing them through a diagnostic concept is more acceptable than before.

For example, it has been reported that many people experience relief when life-management or social difficulties are framed as neurodevelopmental disorders, because such framing makes the challenges seem less like personal "failings" (e.g., Ginapp et al., 2022). Because the only change may be the label used to describe the difficulties, such experiences illustrate how societal tolerance for human variation has narrowed—differences become acceptable mainly when accompanied by a medically sanctioned explanation. At the same time, this demonstrates how profoundly concepts and their associated meanings influence human well-being.

Although such relief may be beneficial at an individual level, the use of medical categories as tools for identity work simultaneously exposes people to problematic power dynamics and perpetuates the broader medicalization of ordinary human traits, contributing further to system overload.

While some psychiatric diagnoses have become socially accepted ways of describing certain life challenges, others remain highly stigmatized and laden with othering assumptions, exposing individuals to discrimination in health care and in other domains of life. In some countries, a psychiatric diagnosis leads directly to restrictions on fundamental human rights—including participation in community life, forming a family, or raising children. WHO (2021) has further emphasized that serious human rights violations remain common in mental health systems worldwide. Beyond stigma, these include coercive practices such as involuntary hospitalization, forced medication, and seclusion. Similar concerns have been raised by UN Special Rapporteurs and the Human Rights Council (Pūras, 2017), which have called for abandoning coercion, overmedication, and other practices that fail to respect autonomy, will, and preferences.

In its 2021 guidance, WHO calls for substantial transformation of mental health services—from policy and legislation to system organization and clinical practice. The guidance highlights the need to shift away from the current reductionist, symptom-focused medical model toward a human-rights-based and person-respecting holistic model.

In recent years, many scholars and experts have likewise argued that a paradigm shift in psychiatry is necessary. They maintain that mental health systems must recognize people's lived experiences and key social and structural determinants far more comprehensively, so that care can be individualized and better integrated into the realities of people's daily lives (e.g., Bracken et al., 2012; Bracken & Thomas, 2005; Hansen et al., 2023; Patel et al., 2023; Rose, 2025; van Os et al., 2019). WHO (2019) has also systematically developed free training materials and resources through its QualityRights initiative to promote person-centered and rights-based approaches. In its 2021 guidance, WHO also presents several practical service-system models from diverse social and cultural contexts where mental health services have been successfully organized in line with these principles.

However, implementing these recommendations has proven challenging (e.g., Gill et al., 2024; Mahdanian et al., 2023). One explanation is social bias: the assumption that such reforms are not needed locally because rights and services appear to be well protected. In reality, these same structures may perpetuate discriminatory practices and restrict people's agency (e.g., Mahdanian et al., 2023; WHO, 2021). In many Western countries, there is also a prevailing belief that human rights, participation, and holistic approaches are already adequately realized, and that system problems result mainly from resource shortages and growing service demand. This increase in demand can also be interpreted as a positive sign of decreasing stigma, further obscuring the need for deeper change.

Many healthcare professionals likewise believe that social dimensions of mental health and people's lived experiences are already sufficiently addressed—for example, through the biopsychosocial model or through routine clinical questioning. New methods are also continually introduced, and these are assumed to address such needs better. This may lead clinicians to believe that criticism of reductionism—and therefore WHO's guidance—does not apply to their practice, even though the guidance explicitly states that many challenges are characteristic of Western systems and cannot be solved by increased resources alone.

A further barrier to change is the lack of practical alternatives and systematic research on them (Gill et al., 2024). WHO's call for holistic approaches risks remaining abstract unless the concept is defined more precisely in contrast to prevalent reductionist models. A challenge is that the term *holism* is used inconsistently in the literature, with no longer a single agreed-upon definition (Jörgenfelt & Partington, 2019).

In medicine, holism typically refers to comprehensive care, attending to multiple dimensions of a person, or applying a broad range of methods. Yet, many of these approaches are in fact reductionist insofar as they attempt to reduce problems to specific individual mechanisms at which interventions are directed.

The concept of holism is also associated with complementary and alternative treatments, which can easily mark it as pseudoscientific and hinder constructive scientific debate. This has impeded the development of a shared theoretical foundation capable of explaining the mechanisms of more holistic forms of mental health practice in relation to prevailing approaches. Alternatives to reductionism have been described, for example, as *critical psychiatry* (Steingard, 2019) or *post-psychiatry* (Bracken & Thomas, 2001; 2005). Although these movements have generated some practical innovations seeking to foreground lived experience and social context, their transformative potential has often been limited as they are easily absorbed back into individualized psychiatric practice and existing power structures (e.g., Rose & Rose, 2023).

Originally, holism was defined as the opposite of reductionism. Addressing the challenges of reductionism therefore requires a more precise and coherent elaboration of a holistic framework.

3.2 The Short History of Holism

In its simplest form, holism refers to examining wholes rather than isolated parts. More commonly, however, it implies a stronger claim: that wholes possess properties not intelligible through components alone—the familiar idea that "the whole is more than the sum of its parts." While reflections on parts and wholes can be traced back to Aristotle, *holism* as a term was introduced by Jan Smuts in *Holism and Evolution* (1926).

According to Smuts (1926), holism is a fundamental organizing principle of nature. A whole does not merely aggregate parts but also shapes their relations, roles, and functions so profoundly that the parts themselves change. The whole thus acts back upon the parts, and their behavior and meaning can be understood only in relation to that larger configuration.

Smuts' idea was later developed within systems theory. In this tradition, biological and social phenomena are seen as dynamic, open systems that cannot be understood by reduction to constituent elements (von Bertalanffy, 1968). Systems exhibit emergent properties arising from interactions among components and therefore require attention to patterns of interaction, larger configurations, and their evolution over time.

Natural systems illustrate this clearly. In ecosystems, the disappearance or reintroduction of a single species can cascade through prey behavior, vegetation, food webs, and habitats, ultimately reshaping landscapes—effects not predictable from a single species in isolation. Likewise, in insect colonies, simple behavioral rules at the micro level generate complex self-organization at the macro level; the meaning of individual actions becomes apparent only within the colony.

To understand how systems regulate themselves, cybernetics complemented systems theory (Bateson, 1967; Wiener, 1948). Cybernetics introduced feedback and homeostasis: systems respond to their own outputs, stabilizing through negative feedback or amplifying change through positive feedback. These ideas deepened systemic thinking by describing *how* wholes maintain, shift, or escalate patterns over time.

Building on these traditions, complexity thinking conceptualized systems as nonlinear, adaptive, and continuously evolving (e.g., Byrne & Callaghan, 2023; Capra, 1996; Holland, 1992). According to these approaches, feedback can generate self-organization and qualitatively novel outcomes that remain partly unpredictable even when lower-level rules are well known.

Systems and complexity theories have been widely applied in the human sciences, where social phenomena are understood as dynamic and relational rather than as the aggregated outcomes of individual actions. Culture and social institutions arise from individuals but simultaneously constrain and shape them, persisting beyond any single person. Families and peer networks likewise form systems in which reciprocal influence makes the whole irreducible to its members. Systems theory therefore became influential in family therapy, shifting focus from isolated individuals to relational patterns.

While systems and complexity traditions clarified *structural* emergence, the human sciences faced an additional question: how meanings and experiences are constituted. This was pursued in phenomenology, which examines lived experience as it presents itself in the lifeworld, without reducing it to external theoretical schemes (Husserl, 1913; 1936). Heidegger (1927) reframed human existence as a contextual being-in-the-world, where meaning emerges through temporality, finitude, and situated agency. In psychiatry and psychotherapy, this shift meant taking subjective experience seriously as a central focus of inquiry (Jaspers, 1968; Parnas et al., 2013).

4E theories further develop phenomenological insights into cognition (Alexander, 2025). The term refers to four closely related perspectives on the nature of mind: embodied, embedded, enactive, and extended cognition. Embodied cognition emphasizes that thinking is shaped by the body and its sensorimotor capacities. Embedded cognition highlights that cognitive processes are situated within and influenced by the surrounding environment and social context. Enactive cognition proposes that cognition emerges through active engagement with the world. Finally, extended cognition suggests that cognitive processes can extend beyond the brain and body to include external tools and structures, such as notebooks, digital devices, or other people.

These perspectives propose that thinking does not occur solely inside the brain. Instead, cognition unfolds through the interplay of body, environment, and action (Alexander, 2025; Gallagher, 2014). From this perspective, mental life is not an isolated inner process but something that happens in the ongoing interaction between a person and their world. For example, catching a ball is not simply the execution of an internal mental calculation. It involves bodily movement, visual perception, timing, balance, and continuous adjustment to the ball's trajectory. The act of "thinking" where the ball will land unfolds through the coordinated interaction of brain, body, and environment. Cognition, in this sense, is something we do with the world, not something that happens only inside the head.

Schütz (1932) brought phenomenology into the social sciences by emphasizing that the lifeworld is not private but shared. Everyday reality is formed through how people interpret situations together. What counts as "normal," "appropriate," or "true" is not simply given but arises through mutual understanding in interaction. This idea laid the foundation for social constructionism. Berger and Luckmann (1966) argued that social reality is continuously produced and maintained through everyday practices—through conversation, institutions, and routines that gradually come to feel self-evident. For example, money, professional roles, or diagnostic categories exist because people collectively treat them as real and act accordingly.

A range of influential thinkers across philosophy, sociology, and psychology have emphasized the role of language, social interaction, and discourse in shaping knowledge. Michel Foucault argued that discursive formations structure what can be said, known, and regarded as true within a given historical period (1965; 1972). Jean-François Lyotard highlighted the fragmentation of grand narratives in late modernity, emphasizing the emergence of multiple, localized forms of knowledge and meaning (1984). Mikhail Bakhtin emphasized the fundamentally dialogical nature of meaning (1984), while Lev Vygotsky demonstrated how higher psychological functions develop through social interaction (1934). Building on these traditions, John Shotter (1993) stressed that meaning is created and transformed in dialogue rather than residing within individuals. Together, these perspectives underscore the view that knowledge and meaning emerge through historically and socially situated discursive practices.

Both phenomenology and constructionism have shaped psychotherapies that foreground lived experience and co-constructed meanings. Existential and humanistic therapies focus on the meanings individuals give to experience (Rogers, 1951), while dialogical and network-oriented postmodern therapy approaches emphasize not-knowing stances and meaning co-creation in relationships (Anderson & Goolishian, 1992; Andersen, 1987; Seikkula & Arnkil, 2006).

In addition to systems-theoretical and phenomenological traditions, another influential model in psychiatry often interpreted as holistic is George Engel's (1977) biopsychosocial model, originally proposed as an attempt to broaden the narrow and strongly reductionist biomedical model. In Engel's framework, human beings are understood as biopsychosocial wholes, such that symptoms or problems cannot be reduced to biological factors alone but emerge from interactions among biological, psychological, and social processes. One practical example is the vulnerability–stress model (Meehl, 1989; Zubin & Spring, 1977), which proposes that illness onset is more likely in individuals with genetic or other biological vulnerabilities, while environmental factors such as stress and adversity increase risk.

Despite its holistic ambition, the biopsychosocial model is in practice often reductionist, because it tends to decompose phenomena into separate biological, psychological, and social components (Bolton & Gillett, 2019). As a result, it may not adequately capture emergent properties of wholes and therefore frequently falls short of holism in its strict sense.

Compared with contemporary biopsychosocial approaches, a conception that comes definitionally closer to holism is the holistic conception of the human being developed by Finnish psychologist and philosopher Lauri Rauhala (1983). In Rauhala's holistic anthropology, the human being is a three-dimensional but unified whole in which bodily, consciousness, and situationality are inseparably intertwined (Backman, 2015; Koivumäki, 2022).

- Bodily refers to the fact that human beings are embodied organisms whose existence depends on biological and physiological structures and processes.
- Consciousness denotes the experiential, psychological, and spiritual dimension of human life—how persons feel, interpret, and understand themselves and their surroundings.
- Situationality describes human existence in relation to environment, time, culture, other people, and life circumstances.

In Rauhala's thought, situationality does not refer only to social factors or life events but to a multilayered being-in-relations with both concrete and ideal realities: time and place, culture and language, history, relationships, values, meaning systems, natural environments, and so forth (Koivumäki, 2022). Through their interaction, an individual's unique and continually changing life situation—and the meanings attached to it—are formed, with their favorability or unfavorability always context-dependent. Mental disorders, in this view, refer primarily to unfavorable modes of consciousness experience, since both the definition of such disorders and the evaluation of helping practices ultimately rest on changes in experience itself (Rauhala, 2002).

Although bodily and biological processes are necessary conditions for conscious experience in Rauhala's framework, experience cannot be reduced to biology alone, because its meaning is always constituted in relation to the other dimensions. Rauhala's anthropology is therefore holist in a strict sense: a human being is not the sum of biological, psychological, and social "parts," but a single, unique whole. Rather than reducing difficulties to disease-caused dysfunctions, attention shifts to the person's unique situation—the whole as such—which should be approached through meanings and context. This entails a move away from methodological monism toward an acknowledgment that different dimensions of existence require corresponding modes of inquiry and their integration.

Taken together, these traditions converge on a view of human beings as relational, situated, and dynamically constituted. Holism thus implies not merely the inclusion of multiple factors, but also a shift in how phenomena are conceptualized and studied: from isolated parts to relational wholes.

3.3 Holism and Its Challenges

3.3.1 *General Challenges*

Holistic frameworks are not without their difficulties. Although Jan Smuts' original formulation of holism has proven useful for describing some natural phenomena, it also contains internal tensions; only later developments in systems theory and its successors provided a more coherent and scientifically robust foundation for understanding how wholes function (Jörgenfelt & Partington, 2019). Yet, systems theory alone was insufficient to address core questions in the human sciences—particularly those concerning how experiences and meanings are constituted. These dimensions were further elaborated in phenomenological philosophy and, subsequently, in social constructionism, both of which come with their own challenges.

A common critique of the more extreme forms of social constructionism is the claim that all aspects of reality—including those described by the natural sciences—are nothing more than products of social interaction and language, and therefore not reducible to any underlying constituents. Under this view, attempts to describe reality become merely additional constructions that themselves reshape the very phenomena they purport to explain. Such a stance leads to radical relativism, where knowledge becomes entirely perspective dependent and competing interpretations cannot be evaluated within any shared framework (Boghossian, 2006).

Although our interpretations of reality are always mediated through socially shaped conceptual schemes—and although we cannot access a fully theory-independent "view from nowhere"—radical social constructionism and the relativism it entails are impractical, particularly in the organization of mental health services. This view risks collapsing all forms of distress into purely linguistic constructs, implicitly assuming that suffering will dissipate once the relevant descriptions are altered. While conceptual reframing can indeed be therapeutically helpful, there is no reason to assume this is universally or causally sufficient. It is also pragmatically necessary to assume that some form of mind- and language-independent reality exists: food does not disappear from the refrigerator when the door is closed and I stop thinking about it or naming it.

Even without embracing radical constructionism, holism itself may sometimes drift toward a form of relativism that emphasizes the uniqueness of wholes without engaging with causal relations among their components. In practice, this can occur when holism is invoked as a rhetorical strategy in situations where the object of study is complex or poorly understood—effectively using holism to sidestep the fact that scientific knowledge has not yet advanced enough to uncover the relevant multicausal or reciprocal mechanisms.

Importantly, the purpose of holism is not to preclude efforts to identify mechanisms operating within a whole. The possibility that a system may possess emergent properties, that its parts derive their significance from the whole, or that the whole can modulate the behavior of its parts does not entail radical relativism, nor does it require the abandonment of reductionist forms of explanation.

A key distinction here is between weak and strong emergence. Weak emergence refers to cases in which a phenomenon appears novel or complex but is, in principle, explainable if all components and their interactions were fully understood (Chalmers, 2006). Weak emergence represents a *practical* rather than a *principled* limitation and is thus compatible with reductionism.

Strong emergence, by contrast, posits that wholes possess properties or causal powers that cannot, even in principle, be derived from their lower-level constituents (Carruth & Miller, 2017). Here, macro-level properties are taken to be ontologically independent from basal physical processes, forming a distinct causal domain. This view approaches an ontological dualism, in which physical processes and irreducible emergent properties lack any transparent relation of derivation or dependence.

The central problem for such dualist or strongly emergent positions concerns causation. If one assumes, for example, a mental domain wholly independent of neural processes, it becomes difficult to explain how this domain could exert causal influence on the brain without violating the causal closure of the physical—that is, the principle that every physical event has a sufficient physical cause. To claim that a mental state causes a change in a neural state would require positing entirely new causal mechanisms, incompatible with established physical laws. Contemporary empirical understanding suggests that the brain is both a necessary and sufficient condition for mental states; no separate nonphysical causal "layer" need be assumed.

Dualism also raises the issue of causal overdetermination, where a single physical event (such as raising one's hand) would be caused simultaneously by a mental event and the corresponding neural configuration, with neither cause depending on the other (Kim, 2006). Although logically possible, such duplication is scientifically implausible and theoretically unnecessary. In nearly all relevant cases, phenomena resembling strong emergence can be explained without appealing to nonphysical causal powers (Bar-Yam, 2004; Chalmers, 2006).

As an alternative to both strong and weak emergence, contextual emergence has been proposed (Silberstein, 2017). On this view, lower-level processes are necessary conditions for higher-level phenomena, but higher-level properties do not fully reduce to them because they arise only from the organization of parts under specific contextual constraints. At the same time, higher-level structures can shape and constrain lower-level phenomena without requiring new physical laws or invoking a dualistic separation between material and nonmaterial domains.

For example, traffic culture does not arise solely from the microlevel characteristics of individual drivers but emerges from interactions across multiple levels: from how people collectively interpret and follow traffic rules and how they relate to one another on the road. The resulting macro-level pattern constrains and guides the behavior of individual drivers without requiring traffic culture to be treated as a separate force or autonomous entity. Rather, it functions as a shared normative framework that arises from people's behavior while simultaneously shaping it.

This perspective highlights that explaining or influencing the behavior of an individual driver requires explanatory models operating at different levels than those needed to understand or modify traffic culture as a whole. Individual behavior cannot be meaningfully understood in isolation from its context. What appears maladaptive or deviant in one environment may be entirely rational in another. For instance, a driver accustomed to the fast-paced and densely interactive traffic of a large city may appear reckless or erratic when driving in a quieter, rule-oriented environment, if their behavior is evaluated without regard to the norms and expectations shaping that context. The intelligibility of behavior therefore depends fundamentally on the situational whole to which it is related.

3.3.2 *The Position of* **Holistic Psychiatry**

In practice, both radical relativism and strong forms of emergence lead to interpretations that are difficult to apply within psychiatry and that generate unnecessary theoretical problems. To avoid these extremes, this book adopts the framework of contextual emergence together with an epistemological position grounded in critical realism. This combination, I argue, makes it possible to develop a pragmatic and clinically workable form of holism.

Critical realism begins from the assumption that reality exists, at least to some degree, independently of our conceptual schemes, observations, and social practices, and that it can be investigated using scientific methods (Bhaskar, 1975). This assumption permits reductive analysis when justified, without collapsing into a purely mechanistic model. At the same time, critical realism recognizes that scientific knowledge is inevitably contextual, socially constructed, and therefore provisional—always open to empirical revision.

Rather than restricting knowledge to what is immediately observable—as in radical positivism—critical realism relies on abductive reasoning, causal modeling, and probabilistic inference. Scientific inquiry thus aims to identify underlying mechanisms, including those that cannot be directly observed but can be inferred from their effects. Experiences, meanings, and other non-observable psychological phenomena are therefore understood as real and as legitimate objects of scientific study.

Because critical realism acknowledges the stratified nature of reality, it supports methodological pluralism: psychological and social phenomena do not need to be reduced to biological processes, nor studied using the same methods as neurophysiology. They can be examined at their own conceptual and methodological level. This makes holism scientifically viable: complex systems can be analyzed as multidimensional and interdependent without denying or oversimplifying the mechanisms that underlie them.

Critical realism also does not exclude reductionism. Scientific progress may reveal that some currently complex phenomena can indeed be reduced to more detailed causal chains. Yet, many of the phenomena labeled as mental disorders are so circular, relational, and context-dependent that it is neither realistic nor theoretically valuable to reduce them to a single latent causal factor (e.g., Kendler, 2016). For instance, bullying may produce anxiety, which alters behavior in ways that reinforce further bullying and mental challenges—a dynamic that does not require positing a hidden underlying "disease entity."

Because the potential feedback loops and relational processes are practically limitless, the aim of this book is not to present holism as a universal explanatory framework. Rather, its purpose is to provide a pragmatic theoretical foundation for organizing services and guiding clinical work in situations where reducing a person's difficulties to a single mechanism is neither realistic nor helpful.

3.4 A Holistic Understanding of Mental Disorders

According to a holistic framework, a phenomenon classified as a mental disorder cannot be understood by examining its constituent parts in isolation. In line with the basic premise of holism, such phenomena display emergent properties that are not found in any single component. Even if these properties could, in principle, be explained through the interaction of lower-level processes as scientific methods advance, the components—and the relations between them—acquire their meaning only within the larger configuration and context to which they belong. In other words, whether a particular psychosocial phenomenon is considered problematic is context-dependent. For this reason, interpreting a psychological or social difficulty as a mental disorder, and understanding the processes through which it develops, always requires situating it within a broader whole rather than reducing it solely to the individual and their attributes.

For example, from a holistic framework, depression is not simply the result of dysregulated neurotransmission, adverse life events, or maladaptive cognitive patterns, even though such mechanisms may contribute to the development of situation what is called "depression." Rather, *depression* names a configuration that arises when a person meets certain diagnostic criteria for a variety of reasons, seeks, or is directed toward care on that basis, and when professionals judge that the criteria are fulfilled. Once established, the diagnosis takes on additional meanings depending on the observer, the situation, the surrounding culture, and the symbolic weight attached to the category.

When a person states that they "have depression," the statement evokes different reactions depending on the listener's assumptions and previous experiences. One person may experience the diagnosis as stigmatizing and avoid disclosing it; another may experience relief and a sense of explanation. One clinician may conceptualize the condition as a disturbance in serotonergic functioning and view medication as essential; another may understand it as a meaning-laden configuration shaped by developmental and relational history and therefore emphasize psychotherapy. A family member may respond with support, while another may withdraw from the topic altogether. These varied reactions and interpretations feed back into the emerging configuration interpreted as depression. In this way, a self-reinforcing and partially unpredictable feedback process arises—an emergent psychosocial configuration described by holistic and complex-systems perspectives.

Because such an emergent configuration cannot be exhaustively reduced to a person's psychological or biological attributes, it is not methodologically meaningful to examine it solely through theories that describe those attributes. This does not imply a dualistic split between mind and body. Rather, from the standpoint of contextual emergence, bodily and psychological processes are *constitutive conditions* for the configuration interpreted as a mental disorder, yet the configuration is not fully intelligible in terms of those processes alone. Its characteristic features arise only in the context in which the components are organized and constrained.

Intuitively, it is already clear to most people that similar experiences or behaviors do not necessarily arise from the same social, psychological, or bodily processes—even within the same person. For instance, an experience labeled "anxiety" may be accompanied by different patterns of neural activity or bodily arousal in different situations even when the experience appears similar. Across individuals, the complexity further multiplies: there is no reason to assume that my experience of anxiety can be reduced to the same social, psychological, or biological processes as yours. Nor can we know with certainty whether we use the same word to refer to phenomenally similar experiences.

Personal developmental history, culture, and historical context shape the meanings we assign to our experiences. Consequently, "anxiety"—or any experiential term—is never fully commensurable across individuals. Even if we apply the same word to broadly similar sensations, our biological dispositions and lived histories shape what elicits the experience and how it manifests.

The brain and the body are continuously shaped by learning and adaptation. Every experience—including reading this sentence—leaves a trace in neural networks; otherwise, it could not be remembered. These changes are always individual because they arise from the unique interplay of previous experiences and environmental conditions.

Although it is intuitively obvious that thoughts, feelings, utterances, and interactions cannot be reduced to identical causal histories across people, this is often forgotten in psychiatric contexts due to the *reification* of diagnostic categories. When psychological and social reactions are reduced to diagnostic labels, they can begin to appear as if rooted in a discrete, biologically defined disorder or latent entity presumed to be the true cause of the difficulties. This lends an unwarranted sense of categorical difference to reactions that would otherwise be understood as dimensional—varying in intensity along continua familiar to all human beings.

Recognizing this helps clarify why experiences classified as mental disorders cannot be straightforwardly mapped onto singular causal mechanisms at the group level. Although the experiences can be severe and highly disruptive, they are not qualitatively distinct from universal human experiences and emotions such as stress reactions, fear, anger, sadness, or shame. Likewise, all people recognize difficulties in executive functioning, interpersonal interaction, and situations where thinking becomes muddled.

Most people also recognize that the classification of psychosocial experiences as problematic depends on cultural norms and contextual expectations. What counts as normal or abnormal is shaped by values, social demands, and shared ideals. For example, hearing voices may be interpreted positively as spiritual communication in one cultural setting and as a symptom of severe brain disease in another. Similarly, impulsivity or high energy may be valued in some social contexts while pathologized as attentional disorder in others.

It is also widely understood that many experiences classified as symptoms of mental disorder can be natural and coherent responses to challenging circumstances, even if their persistence may generate new difficulties. The boundaries of what constitutes a stressful life event, and what emotional responses arise, depend on developmental history and individual predispositions. For example, grief following the death of a loved one may lead one person to withdraw, which reinforces sadness and may eventually meet diagnostic criteria for depression. Another person, drawing on different relational experiences, may seek social contact and thus "recover" without prolonged distress. In both cases, neurotransmitters such as serotonin may be constitutive for emotional experience as they usually are, but the emergent configuration is not intelligible solely in terms of the serotonergic system.

Even when the situation is the same, human reactions differ markedly: one person interprets a social situation as threatening, another as promising. One becomes paralyzed in a crisis, another mobilized. Whether a response is adaptive depends entirely on the context, the expectations attached to it, and the meaning system in which it is situated.

These reactions, together with the meanings attached to them, also influence help-seeking and the type of support received. When a trait is culturally viewed as negative, it tends to evoke shame, which people sometimes attempt to alleviate by externalizing the difficulty through a medical diagnosis. This can bring relief by shifting responsibility away from the individual. In many Western cultures, this is facilitated by a tendency to explain behavior either biologically or morally: the biological model absolves responsibility, whereas the moral model attributes difficulties to personal failure. Both are reductive, as they locate the cause entirely within the individual.

A holistic perspective does not center on blame or responsibility because human difficulties arise from *reciprocally reinforcing, interactional processes* that cannot be reduced to a single person or disorder. This is consistent with the view that symptoms classified as mental disorders lie on a continuum of human experience—differing in degree rather than in kind. Anxiety, for instance, is familiar to everyone, even if the intensity, threshold, and triggers vary.

Anyone can also experience phenomena that might be interpreted as "psychotic" under sufficient stress or exhaustion. Imagine being alone in a remote cabin on a stormy night: branches hitting the window, mice rustling in the corners—many people begin to anticipate threats or perceive ambiguous sounds as meaningful. The more fatigued or stressed one is, the more intense such experiences become. Still, such experiences may have served important evolutive functioning: fear improves arousal and fight-or-flight reaction, increasing odds to survive. In other words, a tendency toward false-positive threat detection may be less costly than failing to respond to an actual threat.

Similarly, many people hold unusual beliefs or behavioral habits that deviate from cultural norms and may resist being questioned, which in certain contexts can be interpreted as psychotic-like. It is worth remembering that without the human mind's capacity for such departures from convention, creativity, spirituality, and scientific innovation would not be possible.

It is also reasonable to assume that people differ biologically—based on temperament, genetics, and development—in how intensely they feel emotions, process information, and respond to situations. These differences do not imply genetic predispositions to discrete disorders but rather variation along dimensions of reactivity that can become vulnerabilities under certain conditions. Combined with the validity problems of psychiatric diagnoses, this helps explain why large-scale genetic studies have not produced clear biomarkers for mental disorders: human traits are highly polygenic, pleiotropic, and environmentally contingent (e.g., Kendler, 2015; Torrey, 2024).

3.4.1 A Holistic Ontology of Mental Disorders

Building on the premises outlined above, it is possible to construct a holistic ontology of what so-called mental disorders consist of and how a holistic framework can be integrated with the prevailing reductionist vulnerability–stress model. Within a holistic framework, vulnerability is not conceptualized as an internal, person-bound characteristic that inevitably leads to a diagnosable disorder. Rather, vulnerability is understood as a susceptibility to certain types of *situations*: situations in which the individual or their close community experiences the conditions as sufficiently adverse for the criteria of help-seeking to be met.

Thus, a disorder does not reside within the individual but in the relationship and interaction between the person and their environment—that is, in the situation at hand. At the same time, it is assumed that individuals vary in their biological and psychological dispositions, which influence the kinds of situations that become adverse for them.

Accordingly, a phenomenon classified as a mental disorder does not exist inside the individual but in the relation between basic dispositions, the environment, and the cultural meaning structures that, under certain conditions, form an unfavorable overall situation from someone's perspective. Such a situation may be brief or long-lasting, fluctuate in intensity, or recur repeatedly. Importantly, an unfavorable overall situation is not a stable property but a temporally evolving relation between personal dispositions, environmental conditions, and cultural meanings.

Figure 3.1 illustrates how biological predispositions, early relational experiences, and later life events interact continuously with micro- and macro-level social factors. The possible variations formed by these interactions are effectively limitless, leading always to some degree of individual specificity. For this reason, such situations can never be fully reduced to discrete components. To avoid relativism, however, several assumptions about linear causal pathways can still be made.

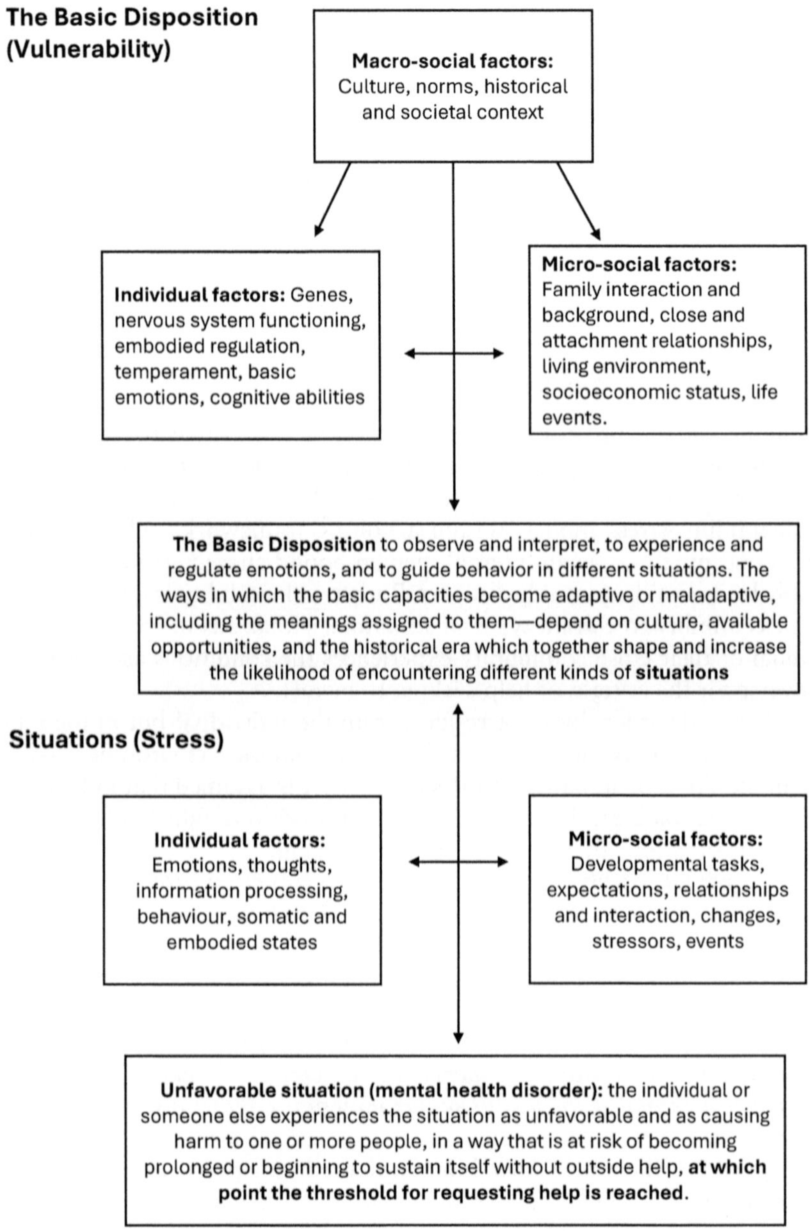

Figure 3.1 From basic dispositions to unfavorable situations: a contextual and developmental framework.

First, genetic factors, prenatal conditions, and early childhood environments shape a person's physiological, psychological, and social dispositions. These include, for example, the intensity of emotional reactions in novel situations, baseline arousal and energy, and basic perceptual and cognitive capacities. Early experiences—particularly those within early attachment relationships—further shape these dispositions. These dispositions, in interaction with features of the immediate environment, influence how the individual acts in their surroundings and how the environment responds: how emotions are expressed and regulated, what kinds of interaction patterns develop, which situations evoke particular reactions, and what the consequences of those reactions are.

Cultural and societal factors determine which reactions are deemed normal or deviant, how they are responded to, and what kinds of life experiences are likely in a given environment. Macro-level contextual structures of emergent systems shape microlevel processes through the meanings, possibilities, and constraints they create for individuals and their close relations. Macro-level factors also influence biological development through available nutrition and living conditions, and they indirectly affect genetic outcomes by shaping societal expectations and boundaries related to forming relationships and reproducing. An individual's dispositions, in turn, influence the extent to which they can meet and operate under these macro-level boundaries and how the environment responds to them.

The reciprocal interaction of biological factors, early conditions, and later experiences forms what is here called *basic disposition*: the set of embodied, psychological, and relational capacities through which the person perceives their environment, interprets events, experiences, and regulates emotions, and guides action in various situations. Basic disposition influences how life events and transitions are experienced, while those experiences influence the kinds of situations the person later encounters. Situations and how one copes with them further shape disposition—increasing or decreasing the likelihood of certain future situations and outcomes.

Consider the following example. Jonathan's mother was genetically prone to heightened emotional reactivity and coped by drinking alcohol, including during pregnancy. Both the prenatal alcohol exposure and the genetic vulnerability contributed to Jonathan being an irritable infant who reacted intensely to novelty. Caring for him evoked difficult emotions in his mother, making daily care overwhelming. A child-protection report was filed, which caused her deep shame because she felt she had failed to meet cultural ideals of motherhood. She coped by drinking again, was reported to authorities, and eventually Jonathan was placed in out-of-home care.

As Jonathan grew older, emotional regulation difficulties persisted. At school, he remained socially capable, even dominant, becoming a central figure in his peer group. Yet, his basic disposition included a heightened sensitivity to anxiety and a tendency to respond to novelty with aggression. This made it less likely for him to succeed academically and more likely for him to gradually withdraw from education and struggle with anxiety in social contexts.

Jonathan's adverse situation may be conceptualized in terms of mental or neurodevelopmental disorders—such as social anxiety disorder, personality pathology, or attention deficit hyperactivity disorder—that emerge through life events and the interplay of psychological, social, and biological mechanisms. Yet, the adverse situation cannot be explained *by* these components alone, nor can the components be fully understood outside the situation. In a different context, both the components and the overall situation could be interpreted very differently. In a prehistoric environment, for instance, dominant and aggressive responses might have increased his status within the group rather than leading to marginalization.

Although culture and context strongly shape what is defined as a problem or disorder, certain phenomena are likely to lead to unfavorable situations across contexts. These include, for example, severe somatic illnesses that disrupt cellular functioning, substance-related harms, and situations in which an individual's embodied reactions and interpretations of reality become so overwhelming that they no longer align with shared social reality. Similarly, states of overwhelming distress in which death comes to be perceived as the only solution almost always represent highly unfavorable and potentially dangerous situations, regardless of cultural context.

At the same time, many traits and behaviors are defined as adverse only within specific historical and cultural contexts. Difficulties associated with individualistic value systems and digitally mediated environments illustrate this contextual dependency. Characteristics such as impulsivity or shyness are more likely to become challenging under conditions of constant self-monitoring, heightened performance expectations, perpetual availability, hyperstimulation, accelerated information flows, and emerging modes of social interaction. These pressures arise from contemporary technological and societal structures rather than from universal vulnerabilities that directly and across contexts threaten basic survival and thus increase the risk of unfavorable situations.

Because certain characteristics and experiences are more likely to predict unfavorable situations within specific historical timeframes—and because unfavorable situations themselves increase the risk of future challenges—phenomena labeled as mental disorders often cluster and appear self-reinforcing. This dynamic is also illustrated by network models of psychopathology (Borsboom, 2017), in which symptoms are conceptualized as mutually interacting nodes that amplify one another without requiring the assumption of an underlying latent disease to which the problems could be reduced. One could theoretically imagine a model that assigns each individual-context configuration a set of probabilities: which pathways lead to particular dispositions, and which dispositions increase susceptibility to specific unfavorable situations.

In practice, however, the number of possible interactions and feedback loops is so vast—and the interactions so multidirectional—that mapping all causal chains is neither feasible nor meaningful from a holistic standpoint. The focus therefore shifts away from locating single causes or reducing problems to discrete components and toward examining the situation itself: the overall configuration in which basic dispositions, early and later relationships, and cultural and societal meaning structures converge at a particular moment in a way that causes harm, restricts agency, and creates a need for support.

Because unfavorable situations classified as mental disorders are inherently unique, there is no single medical solution that is effective for everyone. Consequently, support must be pluralistic, flexible, and responsive to people's immediate and evolving circumstances. Rather than treating presumed psychopathology through predetermined methods, the emphasis shifts toward providing adaptable assistance in unfavorable situations. Central to this approach is the question of meaning: what significance is attributed to a person's experiences, traits, or behaviors? If these do not cause distress or concern to the individual or others, or if people feel able to cope using their own resources or other forms of support, there is no "psychiatric" problem to be addressed. From a holistic perspective, the primary goal of care becomes preserving the agency of individuals and their social networks, enabling them to resolve difficulties themselves and to reduce the risk of future situations in which their own resources may no longer be sufficient.

3.5 The Implications of Holism for Support Practice

A shift from a reductionist to a more holistic framework inevitably affects how mental health care is conceptualized and delivered. Whereas a reductionist approach aims for precise definitions and seeks to break down ambiguous, context-dependent psychosocial difficulties into manageable components to be treated according to predetermined guidelines, a holistic framework approaches such difficulties situationally and case by case, from the perspective of the person's lived experience. Support is thus organized around the individual's unique—and continually changing—lived situation, such that it does not focus solely on the individual and their presumed psychopathology, but more concretely on the challenges of everyday life, the meanings attributed to them, and, when needed, the broader social environment.

First, a holistic framework helps explain why research repeatedly shows that the most influential factors in mental health care are often generic, nonspecific, and common across therapies, rather than the disorder-specific techniques prescribed for particular diagnoses. Psychotherapy, for example, cannot be reduced to a set of techniques, because it is always enacted within a reciprocal interaction in which therapist and client continuously respond to one another. It is therefore unsurprising that the quality of the therapeutic relationship and the therapist's ability to adapt flexibly to the client's needs are among the strongest predictors of favorable outcomes (Wampold, 2015).

Intuitively, most people also recognize that, regardless of the underlying causes of their difficulties, they benefit from being met promptly, understood, and supported in ways that are flexibly adjusted to their immediate situation and needs. What matters most is the experience that something genuinely helps or alleviates distress.

This same non-specificity applies to psychotropic medications. Although their mechanisms of action can be more precisely reduced to neural processes, their "symptom"-relieving effects tend to occur largely irrespective of the original causes of the difficulties. Anxiolytics usually reduce arousal; antidepressants often dampen or modulate affective experience; neuroleptics diminish intense internal stimuli and may induce apathy; hypnotics facilitate sleep; and stimulants enhance alertness, motivation, and concentration for many people, regardless of whether they meet criteria for a specific diagnosis or what the original explanation for their difficulties might be. Consequently, psychotropic medications are used flexibly across diagnostic categories and for a wide range of purposes—pain management, pre-procedural sedation, mitigation of agitation or aggression, and similar uses. Even though certain "symptoms" may suggest which medication could be helpful, actual effects can only be assessed in practice, as individual dispositions and situational factors substantially shape medication response.

Because these generic and nonspecific factors are often the main contributors to effectiveness of care, it would be reasonable for mental health systems to focus on optimizing these factors rather than investing vast resources in artificially reducing psychosocial difficulties into narrow diagnostic categories and targeting treatment in ways that risk overlooking people's real-life needs.

One way to illustrate this is through a thought experiment: imagine that the concept of "mind"—and thus "mental disorders"—did not exist, yet people's distress and need for help remained real. Some might resort to a moral model, blaming individuals for their difficulties and reducing the problem to choices, willpower, or other individual level and thus reductionistic explanations. Most, however, would gravitate toward a more holistic line of inquiry: *what does this person actually need? What are their difficulties connected to? How do they experience their situation? And what concrete forms of support could help?* This line of thinking more closely resembles a holistic framework.

The history of psychiatry includes several practices that are holistic in this sense. Phenomenology has played a substantial role in psychiatry, both in understanding subjectively experienced suffering and in developing therapeutic approaches that emphasize the person's lived experience. Certain therapeutic traditions—such as humanistic (Miller & Rollnick, 2024; Rogers, 1951), existential (Laing, 1965), Gestalt (Perls et al., 1951), and integrative therapies (Norcross & Goldfried, 2019; Wampold, 2015)—also aim for holistic understanding and the flexible application of methods based on changing person's needs. Family therapy (Sexton & Lebow, 2016), originally grounded in systems theory, and later network-oriented therapies (Andersen, 1991; Anderson & Goolishian, 1992) as well as various therapeutic community models (Jones, 1963), are holistic insofar as they focus on treating broader relational and support systems rather than the isolated individual. Recovery-oriented (Anthony, 2000) and participatory approaches (Jones et al., 2021) likewise emphasize a more comprehensive understanding of human challenges and possibilities for coping by highlighting change, strengths, social participation, and the central role of lived experience, empowerment, and meaningful involvement in decision-making and knowledge production.

In practice, however, many approaches intended to be holistic are implemented under the constraints of a reductionist framework and are forced to adapt accordingly—often in ways that reintroduce the very compartmentalization they seek to overcome. A difficulty may be reinterpreted as residing not in the individual but in the family system, leading to referral to family therapy. Similarly, if a person is perceived as needing social services due to financial hardship, the intervention easily becomes narrowly focused on that single domain rather than understanding and addressing the person's lived experience and difficulties holistically within their social reality. Even recovery-oriented practice is often interpreted through a reductionist lens, where a person can "recover" or live a fulfilling life *despite* "mental illness", thereby subtly reinforcing the idea that difficulties still ultimately stem from individual psychopathology.

Despite these challenges, recent efforts have sought to develop more comprehensive ways of understanding "psychopathology," and several authors have proposed new approaches and organizational strategies aimed at acknowledging people's needs more holistically (e.g., Rose, 2025; van Os et al., 2019). Although the clinical applicability of these approaches—and the practical solutions they imply—remains limited, some concrete proposals have been made for designing a more holistic mental healthcare system.

One such contribution is the Power Threat Meaning Framework (Johnstone & Boyle, 2018), which seeks to reconceptualize psychological distress as an understandable response to lived experiences and social contexts rather than as an expression of underlying pathology. Basically, the framework replaces diagnostic categorization with a formulation-based approach that organizes assessment around questions of power, perceived threat, personal meaning, and survival responses, thereby offering an alternative way to guide clinical understanding, collaboration, and intervention without assuming disorder-specific causal mechanisms.

Another concrete illustration of a more holistic organization of care is found in the problem-oriented medical records (POMR) approach, further developed in mental health care through the Problem–Resources–Goals Oriented (PRoGO) framework, proposed as an alternative to contemporary diagnosis- and specialty-driven models of medicine, in which assessment and treatment are fragmented across medical specialties, each responsible for its own narrowly defined domain. Instead of organizing treatment and resources according to diagnostic categories and predefined care pathways, POMR/PRoGO structures care around each person's actual needs, resources, and personal goals (Leucht et al., 2025). Similar proposals elsewhere likewise call for a shift away from reductionist, top-down, and diagnosis-led service structures toward bottom-up, process-oriented systems that adapt to individual needs in case-by-case manner rather than the reverse (e.g., Maj et al., 2020; 2021; van Os et al., 2019).

A related early example is *need-adapted treatment* for psychosis, where planning and decision-making occurred in joint meetings rather than being determined by diagnostic labels or predefined criteria (Alanen, 2009). This work later informed the development of the Open Dialogue approach in Finnish Western Lapland—a system-level reorganization that de-emphasized specialized units and instead concentrated resources on arranging immediate dialogical meetings (Bergström et al., 2025). From the outset, meetings included everyone relevant to the situation. Practitioners adopted a not-knowing stance and engaged in dialogical processes aimed at constructing a shared meaning-making that could guide flexible planning and allocation of resources.

Open Dialogue has been highlighted by WHO (2021) as an example of a holistic service model and has been implemented or piloted in several countries (Pocobello et al., 2023). Yet, its transferability has proven challenging, particularly where surrounding service systems remain organized according to reductionist principles (Bergström et al., 2025). Additionally, the demands of evidence-based medicine have required that approaches such as Open Dialogue be operationalized and validated using reductionist research designs. This creates a risk that originally holistic models become reified as one more predefined intervention to be applied whenever certain criteria are met, thereby obscuring their underlying principles.

At the same time, the core idea of dialogical practice—reciprocal engagement with the perspectives of others and the co-creation of meaning and understanding through expanding, rather than closing, the conversation—is not dependent on any single method (Arnkil, 2019; Bergström et al., 2025; Seikkula, 2025). One path toward a genuinely case-based, perspective-sensitive, and bottom-up care process is the reorganization of services so that, especially at critical junctures, the likelihood of high-quality dialogical encounters is maximized. Such encounters strengthen alliances, enhance trust, and support the formation of a shared understanding of the current situation. In this context, shared understanding does not imply consensus or the reduction of differences; rather, it refers to a polyphonic understanding in which multiple perspectives can coexist and inform further action. In this way, the common factors known to drive therapeutic effectiveness can be optimized at the system level, allowing care to be tailored on a case-by-case basis.

In the holistic system described in this book, the fundamental unit of care is dialogical space (Arnkil, 2019): a relational setting in which the person, their close network, and practitioners can meet reciprocally and polyphonically. Dialogue refers to interaction in which each participant can articulate their experiences and perspectives openly, and where active listening is as central as speaking. Thus, dialogue does not simply refer to a friendly or everyday conversation, but to a relational process in which participants orient to one another's utterances and allow different perspectives to remain present without prematurely resolving them. Therefore, dialogue does not aim for a single correct formulation or for prematurely closing the conversation; instead, themes remain open, and participants orient toward one another's utterances. This enables the emergence of new shared meanings. Its opposite is monologue, where one voice dominates and exerts one-way influence—typically from an expert position.

A dialogical space allows the situation to be viewed simultaneously from multiple vantage points and facilitates solutions grounded in the person's everyday life and social networks. In mental health system—and particularly within a reductionist framework—such a space does not arise accidentally. Its conditions must be actively supported by organizing the environment, time, participants, and interaction structure in ways that increase the likelihood of genuine dialogue and, consequently, shared understanding. Thus, dialogical space is not an abstract ideal or a communication technique, but a space that is actively *co-generated* in concrete situations.

Practically, this means that all key people are brought together promptly in a safe environment, that there is ample room for different perspectives, and that a shared understanding can form the basis for subsequent steps. To support this, practitioners must adopt a stance of curiosity and avoid premature certainty, pathologizing, and reductive language or interpretations that define the situation unilaterally.

The preconditions for dialogical space are presented in Figure 3.2 (see also Arnkil, 2019). In the holistic system outlined here, service reorganization aims to increase the likelihood that these conditions are met at the beginning of support process and during critical transitions.

The underlying assumption is that the emergence of a dialogical space can itself alleviate situations what is currently understood or operationalized as a mental disorder. This assumption rests on the observation that such situations are often maintained by the meanings attached to experiences, by relational patterns, and by the accumulation of concerns. Moreover, dialogical space fosters shared understanding and provides an integrated picture that can guide flexible tailoring of more reductionist interventions—whether these involve activating personal and social resources or drawing on specific medical or psychosocial tools. Because dialogical work builds strong alliances, it aligns with the common therapeutic factors known to be central to effective psychotherapy and thus can be expected to have intrinsic therapeutic value.

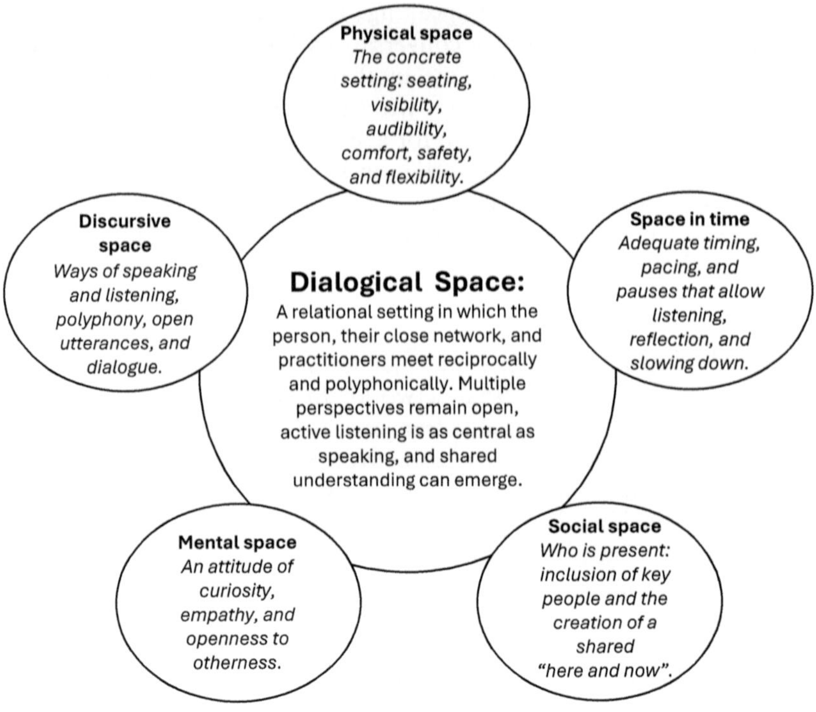

Figure 3.2 Dialogical space.

When situations are severe, prolonged, or recurrent, this dialogical foundation can be complemented by more traditional, reductionist strategies—such as medication or other targeted interventions—aimed at influencing the person's distress, context, and/or basic dispositions more directly. What changes, however, is the sequence: the process begins with understanding and addressing the overall situation, and reductionist assessments or interventions are employed only when needed. Through dialogical space, support can progress stepwise to more specific interventions grounded in shared understanding. In this sense, the holistic system resembles a staged approach (e.g., McGorry et al., 2007), in which severity guides the level of intervention, moving from lighter to more intensive options.

Figure 3.3 illustrates how a holistic dialogical space functions as the primary and initial response to an unfavorable situation. Within the dialogical space, shared reflection and the optimization of common therapeutic factors support the development of a shared understanding of the situation, its dynamics, and the person's needs. In many cases, this dialogical process alone is sufficient to change the situational configuration and promote improvement, without the need for additional interventions.

When the situation is severe, prolonged, or recurrent, the shared understanding developed within the dialogical space provides the basis for introducing additional, need-based interventions. These interventions may be targeted at different levels of the situation—including individual factors (e.g., emotions, cognition, behavior, and somatic health) and micro-social factors (e.g., relationships, developmental demands, and social stressors). At this stage, more reductionistic approaches (such as symptom-focused, psychological, or biological interventions) can be applied selectively and purposefully, guided by the situational understanding rather than replacing it.

The different line types in the figure illustrate the underlying logic of care trajectories. Solid arrows indicate situations that improve within the dialogical space through shared understanding and relational support. Dotted arrows represent the introduction of time-limited, need-based interventions when additional support is required to stabilize or improve the situation. Dash-dotted arrows indicate situations that become long-lasting or recurrent, where longer-term, structured support is arranged in line with the person's needs, context, and evolving situational dynamics.

Across all trajectories, the dialogical space remains the integrative core, ensuring that reductionistic interventions at different levels are coordinated within a holistic, situational framework rather than applied as isolated or default responses.

The primary goal of a holistic system is therefore to activate real-life networks, strengthen agency, and concentrate resources on encounters that illuminate and alleviate the situation as a whole. Dialogical space can be revisited flexibly whenever the process stagnates or reaches a turning point.

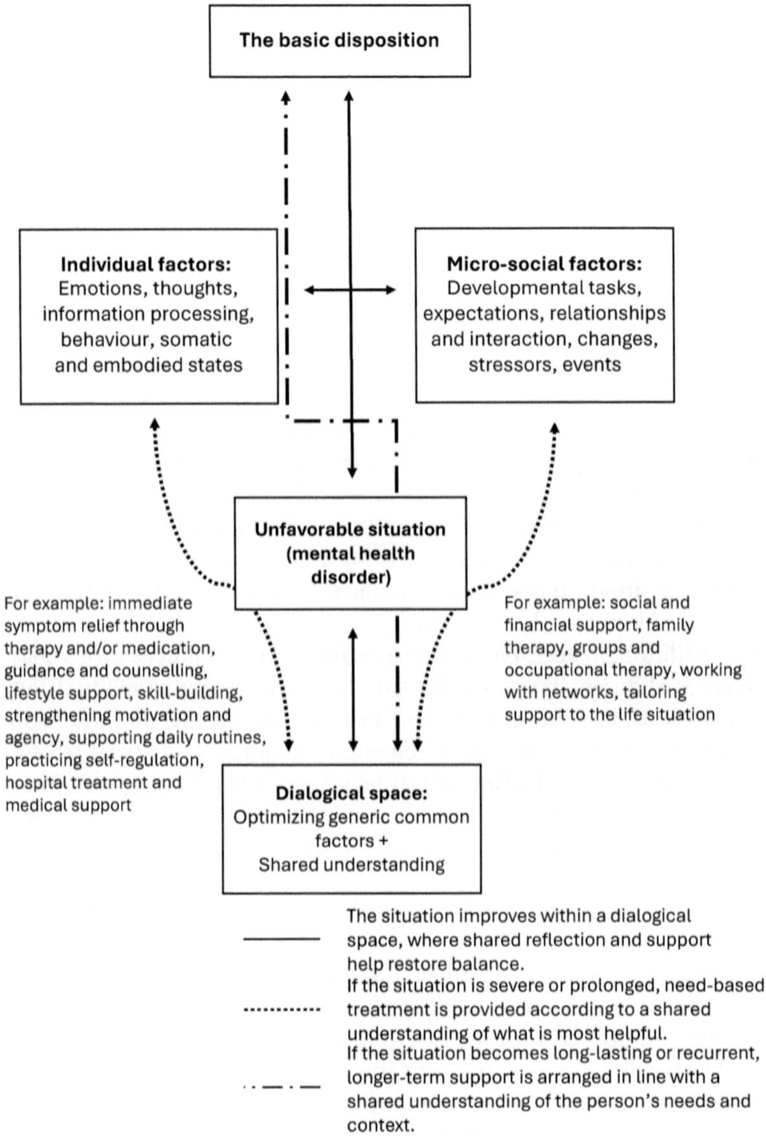

Figure 3.3 Dialogical space as the integrative core of a holistic care process.

3.6 Summary of the Holistic Framework

Within a holistic framework, whole situations classified as mental disorders are examined as they present themselves, without immediate need to reduce them to isolated components or to treat them as signs of an underlying disease entity. The approach is guided by the basic premise of holism: the whole is more than the sum of its parts. Interactions across different levels generate emergent phenomena that cannot be understood by analyzing their components in isolation.

A situation interpreted as a mental disorder is, in this view, an emergent, multilayered, and relational process arising from ongoing interactions between the biological organism, the meaning-making individual, and the social environment. This framework aligns with models such as the 4E/5E approach (Rose, 2025), complexity theory in psychopathology (Olthof et al., 2023), and the network model (Borsboom, 2017), all of which posit that biological, psychological, and social processes can self-organize into observable symptom configurations without requiring a single latent variable—such as a disease—to explain the pattern.

The holistic perspective is also compatible with the growing dimensional understanding of mental phenomena. From this standpoint, symptoms associated with mental disorders are not viewed as categorical indicators of disease but as variations along continua of normal human experience. Where a particular experience is located along this continuum—and whether it becomes defined as a disorder—depends on the degree of harm it produces, which is itself shaped by the person's environment and context.

Accordingly, what is called a mental disorder is understood primarily as an unfavorable situation in which one or more people are concerned about an individual's ability to cope. "Situation" here refers not merely to life conditions or discrete events but also to the overall configuration in which basic dispositions, social relationships, cultural meanings, and environmental expectations intertwine to produce harm. For this reason, a holistic framework does not begin by decomposing phenomena into separate causal factors to be matched with prespecified, top-down interventions. Instead, it proceeds on the principle of need-adapted, case- and context-specific support, where the form of help emerges from the person's unique and evolving circumstances—essentially from the bottom up.

The holistic framework also clarifies phenomena that appear puzzling from a reductionist standpoint. For example, it provides an alternative explanation for the correlations observed among mental disorders, which have led to theories of a general psychopathology factor (the latent *p*-factor) (Caspi et al., 2014). Instead of positing a hidden causal entity, a contextual and emergent model predicts that certain sets of basic dispositions together with certain cultural and relational contexts increase the likelihood of situations diagnosable as mental disorders.

Similarly, the long-standing finding that major psychotherapy modalities produce comparable outcomes becomes less surprising when therapy is understood as a complex, reciprocal interaction. In such processes, the quality of the therapeutic alliance, the experience of being helped, and expectations of benefit often outweigh technique-specific effects. Likewise, psychotropic medications are known to have broad, nonspecific influences on neural processes and behavior, even when no clear neurobiological abnormality is identifiable. From a holistic viewpoint, these general symptom-relieving effects may be meaningful regardless of whether they target specific underlying mechanisms. This helps explain why medications can be effective across diagnostic categories and why chemically distinct drugs may produce similar outcomes.

The aim of the holistic framework is therefore to optimize context-sensitive and nonspecific mechanisms of change, while acknowledging that people benefit from very different forms of support, as their situations are always unique in important respects. Because phenomena interpreted as mental disorders are, by definition, experiential and their etiologies often poorly understood, support should focus primarily on alleviating distress and addressing concerns rather than on establishing definitive causal explanations. Once distress has subsided and people's sense of agency has been sufficiently restored for the situation to feel manageable, it is no longer necessary to conceptualize the situation as a disorder requiring a mental health system response.

Accordingly, this book adopts the term *helping in unfavorable situations* rather than treatment or care. While psychiatric services have traditionally been divided into medical interventions on the one hand and broader mental health services on the other, the holistic framework presented here uses the term *mental health system* to cover the full range of phenomena that, in contemporary societies, are directed toward any form of mental health–related support. This does not exclude medical assessment or intervention when these are needed. Rather, it enables medical expertise to be integrated flexibly alongside psychological, social, relational, and community-based forms of support, according to the demands of each situation.

For this reason, the central task of a holistic system is to establish the most constructive possible relational and collaborative environment between those seeking help and those involved in providing it. Such relationships form the basis for flexibly tailoring support processes and for safely exploring what may be effective in a given context. This kind of collaboration emerges within dialogical space, which, in a more holistic system, can be understood not merely as a method but also as the primary goal of support work itself.

References

Alanen, Y. O. (2009). Towards a more humanistic psychiatry: Development of need-adapted treatment of schizophrenia group psychoses. *Psychosis, 1*(2), 156–166. https://doi.org/10.1080/17522430902795667

Alexander, C. (2025). What is 4E cognitive science? *Phenomenology and the Cognitive Sciences*. Advance online publication. https://doi.org/10.1007/s11097-025-10055-w

Andersen, T. (1987). The reflecting team: Dialogue and meta-dialogue in clinical work. *Family Process, 26*(4), 415–428. https://doi.org/10.1111/j.1545-5300.1987.00415.x

Anderson, H., & Goolishian, H. (1992). The client is the expert: A not-knowing approach to therapy. In S. McNamee & K. J. Gergen (Eds.), *Therapy as social construction* (pp. 25–39). Sage Publications, Inc.

Anthony, W. A. (2000). A recovery-oriented service system: Setting some system level standards. *Psychiatric Rehabilitation Journal, 24*(2), 159–168. https://doi.org/10.1037/h0095104

Arnkil, T. E. (2019). Co-generating dialogical spaces: Challenges for open and anticipation dialogues and dialogical practices in general. *International Journal of Collaborative-Dialogic Practices, 9*(1), 37–50.

Backman, J. (2015). Situationaalinen säätöpiiri: Rauhalan filosofinen kädenjälki. In V. Tökkäri (Ed.), *Kokemuksen tutkimus V : Lauri Rauhala 100 vuotta* (pp. 73–102). Lapin yliopistokustannus. https://urn.fi/URN:ISBN:978-952-310-969-8

Bakhtin, M. (1984). *Problems of Dostoevsky's poetics* (Vol. 8). Manchester University Press.

Ballout, S. (2025). Trauma, mental health workforce shortages, and health equity: A crisis in public health. *International Journal of Environmental Research and Public Health*, 22(4), 620. https://doi.org/10.3390/ijerph22040620

Bar-Yam, Y. (2004). A mathematical theory of strong emergence using multiscale variety. *Complexity, 9*(6), 15–24.

Bateson, G. (1967). Cybernetic explanation. *American Behavioral Scientist, 10*(8), 29–32. https://doi.org/10.1177/000276420100808

Berger, P. L., & Luckmann, T. (1966). *The social construction of reality*. Penguin.

Bergström, T., Kurtti, M., Duthie, A., Valtanen, K., & Seikkula, J. (2025). Open dialogue. In O. Smoliak, E. Tseliou, T. Strong, S. Bava, & P. Muntigl (Eds.), *The Routledge international handbook of postmodern therapies* (pp. 174–185). Routledge. https://doi.org/10.4324/9781003376231-14

Bhaskar, R. (1975). *A realist theory of science*. Verso.

Boghossian, P. (2006). *Fear of knowledge: Against relativism and constructivism*. Oxford University Press.

Bolton, D. & Gillett, G. (2019). *The biopsychosocial model of health and disease: New philosophical and scientific developments*. Palgrave Macmillan.

Borsboom, D. (2017). A network theory of mental disorders. *World Psychiatry : Official Journal of the World Psychiatric Association (WPA)*, *16*(1), 5–13. https://doi.org/10.1002/wps.20375

Bracken, P., & Thomas, P. (2001). Postpsychiatry: A new direction for mental health. *British Medical Journal, 322*, 724–727.

Bracken, P., & Thomas, P. (2005). *Postpsychiatry: Mental health in a postmodern world*. Oxford University Press.

Bracken, P., Thomas, P., Timimi, S., Asen, E., Behr, G., Beuster, C., Bhunnoo, S., Browne, I., Chhina, N., Double, D., Downer, S., Evans, C., Fernando, S., Garland, M. R., Hopkins, W., Huws, R., Johnson, B., Martindale, B., Middleton, H., Moldavsky, D., ... & Yeomans, D. (2012). Psychiatry beyond the current paradigm. *The British Journal of Psychiatry: The Journal of Mental Science, 201*(6), 430–434. https://doi.org/10.1192/bjp.bp.112.109447

Byrne, D., & Callaghan, G. (2023). *Complexity theory and the social sciences: The state of the art*. Routledge.

Capra, F. (1996). *The web of life: A new scientific understanding of living systems*. Anchor Books.

Carruth, A. D., & Miller, J. T. M. (2017). Strong emergence. *Philosophica, 91*, 5–13.

Caspi, A., Houts, R. M., Belsky, D. W., Goldman-Mellor, S. J., Harrington, H., Israel, S., Meier, M. H., Ramrakha, S., Shalev, I., Poulton, R., & Moffitt, T. E. (2014). The p factor: One general psychopathology factor in the structure of psychiatric disorders?. *Clinical Psychological Science : A Journal of the Association for Psychological Science*, 2(2), 119–137. https://doi.org/10.1177/2167702613497473

Chalmers, D. J. (2006). Strong and weak emergence. In P. Clayton & P. Davies (Eds.), *The re-emergence of emergence: The emergentist hypothesis from science to religion* (pp. xx–xx). Oxford University Press.

Engel, G.L. (1977). The need for a new medical model: A challenge for biomedicine. *Science, 196*(4286), 129–136.

Foucault, M. (1965). *Madness and civilization: A history of insanity in the age of reason* (R. Howard, Trans.). Random House.

Foucault, M. (1972). *The archaeology of knowledge* (A. Sheridan, Trans.). Pantheon Books.

Gallagher, S. (2014). Phenomenology and embodied cognition. In L. Shapiro (Ed.), *The Routledge handbook of embodied cognition* (pp. 9–17). Routledge.

Gill, N., Drew, N., Rodrigues, M., Muhsen, H., Morales Cano, G., Savage, M., Pathare, S., Allan, J., Galderisi, S., Javed, A., Herrman, H., & Funk, M. (2024). Bringing together the World Health Organization's QualityRights initiative and the World Psychiatric Association's programme on implementing alternatives to coercion in mental healthcare: A common goal for action. *BJPsych Open*, *10*(1), e23. https://doi.org/10.1192/bjo.2023.622

Ginapp, C. M., Macdonald-Gagnon, G., Angarita, G. A., Bold, K. W., & Potenza, M. N. (2022). The lived experiences of adults with attention-deficit/hyperactivity disorder: A rapid review of qualitative evidence. *Frontiers in Psychiatry, 13*, 949321. https://doi.org/10.3389/fpsyt.2022.949321

Guerrero, Z., Kågström, A., Aliev, A., Tomášková, H., Yon, Y., Lazeri, L., Reinap, M., Redlich, C., Tijerino Inestroza, A. M., Maurer, J., & Winkler, P. (2024). Mental health plans and policies across the WHO European region. *Global mental health (Cambridge, England)*, *11*, e110. https://doi.org/10.1017/gmh.2024.88

Hansen, H., Gutierrez, K. J., & Garcia, S. (2023). Rethinking psychiatry: Solutions for a sociogenic crisis. *Daedalus, 152*(4), 75–91. https://doi.org/10.1162/daed_a_02032

Heidegger, M. (1927/2010). *Being and time* (J. Stambaugh, Trans.). State University of New York Press.

Holland, J. H. (1992). Complex adaptive systems. *Daedalus, 121*(1), 17–30.

Husserl, E. (1913/2012). *Ideas: General introduction to pure phenomenology* (W. R. B. Gibson, Trans.). Routledge.

Husserl, E. (1936/1970). *The crisis of European sciences and transcendental phenomenology* (D. Carr, Trans.). Northwestern University Press.

Jaspers, K. (1968). The phenomenological approach in psychopathology. *The British Journal of Psychiatry, 114*(516), 1313–1323. https://doi.org/10.1192/bjp.114.516.1313

Johnstone, L. & Boyle, M. with Cromby, J., Dillon, J., Harper, D., Kinderman, P., Longden, E., Pilgrim, D. & Read, J. (2018). *The power threat meaning framework: Towards the identification of patterns in emotional distress, unusual experiences and troubled or troubling behaviour, as an alternative to functional psychiatric diagnosis.* British Psychological Society.

Jones, M. (1963). The therapeutic community. In A. Deutsch & H. Fishman (Eds.), *The encyclopedia of mental health* (Vol. 6, pp. 1992–1999). Franklin Watts.

Jones, N., Atterbury, K., Byrne, L., Carras, M., Brown, M., & Phalen, P. (2021). Lived experience, research leadership, and the transformation of mental health services: Building a researcher pipeline. *Psychiatric Services (Washington, D.C.), 72*(5), 591–593. https://doi.org/10.1176/appi.ps.202000468

Jörgenfelt, C., & Partington, H. (2019). A critical analysis of J. C. Smuts' theory of holism. *European Journal of Integrative Medicine, 31*, 100980. https://doi.org/10.1016/j.eujim.2019.100980

Kendler, K. S. (2016). The nature of psychiatric disorders. *World Psychiatry: Official Journal of the World Psychiatric Association (WPA), 15*(1), 5–12. https://doi.org/10.1002/wps.20292

Kim, J. (2006). Emergence: Core ideas and issues. *Synthese, 151*(3), 547–559.

Koivumäki, P. (2022). Eletty elämäntilanne päihdessosiaalityössä: filosofinen analyysi Rauhalan ihmiskäsityksen situaation käsitteestä. *Janus: sosiaalipolitiikan ja sosiaalityön tutkimuksen aikakauslehti, 30*(2), 124–139. https://doi.org/10.30668/janus.107625

Laing, R. D. (1965). *The divided self: An existential study in sanity and madness.* Penguin Books.

Leucht, S., König, B., di Francesco, A., Rodolico, A., Priller, J., Böge, K., Strube, W., Gensichen, J., Bechmann, P., ElDeeb, A., Hasan, A., Moritz, S., Jäger, M., Leucht, C., van Os, J., & Davis, J. M. (2025). Enhancing mental health care: A problem, resources and goals oriented multidimensional framework (PRoGO). *European Archives of Psychiatry and Clinical Neuroscience.* Advance online publication. https://doi.org/10.1007/s00406-025-02045-5

Lyotard, J.-F. (1984). *The postmodern condition: A report on knowledge* (G. Bennington & B. Massumi, Trans.). University of Minnesota Press.

Maj, M., Stein, D. J., Parker, G., Zimmerman, M., Fava, G. A., De Hert, M., Demyttenaere, K., McIntyre, R. S., Widiger, T., & Wittchen, H. U. (2020). The clinical characterization of the adult patient with depression aimed at personalization of management. *World Psychiatry: Official Journal of the World Psychiatric Association (WPA)*, *19*(3), 269–293. https://doi.org/10.1002/wps.20771

Maj, M., van Os, J., De Hert, M., Gaebel, W., Galderisi, S., Green, M. F., Guloksuz, S., Harvey, P. D., Jones, P. B., Malaspina, D., McGorry, P., Miettunen, J., Murray, R. M., Nuechterlein, K. H., Peralta, V., Thornicroft, G., van Winkel, R., & Ventura, J. (2021). The clinical characterization of the patient with primary psychosis aimed at personalization of management. *World Psychiatry: Official Journal of the World Psychiatric Association (WPA)*, *20*(1), 4–33. https://doi.org/10.1002/wps.20809

Mahdanian, A. A., Laporta, M., Drew Bold, N., Funk, M., & Puras, D. (2023). Human rights in mental healthcare; A review of current global situation. *International Review of Psychiatry (Abingdon, England)*, *35*(2), 150–162. https://doi.org/10.1080/09540261.2022.2027348

McGorry, P. D., Purcell, R., Hickie, I. B., Yung, A. R., Pantelis, C., & Jackson, H. J. (2007). Clinical staging: A heuristic model for psychiatry and youth mental health. *The Medical Journal of Australia*, *187*(S7), S40–S42. https://doi.org/10.5694/j.1326-5377.2007.tb01335.x

Meehl, P. E. (1989). Schizotaxia revisited. *Archives of General Psychiatry*, *46*(10), 935–944.

Miller, W. R., & Rollnick, S. (2024). Why motivational interviewing is a person-centered approach. *Sucht: Zeitschrift für Wissenschaft und Praxis*, *70*(2), 97–101. https://doi.org/10.1024/0939-5911/a000862

Norcross, J. C., & Goldfried, M. R. (Eds.). (2019). *Handbook of psychotherapy integration* (3rd ed.). Oxford University Press. https://doi.org/10.1093/med-psych/9780190690465.001.0001

OECD. (2021). *A new benchmark for mental health systems: Tackling the social and economic costs of mental Ill-health*. OECD Publishing. https://doi.org/10.1787/4ed890f6-en

Olthof, M., Hasselman, F., Oude Maatman, F., Bosman, A. M. T., & Lichtwarck-Aschoff, A. (2023). Complexity theory of psychopathology. *Journal of Psychopathology and Clinical Science*, *132*(3), 314–323. https://doi.org/10.1037/abn0000740

Parnas, J., Sass, L. A., & Zahavi, D. (2013). Rediscovering psychopathology: The epistemology and phenomenology of the psychiatric object. *Schizophrenia Bulletin*, *39*(2), 270–277. https://doi.org/10.1093/schbul/sbs153

Patel, V., Saxena, S., Lund, C., Kohrt, B., Kieling, C., Sunkel, C., Kola, L., Chang, O., Charlson, F., O'Neill, K., & Herrman, H. (2023). Transforming mental health systems globally: Principles and policy recommendations. *Lancet (London, England)*, *402*(10402), 656–666. https://doi.org/10.1016/S0140-6736(23)00918-2

Perls, F. S., Hefferline, R. F., & Goodman, P. (1951). *Gestalt therapy: Excitement and growth in the human personality*. Julian Press.

Pocobello, R., Camilli, F., Alvarez-Monjaras, M., Bergström, T., von Peter, S., Hopfenbeck, M., ... & el Sehity, T. J. (2023). Open Dialogue services around the world: A scoping survey exploring organizational characteristics in the implementation of the Open Dialogue approach in mental health services. *Frontiers in Psychology, 14,* Article 1241936. https://doi.org/10.3389/fpsyg.2023.1241936

Pūras, D. (2017). *Report of the Special Rapporteur on the right of everyone to the enjoyment of the highest attainable standard of physical and mental health* (A/HRC/35/21). The United Nations Human Rights Council. https://undocs.org/A/HRC/35/21

Rauhala, L. (1983). *Ihmiskäsitys ihmistyössä*. Gaudeamus.

Rauhala, L. (2002). Minikurssi mentaalisten ongelmien ymmärtämiseksi. *Tieteessä Tapahtuu, 20*(6), 21–26. https://journal.fi/tt/article/view/57918

Read, J., Haslam, N., Sayce, L., & Davies, E. (2006). Prejudice and schizophrenia: A review of the 'mental illness is an illness like any other' approach. *Acta Psychiatrica Scandinavica, 114*(5), 303–318. https://doi.org/10.1111/j.1600-0447.2006.00824.x

Rogers, C. R. (1951). *Client-centered therapy: Its current practice, implications, and theory*. Houghton Mifflin.

Rose, N. (2025). 5E mental health? Notes on an emerging style of thought. *Transcultural Psychiatry, 62*(3), 325–340. https://doi.org/10.1177/13634615251327862

Rose, D., & Rose, N. (2023). Is 'another' psychiatry possible?. *Psychological Medicine, 53*(1), 46–54. https://doi.org/10.1017/S003329172200383X

Schütz, A. (1932/1967). *The phenomenology of the social world* (G. Walsh & F. Lehnert, Trans.). Northwestern University Press.

Seikkula, J. (2025). *Why dialogue does cure: Explaining what makes dialogue unprecedentedly effective in difficult crises*. Springer Nature Switzerland AG. https://doi.org/10.1007/978-3-031-91294-8

Seikkula, J., & Arnkil, T. E. (2006). *Dialogical meetings in social networks*. Karnac Books.

Sexton, T. L., & Lebow, J. (Eds.). (2016). *Handbook of family therapy: The science and practice of working with families and couples*. Routledge.

Shotter, J. (1993). *Conversational realities: Constructing life through language*. Sage.

Silberstein, M. (2017). Strong emergence no, contextual emergence yes. *Philosophica, 91*(1), 1–30.

Smuts, J. C. (1926). *Holism and evolution*. Macmillan and Co.

Steingard, S. (Ed.). (2019). *Critical psychiatry: Controversies and clinical implications*. Springer.

Torrey E. F. (2024). Did the human genome project affect research on Schizophrenia?. *Psychiatry research, 333*, 115691. https://doi.org/10.1016/j.psychres.2023.115691

van Os, J., Guloksuz, S., Vijn, T. W., Hafkenscheid, A., & Delespaul, P. (2019). The evidence-based group-level symptom-reduction model as the organizing principle for mental health care: Time for change? *World Psychiatry, 18*(1), 88–96. https://doi.org/10.1002/wps.20609

von Bertalanffy, L. (1968). *General system theory: Foundations, development, applications*. George Braziller.

Vygotsky, L. S. (1934/1986). *Thought and language* (A. Kozulin, Ed. & Trans.). MIT Press.

Wampold B. E. (2015). How important are the common factors in psychotherapy? An update. *World psychiatry: official journal of the World Psychiatric Association (WPA), 14*(3), 270–277. https://doi.org/10.1002/wps.20238

Wiener, N. (1948). *Cybernetics: Or control and communication in the animal and the machine*. MIT Press.

World Health Organization. (2018). *Mental health atlas 2017*. World Health Organization.

World Health Organization. (2021). *Guidance on community mental health services: Promoting person-centred and rights-based approaches*. World Health Organization. https://creativecommons.org/licenses/by-nc-sa/3.0/igo/

World Health Organization. (2019). *Human rights: WHO QualityRights core training – For all services and all people. Course guide*. World Health Organization. https://apps.who.int/iris

Zubin, J., & Spring, B. (1977). Vulnerability: A new view of schizophrenia. *Journal of Abnormal Psychology, 86*(2), 103–126.

Part II

Practice

Building on the theoretical framework established in the previous part, this part turns to practice. Its focus is not on individual techniques or therapeutic schools, but on how mental health care can be organized in a way that consistently aligns with the holistic framework. The central question is how services can be structured so that unfavorable situations are met as wholes, rather than fragmented into diagnoses, referrals, and narrowly defined interventions.

The part begins by elaborating on dialogical space as the foundational event of holistic practice and then examines how this logic extends to service organization, resource allocation, professional roles, leadership, financing, and legislation. The chapters address concrete institutional constraints and show how a holistic framework can be implemented within—and gradually transform—existing systems. Particular attention is paid to responsibility, continuity, and the reduction of fragmentation across service pathways. Together, the chapters outline how a holistic framework reshapes everyday clinical work and the broader architecture of the mental health system.

All of the principles outlined in this part follow from the theoretical framework of holism developed in the previous chapter. They describe how mental health practice and service organization might be structured if one seeks to implement this framework in a consistent manner. These proposals are intended as a theoretically informed model rather than as clinical guidelines or prescriptive standards. Their practical application requires further empirical research, contextual adaptation, and iterative development, which are discussed in the final part of this book.

DOI: 10.4324/9781003777939-6

Chapter 4

Dialogical Space

In a holistic system, service structures and resources are reorganized to increase the likelihood of entering a dialogical space. The central task of the mental healthcare system is therefore to facilitate immediate meetings with individuals and, when appropriate, their networks. These meetings may include the person's close relationships as well as other relevant actors, enabling a shared understanding of the current situation to emerge. On this basis, the treatment process can be designed and organized on a case-by-case basis, built from the bottom-up around the concrete circumstances of people's lives.

This approach differs from reductionist mental healthcare system, whose primary aim is symptom reduction according to group-level treatment guidelines applied from the top-down. Because this requires a unidirectional definition or reduction of the problem, considerable resources are devoted to thorough assessment, finding the "right" place of treatment, and trying out predefined interventions that are selected on the basis of this initial definitional work.

A holistic system, by contrast, seeks to understand situations as wholes and to respond to them contextually without needing to reduce them to constituent parts through extensive assessment processes. Because psychosocial challenges—those commonly defined as mental health problems or psychiatric disorders—are always somehow embedded in social contexts and life situations in which they become problems in the first place, the most essential investment is in participatory helping practices that can be brought into people's actual living environments, outside the formal mental healthcare system.

The basic principle of the holistic system is illustrated in Figure 4.1. Regardless of the nature or presumed etiology of the problem, the core task of psychiatric and broader mental healthcare system is to organize, at the initial and change phases of treatment, a dialogical space from which a tailored, case-specific helping process can be planned and implemented. Because one cannot remain indefinitely in a dialogical space,

DOI: 10.4324/9781003777939-7

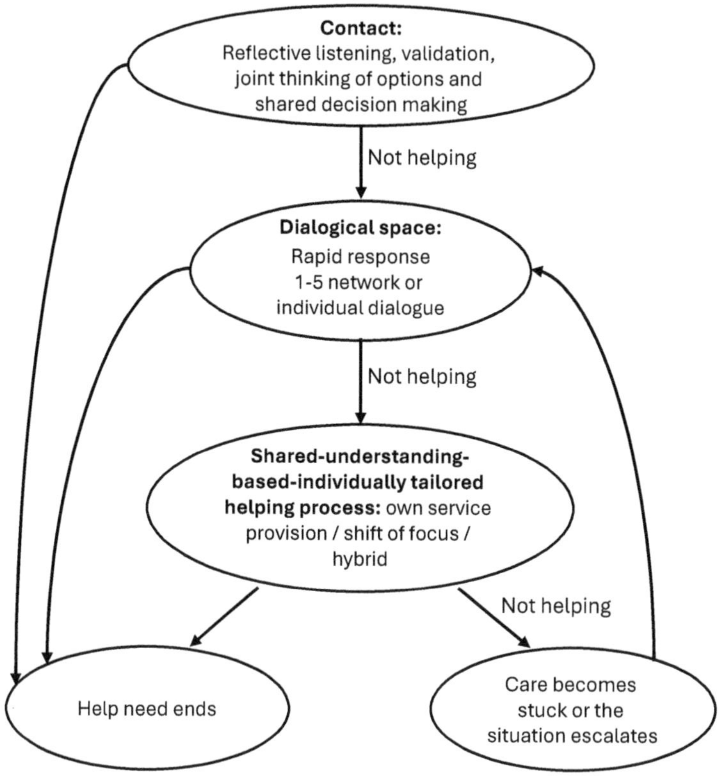

Figure 4.1 The basic organizing principle of a holistic system.

a target endpoint can be set to make the process more predictable and goal-directed. In situations of impasse or difficulty, the process can always return to the dialogical phase, from which the helping process can be reorganized. The starting point is the flexible trialing of different care and support strategies and the assessment of what, in the given situation, feels workable and relieving of worry or distress from the perspective of the people involved. The aim is to proceed in small steps—starting "where movement is possible"—to keep the process as simple and thus as manageable as possible.

The holistic system described here is largely based on the Open Dialogue approach (Bergström et al., 2025) as incorporated into the World Health Organization's (WHO, 2021) guidelines. The origins, development, and research findings of the Open Dialogue are discussed in more detail in the research section. In here, the Open Dialogue should not be seen as a sharply defined method, but rather as an example of how the entire service system can operate in a process-oriented way that supports holistic and dialogical helping processes. This way of thinking is closer to the approach's original idea, which was grounded in a needs-adapted and flexible approach but has, over time, been methodologies largely due to reductionist demands—particularly for producing research evidence and enabling broader implementation. If the starting points of the service system are themselves holistic, the approach can remain closer to its original ideal and is easier to sustain, as it does not need to conform to the operational logic of a reductionist system. Moreover, a holistic ontology already directs mental health services to organize themselves in this direction.

To illustrate the functioning of a holistic system, the tasks of workers in both basic and specialized mental health services are divided here into two central roles: service coordinators and facilitators of care processes. The majority of personnel resources in psychiatric and mental health services are directed toward these roles. In practice, however, a holistic service system may use a range of professional titles, and job descriptions may also include more reductionist or specialized clinical interventions. What is essential is not the titles themselves, but the systematic shift in work focus and resource allocation away from specialized treatments and services toward more generic, situational, and dialogically constructed helping processes. The aim is to draw flexibly on specialized expertise when needed, while maintaining a primary operational logic grounded in perceiving situations holistically, facilitating processes, and providing participatory support for the person's network. The more detailed changes in professional roles, organizational structures, and workflows are presented in Chapter 6.

The following section outlines the organization of a dialogical space step by step, beginning with initial contact, service coordination, and the arrangement of a dialogical meeting, and proceeding to maintaining dialogue and coordinating the helping process after the dialogical phase.

4.1 Initial Contact and Rapid Response

For the emergence of a dialogical space, it is important that people are able to define for themselves the timeframe within which help should be organized. This is particularly crucial when the person contacting services is concerned about their own or someone else's life; in such cases, help should be arranged as soon as it is requested.

A rapid response serves several purposes. First, it can in many situations prevent problems from becoming prolonged or more complex, which would make helping more difficult at later stages. In line with a holistic ontology, the fact that someone is worried or experiences a psychological or social challenge as a problem is already, in itself, something that warrants "treatment." Second, people are often most ready for change and for accepting help precisely at the moment when they feel worry or distress. If this "window" is missed, they may begin to adapt to and normalize a challenging situation, which decreases their readiness for change.

Third, an immediate response helps all parties grasp the current factors that are most likely generating or maintaining the difficulties. For one person, something sudden and distressing may have occurred, while another may have endured long-term strain that has culminated in a request for help at that specific moment. Someone else may have struggled with difficulties for a long time, but in a particular situation, these have become more visible to others, triggering concern and prompting help-seeking. When the request for help is met immediately, the recent events that have led to worry or distress are still fresh in mind, making it more likely that professionals can gain an early understanding of what may be at stake.

To ensure an immediate response, service coordination must be as simple as possible and service stratification as minimal as possible. In practice, this means that neither professionals nor service users should need to determine, in the early stages of help-seeking, what the "right" service or place of treatment might be. In a holistic helping system, service coordination should therefore occur through a single point of contact, with the basic assumption that, regardless of the situation, the person has reached the correct place.

The contact channel must be centralized so that resources can be organized rapidly and efficiently. At the same time, it must be easily accessible for those who find face-to-face contact or using their real name challenging. Accessibility can be improved by providing options for text-based communication or mobile applications alongside in-person and telephone contact. The contact channel must be available around the clock to ensure accessibility and rapid response.

To lower the threshold for making contact, public guidance must be as broad as possible. For example, people can be instructed to use this channel if they feel that their own or a loved one's situation is causing concern that requires outside support.

Example of an Initial Contact—Quiet Elias

Elias is naturally shy, and social situations make him anxious. Recently, the anxiety has become so intense that he has no longer been able to study properly. He has also begun avoiding people, which has weakened his friendships. Public places, in particular, have become difficult for him. One day, Elias experiences a panic-like episode while grocery shopping. He abandons his purchases and rushes home. Distressed, he calls a service coordinator.

During the call, Elias describes his situation. The service coordinator listens, asks clarifying questions, and reflects back on what she has heard, and how distressing Elias's situation sounds. At the same time, she notes that it is also positive that, despite the anxiety, Elias has still been able to continue his studies and spend some time with friends.

Elias feels that the conversation itself already brings some relief. He thinks it would be helpful to consider more carefully what should be done next. The service coordinator agrees and asks when and in what way Elias would like to meet. She explains that the meeting can be arranged at the outpatient clinic, at Elias's home, or in another environment that he prefers. Elias feels that meeting at home would be easiest for the first time and suggests that the meeting should take place within a week. The service coordinator agrees and promises to make the arrangements. She encourages Elias to get in touch again at a low threshold if things get worse and he would like to meet earlier.

The service coordinator then asks whether Elias would prefer to meet alone or whether it might be helpful to invite someone close to him. Elias is unsure but mentions that his brother has been supportive and that he admires his brother's confidence in social situations. The service coordinator encourages Elias to consider whether his brother might join the meeting, if that feels right for him.

Because, in a holistic system, the act of making contact—and the response to it—is one of the most important "interventions," the contact channel should be answered by a real person. The service coordinator's task is to respond immediately in whatever form the contact has been made. The key is to listen in such a way that the person contacting services gains a sense of being met directly and without delay. This requires asking open and clarifying questions about the issues the caller has themselves raised. The service coordinator also inquiries about the person's own view of what kind of help they are seeking and within what timeframe.

Although active listening often leads to a shared understanding of the situation and possible ways forward, the service coordinator's task is not to interpret or define the situation any further. Instead, alongside active listening, their primary role is to decide together with the caller whether they wish to have a meeting and, if so, what an appropriate timeframe for such a meeting would be.

Example of an Initial Contact—Exhausted Sarah

Sarah has long struggled with feelings of exhaustion and fatigue. One day, she suddenly bursts into tears in the middle of her workday. A colleague sees this and encourages Sarah to contact a service coordinator. Sarah feels, however, that she does not have the strength to make a phone call. Together, they decide to write a message describing Sarah's situation, which they send to the service coordinator.

The service coordinator replies, thanking her for the message and suggesting that it might be helpful to talk in more detail. She asks whether she could call Sarah, or whether Sarah would prefer to come in for a meeting. If needed, the conversation can also continue by text. Sarah gives permission for a phone call.

During the call, the service coordinator first asks general questions about Sarah's life. Sarah is initially quiet but gradually begins to describe the strain and feelings of inadequacy she experiences particularly at work. The service coordinator listens, summarizes what Sarah has said, and asks whether she would like to meet in person, continue the conversation, and think together about what might help improve her situation. Sarah feels this might be worth trying.

The service coordinator also suggests that someone important to Sarah—such as the colleague who helped write the message—could join the meeting. Sarah hesitates but agrees to consider it. The service coordinator emphasizes that the decision can be made later and that the meeting can take place with whatever group Sarah herself chooses. She explains that the meeting can be arranged, for example, at Sarah's home, at her workplace, or at the outpatient clinic. Sarah feels the outpatient clinic would be the easiest option.

The service coordinator then considers what timeframe would be appropriate for arranging the meeting. Sarah says that she cannot cope at work right now but is otherwise managing. They agree to try to arrange the meeting within a few days and that a doctor will also participate. Before the meeting, the service coordinator consults the doctor, who may contact Sarah to write a short sick leave certificate until the meeting takes place. Finally, the service coordinator encourages Sarah to reach out again at a low threshold if the situation worsens and an earlier meeting becomes necessary.

4.2 Organizing the Meeting

In many situations, responding to a request for help, hearing a person's distress, and jointly considering possible solutions in the manner described above may constitute a sufficient intervention, and no further assistance is necessarily required. It is also possible that the mere knowledge of the existence of such a contact channel creates a sense of safety for a large part of the population and reduces the need for people to make contact in the first place.

Example of Responding—Maria's Relationship Difficulties

Maria has long struggled with difficulties in her relationship. She repeatedly ends up in conflict with her partner and feels that the situation has become almost unbearably distressing. Maria contacts a service coordinator, who listens to her describe what has been happening. She reflects and summarizes Maria's words, invites her to elaborate, and asks how different everyday situations have felt, how it feels to talk about all this now, and how Maria has been coping overall. Maria also mentions things that support her well-being, and the service coordinator highlights and reinforces the importance of these strengths.

Together, they consider how conversations with her partner could be approached in a more constructive way, and how Maria feels about the idea of her partner hearing this discussion. The service coordinator then asks whether Maria would like to continue the conversation at another time—either alone or together with her partner, at home or at the outpatient clinic, in whichever setting Maria would feel safest. However, Maria feels that this conversation has already eased her distress and helped her view the situation in a way that no longer feels as overwhelming.

The service coordinator reminds her that she is welcome to get in touch again at a low threshold if she changes her mind. After the call, Maria notices that she can approach her partner somewhat more calmly. A few days later, they are able to speak more constructively, and the situation gradually begins to improve without the need for further intervention.

If, however, people themselves wish to continue the conversation, or if the service coordinator becomes concerned about the situation, they will begin organizing a meeting.

The starting point for arranging the meeting is that already the first meeting should include everyone who is in some way affected by the situation. To determine this, the service coordinator actively asks the person contacting services who belongs to their close network and who it would be useful to invite. If, during the contact, it becomes apparent that the situation might also benefit from other forms of expertise—such as occupational health, social services, or medical professionals—this is noted. What is essential is that the person is not immediately directed to other services unless the situation involves, for example, a medical emergency requiring somatic hospital care or another urgent health issue.

A second guiding principle is to organize the meeting in a location where the participants feel safest. For some, this may be their home; for others, a hospital or outpatient clinic. Some may prefer to meet remotely. During the initial contact, the service coordinator discusses these options and records any preferences.

People often feel reluctant to burden their loved ones with their problems. Especially in such cases, the service coordinator must be proactive and encourage them to invite close others by, for example, reminding them that uncertainty is often what burdens loved ones most. The service coordinator must also emphasize that close network members are not being assessed or judged; rather, they are collaborators in thinking together about how the situation can begin to be addressed.

Example of Service Coordination—Tim and the Feeling of Shame

Tim is a young man who has used cannabis occasionally for several years. During one episode of use, he began hearing mocking voices that felt so real that he called his mother in distress. Later, his mother encouraged Tim to contact a service coordinator.

Tim calls the service coordinator, feeling ashamed, and explains his situation. He mentions that he sometimes hears voices even when sober. The service coordinator asks more about the voices: what they say and how they feel to Tim. He describes the voices as distressing because they mock and belittle him. The service coordinator validates the experience by noting that hearing such voices must be very burdensome and thanks Tim for having the courage to talk about them. Together, they reflect on why the voices might be so mocking in tone.

The service coordinator suggests that it would be helpful to continue the conversation, and Tim agrees. She asks whether Tim has close others who could be invited to the meeting and who might support him. Tim mentions his mother but says he feels too ashamed about what has happened and does not want to worry her any further. The service coordinator reflects Tim's concern and acknowledges that this is completely understandable. At the same time, she asks how it might feel if his mother were present or heard the conversation in a similar way to how she, the coordinator, is hearing it now. Tim pauses to think and says that perhaps it would not be such a bad idea after all. He agrees to consider it further.

Although the inclusion of close others is encouraged, the service coordinator must recognize that meeting with family, friends, or professionals—or having professionals enter one's personal living environment—requires courage and trust. For this reason, the service coordinator explains already during the first contact that the person may also attend the meeting without their network and that it can be arranged in a neutral location, such as a hospital or an outpatient clinic. It is also explained that future meetings can be organized flexibly with different constellations of people, depending on the situation and the person's needs.

Example of Service Coordination—Paula and Ron's Conflict-Prone Situation

Paula has long been worried about her partner Ron, who lost his job and whose alcohol use has increased. When intoxicated, Ron behaves impulsively and threateningly toward Paula. In addition, the family's financial difficulties strain daily life to the point that Paula feels increasingly hopeless. Eventually, she finds herself thinking about suicide and is frightened enough by the thought that she decides to contact a service coordinator.

During the call, Paula speaks primarily about her own distress and is initially too afraid to mention her husband, as she greatly fears his impulsiveness. The service coordinator asks more questions and thinks aloud about what might be contributing to Paula's difficult feelings. Gradually, Paula dares to talk about the financial stress and her husband's drinking. The service coordinator validates Paula's experience, noting that it makes the situation understandable, and wonders whether it might be helpful to meet with Ron as well. The suggestion frightens Paula, who does not want her husband to know about the contact. She also hesitates about meeting on her own.

The service coordinator reassures her and suggests that Paula could first come alone to talk so that they can consider the situation together. She reflects on Paula's circumstances and notes that they sound so overwhelming that it would probably be best to meet as soon as possible—perhaps even the next day. Paula hesitates, as it is difficult for her to get to the outpatient clinic, and a home visit does not feel possible because of her husband. The service coordinator asks about Paula's daily routines and suggests that they could meet in a nearby park where Paula often goes for walks. She also reflects aloud that it is always possible to seek help from, for example, addiction or social services, arranging for a professional from those services to join a meeting if needed—but she does not pressure Paula, instead leaving the option open for the future.

After the call, the service coordinator records Paula's concerns and the potential need for additional support. She forwards Paula's contact information and the agreed time to the meeting facilitator, who sets out the next day to meet Paula for a walk in the park.

Once the service coordinator has clarified the timeframe as well as the preferences regarding who should attend the meeting and where it should take place, they begin assembling the working team. In practice, this means identifying at least two professionals—namely, the facilitators—using an electronic calendar or another agreed-upon method.

If the situation concerns an existing treatment process that has reached a crisis or impasse, or if previously concluded treatment needs to be restarted, the service coordinator will primarily seek to invite the facilitators who were previously involved in the case. An exception is when the person contacting services requests a change of workers. In such cases, the service coordinator explores the reasons for this request and identifies professionals within the services who better match the person's preferences—for example, regarding gender, age, experience, or interpersonal compatibility.

Example of Service Coordination—Dissatisfied Jonah

Jonah calls service coordination in anger. He explains that he has been in treatment for several months but feels that nothing is progressing. He finds one of the facilitators particularly irritating.

The service coordinator listens to Jonah, reflects and summarizes what he says, and asks clarifying questions: how long he has felt this way, whether the experience started immediately, and how he feels the treatment has gone overall. She also explores what exactly irritates him about this particular worker and how he gets along with the other staff members.

Jonah explains that this worker's mannerisms remind him of another relationship from his past, which makes it difficult for him to speak openly in the worker's presence. The service coordinator validates his experience and thanks Jonah for the courage to share it—this helps the staff consider what would be most useful for him at this stage. It becomes clear that the facilitators are likely unaware of how Jonah has been feeling, as he has not dared to tell them directly.

The service coordinator and Jonah then consider how the issue could be brought up safely with the facilitators. They eventually agree that the service coordinator could facilitate a joint discussion in which Jonah's concerns can be voiced and the workers can better understand his experience.

Once the facilitators have been selected, they confirm the schedule, meeting location, and participants with those involved. If the participants find it difficult to invite family members or other relevant parties themselves, the professionals can make the invitations on their behalf. In such cases, it is important to emphasize that the invitation does not include details about the concerns or previous conversations; rather, the focus is placed on the present situation and on the invitees' perspectives and willingness to participate.

The facilitators do not pressure anyone to attend and make clear that meetings can be arranged in different constellations. At this stage, they do not interpret or define the situation; instead, they simply agree on the practical arrangements necessary for organizing the meeting.

Example of Service Coordination—Carl's Crisis

A worried mother calls the service coordinator. She explains that her son, Carl, has been isolating himself in his room for several days and no longer agrees to open the door. Even earlier, he had been behaving oddly and talking about some kind of "syndicate" that, according to him, is monitoring him and intends to harm him. The service coordinator validates the mother's concern, acknowledges that the situation sounds difficult, and thanks her for reaching out. She reflects that it would be important to meet as soon as possible, preferably at the family's home. The mother says she has suggested this to Carl, but he refused sharply and behaved threateningly. The service coordinator proposes that they could first meet with the mother alone. She agrees. The coordinator promises they will be in touch shortly to arrange a specific time.

After the call, the service coordinator checks the staff calendars and notices that nurse Matt and psychologist Jane would be available that afternoon to visit the mother at home. The physician, Sonia, also has a couple of short time slots during which she could join the conversation by phone if needed. The coordinator sends a message to the staff, explaining the urgency of the situation.

The facilitators call the mother, ask how she is coping, and confirm whether it would be acceptable for them to come. The mother asks what she should tell Carl about the meeting. The facilitators reply that it is good to mention it, but of course he does not have to participate, and she can say that as well. They also ask whether it might be helpful to invite other people. The mother says that Carl has been close to his grandfather, who lives next door, but she is unsure how to raise the matter with him. The facilitators agree that they can contact the grandfather themselves. She provides the contact information.

They call the grandfather, explain that there is concern about Carl, and suggest a meeting. The grandfather says that he, too, has been worried for some time and is willing to join the meeting.

4.3 Preparing and Orienting to the Meeting

A prerequisite for the emergence of a dialogical space is that professionals and experts occupying positions of authority adopt a not-knowing and wondering stance during the meeting. This stance enables active listening and a more polyphonic conversation in which no single voice or interpretation begins to dominate. Such a stance is also characteristic of many psychotherapeutic approaches, as it allows for a more equal and exploratory collaborative relationship that provides a strong foundation for working alliance. Moreover, it reduces the influence of preconceptions that shape and reinforce interpretations, thereby enabling a more open and respectful attitude as well as the kind of learning that is essential for implementing needs-adapted care.

Maintaining a not-knowing stance is, however, challenging. It may evoke feelings of uncertainty in workers, and various issues related to professional roles and responsibilities often steer them toward a more expert-driven position. To support the not-knowing stance, facilitators work as a team or pair, so that responsibility for the treatment does not fall too heavily on one person and so that uncertainty becomes easier to tolerate. Working in pairs or teams also enables more polyphonic dialogue and ensures that at least one facilitator is likely to be reachable between meetings should the situation escalate or require a reorganization of care.

To safeguard the not-knowing stance, facilitators do not interpret the situation or create treatment plans on the basis of preliminary information. Instead, they aim to enter the meeting with as open a mind as possible, trusting that solutions and perspectives will emerge in interaction with those seeking help. An exception to this principle concerns severe situations where the initial contact already indicates the need for medication, hospital care, or sick leave; in such cases, a physician may be invited to the meeting. Even then, no further interpretation or advance planning is done prior to the meeting, thus preserving the option that the situation may calm during or between meetings, making the pre-anticipated interventions unnecessary at that stage.

4.4 The Meeting

4.4.1 Opening

Phases of the meeting are presented in Table 4.1. The facilitators' first task is to establish as ordinary and natural a connection as possible with all participants, since people may feel tense at the beginning of a meeting. They may, for instance, lighten the atmosphere by commenting on current events, the weather, or other general topics that are not directly related to the meeting and do not evoke strong emotions.

If the facilitators are visiting people in their home, they ask the participants—or follow their lead—regarding which room the meeting should take place in and how they would like to arrange the space. If the meeting is held at the facilitators' unit, they ensure that there are enough seats for everyone and guide participants to sit in a circle so that all can see and hear one another, with no tables, computers, or other objects placed between them.

Example of Orienting—Carl's Crisis (Continued)

Nurse Matt and psychologist Jane are on their way to Carl's home. Earlier that morning, his mother had contacted services, worried about her son's strange and increasingly withdrawn behavior. On the way there, Matt and Jane do not speculate about or plan the meeting in advance; instead, they talk casually about everyday matters.

When they arrive, Carl's mother opens the door. She looks tired and concerned. Matt and Jane introduce themselves, compliment the well-kept yard, and exchange a few words about the rainy weather. They follow the mother into the kitchen, where two men are sitting at the table. Matt and Jane greet them as well and sit down where the mother indicates. She asks whether they would like some coffee, and both respond affirmatively.

Table 4.1 Phases of dialogue

Phase	*Description*
Opening	A safe and natural atmosphere is established. The facilitators introduce themselves and explain the purpose of the meeting, the situation that led to it, and how much time they have reserved for the meeting. Participants are then invited to introduce themselves and describe their relationship to the situation. They are given space to determine what they wish to talk about and how they would like to use the meeting. If needed, the facilitators help to focus the discussion.
Joining	The facilitators follow the flow of the conversation and continually join with what participants bring forward. They build on what the previous speaker has said, ask open and clarifying questions, and create space for multiple perspectives. Active listening is shown through repetition, summarizing, and reflective comments. The aim is to engage all participants, support the emergence of different viewpoints, and deepen shared understanding.
Closing	The key issues that have emerged in the dialogue are summarized, and decisions about next steps are made collaboratively. These decisions are based on the shared understanding developed during the meeting and are agreed upon openly with everyone present. Simple and concrete action plans are preferred. If the situation remains unresolved, additional dialogical meetings or need-adapted crisis support may be arranged, followed by a renewed dialogical process.

4.4.2 *Entering into Dialogue*

Once everyone has settled, the facilitators introduce themselves and briefly describe the context and background of the meeting. For example, they might note that someone had made contact because they were worried about someone, and that the meeting was arranged so that everyone could consider together how best to be of help. The background can also be explored through an open, wondering question: who made contact, what the main concern was, and why it was felt necessary to organize a meeting.

If the meeting includes participants who have not met before, a round of introductions is held, during which each person states their name and, for instance, their relationship to the individual about whom there is currently the most concern. After the introductions, the facilitators may pose an open question—typically to the person who made contact—such as: *What do you think would be most important to begin with? How would you like to use this time together? Or what would you consider to be the best possible outcome of this meeting?* Often, the central theme emerges during introductions, and the dialogue continues naturally from there.

From this point on, the facilitators' primary task is to follow and connect with the themes that the participants themselves bring into the conversation. In practice, this occurs through open and clarifying questions as well as reflective repetition. A facilitator may ask someone to elaborate on a topic that has arisen or ask questions such as: *What thoughts or feelings did this bring up for you? What happened in that situation? How did you understand it?* Likewise, they may ask others in the network: *What thoughts or feelings does this evoke for you? What is it like to hear this? She said... I would be interested to hear more about... Would you like to say something about this?*

The goal is to create a polyphonic dialogue among those affected by the unfavorable situation. For this reason, facilitators avoid introducing their own themes, questions, or interpretations. However, they are not passive listeners; they actively encourage people to speak as openly as possible and to reflect on the situation from various angles. Facilitators keep interpretations as open as possible and emphasize that the same issues can be understood in many different ways—hence, all perspectives are important to hear. Open and clarifying questions are linked to the ongoing discussion through first-person expressions, such as: *When I listen to you, I find myself wondering..., Could it be that..., When you said that, I found myself thinking/feeling....* In this way, the expert and power positions are softened, encouraging a more polyphonic and participatory dialogue.

Facilitators also aim to keep the broader relational network present in the dialogue even when its members are not physically there. For instance, through circular questioning, they may ask: *If this person were listening to our conversation right now, what do you think they might think or feel?* At the same time, they encourage participants to reflect on what might become possible if that person were to join a meeting in the future.

Example of Beginning the Dialogue—Carl's Crisis (Continued)

Once everyone has been served coffee and Carl's mother has also taken a seat at the table, Matt and Jane reintroduce themselves and briefly explain how much time they have and how the meeting came about. They tell the family that the mother had contacted services that morning because she was worried about her son Carl, who had refused to come out of his room and about whom there had been concerns for some time. According to the service coordinator, the situation sounded serious enough that it would be important to meet quickly. After this, Matt and Jane invite the others to introduce themselves as well. It becomes clear that one of the men is the grandfather and the other is Carl's father. Jane clarifies whose side of the family the grandfather is from, noting that she understood from the phone call that he lives next door. The grandfather replies that he is the mother's father and confirms that he lives nearby.

Once the introductions are complete, Matt asks how the family is doing at the moment and what they feel is most important to begin with. The mother starts by describing how she has been worried about her son for a long time: his behavior has been strange, and at times his speech frightening. Jane reflects back on what she has heard, asks clarifying questions, and then turns to the father and grandfather. Both say they have been concerned as well. The father mentions that Carl has always had few friends and was bullied at school, which has contributed to his worry. Matt summarizes their concerns and asks the mother what thoughts or feelings their comments evoke in her. She nods, says she shares their long-standing concern, and begins to cry.

Jane reflects the mother's expressed emotion, validating it by noting how heavy the situation must feel. She asks whether there might be some paper or tissues for the mother. The father brings some and then spontaneously continues by sharing how the situation has felt for him. Matt reflects his words back and asks the mother what she feels when hearing her husband's perspective. The mother says she is surprised—she had not realized he felt the same way because they had hardly talked about it. Matt repeats this and asks the father how he understands it. The father says he recognizes the same pattern and wonders aloud what it might be related to. Jane reflects that the father has been thinking about what it could be connected to. The mother responds by sharing her own thoughts.

After a moment, Matt asks the grandfather how the conversation has sounded to him. The grandfather describes his relationship with the family: he notes that the parents have always worked hard, and that he has therefore spent a great deal of time with Carl. He says he is surprised by what has happened to the boy, as Carl has usually been in good spirits when spending time with him. Matt repeats this and asks the mother and father what they think about the grandfather's comment.

The mother and father say they feel guilty about having worked so much. Matt summarizes their feelings and invites everyone to consider what Carl might think—or perhaps say—if he were sitting at the table listening to the conversation. The mother thinks that Carl would not blame them; that would not be like him. The grandfather agrees, adding that the bullying must have left its mark on Carl, even though he has always acted as if he is coping. Carl has had little contact with peers and is surely lonely.

Suddenly, the father asks whether Carl might have developed psychosis and expresses concern about whether he will ever be the same again.

4.4.3 Reflection and Maintaining the Dialogue

In addition to open, clarifying, and circular questions, dialogue is maintained through reflective practice, involving the repetition and summarizing of what has been said. When a facilitator repeats a sentence either word for word or in a slightly modified form, they demonstrate that they are listening and offer the speaker an opportunity to view their own message from a slight distance, which often deepens the narrative. Repetition also helps to pace the conversation and, when necessary, to slow it down. By summarizing what has been discussed so far and then posing an open follow-up question, the conversation can move more deeply into a particular theme.

Facilitators may also reflect on what they have heard with each other, either flexibly during the conversation or in a separate reflective moment. If, for example, the discussion becomes stuck or emotionally overwhelming, a facilitator may summarize what has been said, share the thoughts it evokes in them, and then ask others what they think. Reflection can also be carried out by asking permission to speak briefly with one another while the participants listen. In such cases, it is emphasized that everyone will have an opportunity to comment on what they have heard immediately after the reflection.

During reflection, the facilitators turn toward each other and, in order to protect their listener position, speak as if the others in the room were not present. Their focus is on what has been heard and raised during the meeting. They may offer perspectives or interpretations, but always in the first-person mode and in ways that leave space for differing viewpoints: *It sounded to me as if..., I had the feeling that..., I found myself thinking that when they..., When I listened to her, I felt that....*

Example of Reflection—Carl's Crisis (Continued)

Nurse Matt asks the family whether it would be acceptable for him and Jane to think aloud for a moment while the family simply listens. The family members nod. Matt then turns toward psychologist Jane and asks what thoughts have arisen for her while listening to the family's conversation.

Jane reviews the concerns the family has expressed by summarizing the key points of the discussion and says that she was moved by what she heard. She notes that the family's care and concern for Carl were clearly evident, and that she herself felt very sad hearing about the bullying and how alone Carl has been. Matt nods and says he felt similarly. He adds that he also found himself thinking about the parents' guilt—and also their sense that Carl might not actually blame them. He further reflects that the grandfather has obviously been an important figure for Carl, and that it is valuable that he is present to consider together how to proceed. To Matt, the parents' and grandfather's comments conveyed an overall very positive picture of Carl, which perhaps also explains why the situation and Carl's recent behavior feel so confusing to them now.

Jane agrees and then asks Matt what thoughts he had in response to the father's earlier question about psychosis. Matt replies that it is of course difficult to answer because they have not yet met Carl, but the situation does indeed sound worrying. Jane continues by noting that *psychosis* can mean many different things and does not necessarily tell them precisely what is going on here. She suggests that it might be more useful to focus for now on how to move forward in the situation. Matt nods and says he partly agrees; however, as he listened both to the family's concerns and to Jane's reflections, he felt that one option might be to contact a physician and discuss a medication that could help if Carl is feeling extremely distressed—and given that he appears to have been awake for several nights, as the family suspected. Jane nods and says this also crossed her mind, though she feels it would be important to meet Carl and hear his perspective before considering medication. Matt agrees fully but adds that they could still request a medication to have on hand for the night, to be used if necessary; still, he thinks it would be important to ask the family and otherwise hear what they make of their reflective discussion.

Matt and Jane then turn back to the family and ask what thoughts arose for them. The mother says she feels that the professionals truly listened to and understood them. She agrees that medication might help but doubts that Carl would agree to take it. The father concurs and wonders whether it might still be possible to involve Carl in thinking this through. The grandfather says he is willing to go and ask Carl himself.

It is important that facilitators avoid pathologizing interpretations from expert position that might overly shape the content of the conversation or steer treatment decisions prematurely. Instead of adopting illness-based frameworks, the emphasis is placed on situational and current themes, and on hearing each person's lived experience as it is. If a participant has expressed an illness-based interpretation, it can be reflected on polyphonically, for example, by saying: *He interpreted this as a symptom of illness, but at the same time it sounded quite understandable in light of the situation.* After this, one might ask, for instance, the co-facilitator: *What thoughts did that bring up for you?*

Reflection may also include preliminary thoughts about treatment, but always in the first-person mode, and in ways that invite discussion and leave room for disagreement. Polyphony can be strengthened by asking the other facilitator why a particular interpretation or thought about treatment occurred to them.

Through reflection, challenging themes can be raised in a respectful manner and different perspectives can be brought into the conversation. Facilitators may, for example, reflect on a particular theme that has emerged and consider it from the viewpoints of different participants. They might say: *I had a certain feeling about that, and in this meeting, I would be interested to hear more about what it brought up for her. What was it like for you to listen to them?*

The aim of reflection—as with the meeting more generally—is to safeguard a maximally polyphonic dialogue in which perspectives and interpretations remain open for as long as possible. During both reflective moments and the ongoing dialogue, facilitators may think aloud that if someone has been quieter, it would be important to hear their perspective. Likewise, facilitators may, when necessary, distribute turns or use other means to structure the dialogue if some voices start to dominate too strongly.

A reflective exchange between facilitators typically lasts a few minutes, and there may be one or several such moments during a meeting depending on the situation. After the reflection, the facilitators turn back to the participants and give each person an opportunity to comment on what they have heard. They then continue as before—connecting with whatever the previous speaker has said and encouraging dialogue through open, clarifying, and circular questions, as well as through repetition and summarizing as described in dialogue tools (Table 4.2).

4.4.4 *The Immediate Effect of Dialogue*

A central task of the facilitators is to slow the pace of the meeting, thereby calming the overall atmosphere. The rhythm of the conversation can be slowed through repetition, questioning, and allowing space for pauses or for quieter voices to emerge. When the overall tone becomes calmer, distress and anxiety often ease, and the dialogue becomes more constructive. The aim is to increase participants' curiosity toward one another so that they can approach differing perspectives and experiences with greater openness and, when needed, with a bit more distance. For this reason, experiences that might initially appear incomprehensible—such as those interpreted as psychotic—are still heard and treated as part of the conversation.

Often, simply ensuring that a person in acute psychosis does not have to defend or justify their experiences reduces the intensity of those experiences. In other words, the person tends to speak less about matters interpreted as psychotic. This also allows for better contact with the person, which in turn often eases the worry and distress of loved ones, helping the network's ability to communicate improve immediately. As a result, it becomes easier to form an overall understanding of the person's life situation, making even strange or perplexing experiences appear more comprehensible in context. This supports a more positive and compassionate stance toward the person—even in situations where their difficulties are not easily relatable.

In a similar way, the relationship can improve through dialogue even when the person has, for example, initially refused the involvement of close others. As the person begins to feel heard, the alliance and trust develop, making it more likely that they will allow loved ones to participate in future meetings—if such involvement is still needed.

Table 4.2 Dialogical tools for different situations

Principle	Tools	Purpose and focus	Examples
Guiding principles			
Linking expressions to what came before	Linking and receptive comments	To maintain a shared, coherent dialogue that builds on what has been said or done; to construct understanding through connection	"Earlier you mentioned… could you clarify?" "I was thinking about what you said a moment ago…" "Related to what you shared…"
Situational sensitivity and flexibility	Gentle steering of the direction of the conversation	To ensure the meeting serves participants; to proceed according to what matters in the moment	"Now we have talked about… I wonder if there is also something else that…"
Simplicity and slowness	Using the participants' language and simple expressions	To adapt the language to that of the participants; to use simple formulations and small steps	"She said it felt like…" "He expressed that…"
Basic situations			
Starting the dialogue/ opening the space	Open-ended questions	To explore what participants wish to talk about; to bring out their perspectives	"Where would it be most important to begin?" "How would you like to use this time?" "What do you hope for from this meeting?"
Deepening the dialogue and understanding	Clarifying and open-ended questions	To clarify and deepen the dialogue; to demonstrate active listening; to build shared understanding	"Could you tell me more?" "Did I understand correctly that…?"
Regulating the rhythm of the dialogue and active listening	Repetitions and summaries	To show active listening and regulate the pace; to encourage further elaboration	"You said that…" "Yes, she said… How does that feel for you?"
Bringing forward multiple perspectives and understanding relationships	Circular and open-ended questions	To help participants see interactional patterns and relational dynamics; to foster polyphony	"You mentioned that… what do you think *she* might be thinking?" "What might he say if he had heard this?"

Strengthening polyphony and keeping interpretations open	Reflection	Professionals reflect aloud on what they have heard; increases transparency, trust, and polyphony	"When I heard that, I felt…" "I found myself wondering…" "I was thinking… but I may be mistaken."
Structuring the content and ending the dialogue	Summaries	To organize complex themes and synthesize the content; to plan next steps based on the joint understanding	"It sounds to me that the most important issues are…" "Today we talked about… And based on that, I'm thinking that…"
Challenging situations			
The conversation does not start/participants withdraw	Metacommunication and returning to earlier themes	To activate participants by returning to the purpose of the meeting; to propose concrete themes based on prior information	"She contacted us and hoped that… I'm wondering how this feels for you now?" "How could this time be helpful for you?" "What do you think she might have been worried about?"
Conversation stalls/ does not progress	Reintroducing or revisiting themes; asking for concrete everyday examples; focusing on easier topics	To maintain the flow of the conversation by returning to earlier themes or activating them; to ask for concrete illustrations; to shift toward everyday topics that are easier to approach	"What part of this feels especially important to you?" "In what situations does this happen / how has it shown up lately?" "You said that… when exactly did this…?" "You mentioned … I'd be interested to hear more about that."
Dominant, confused, or attacking voices	Setting boundaries and structure for turn-taking and reflective work	To protect polyphony, balance the dialogue, and calm the interaction; to ensure everyone has space to be heard	"This is an important point, and for that reason I'd also really like to hear what she…" "Would it be okay if I allocated speaking turns for a moment…?" "Let's return to this, but first let's hear…"

Example of the Effect of Dialogue—Carl's Crisis (Continued)

To the parents' surprise, Carl arrives at the table accompanied by his grandfather. Outwardly he appears relatively calm. Carl says he has been listening to the whole time and insists that he will not take any medication—*that is exactly what the syndicate wants*, he says. The father tries to interject, saying that there is no such thing as a syndicate. Carl raises his voice and begins arguing with him.

Nurse Matt introduces himself and says that he is genuinely glad Carl has joined the conversation. He adds that it feels important that Carl heard the earlier discussion and is voicing his opinion about medication. Matt then asks Carl whether he understood correctly that Carl fears someone wants to harm him. Carl nods and begins vividly describing how the syndicate is persecuting him in various ways and trying to poison him. Matt repeats his words and reflects aloud that it indeed sounds heavy and frightening. Psychologist Jane nods, introduces herself, and says she would like to hear more about Carl's concerns—but only if it feels safe for him to talk about them. Carl hesitates for a moment but then continues describing his experiences.

Matt repeats what Carl says and encourages him to tell more. He also asks the others whether they have heard Carl express these concerns before. The mother says that Carl has been talking about similar things for several days. Carl snaps that he *has* tried to ask for help, but no one believes him. Jane calmly repeats Carl's words and reflects on what kind of help he might hope for, and whether they could think it through together now—*which is why they have come*.

Carl suddenly bursts into tears and says he just wants to be left in peace and allowed to sleep—he has not slept in days because the syndicate makes constant noise. Jane acknowledges that this sounds extremely overwhelming and asks what might help Carl to rest. Carl does not know. The parents begin suggesting different solutions, but Carl grows more agitated, and the conversation becomes tense again.

Matt gently intervenes and asks the family for permission for him and Jane to think aloud together once more. He summarizes for Jane what Carl has said about his fears and his need for peace and rest. Jane replies that she heard the same, and she found herself wondering what they—and the parents—could do to meet Carl's need, but Carl seemed to get agitated when they discussed it. Matt asks Jane whether they might still try to consider it together. Jane and Matt then turn back to the family and invite them to share their thoughts.

Gradually, as the discussion continues, the tension begins to ease. Carl says he is extremely tired and simply wants to rest for a while without disturbance. It is agreed that the main goal for the evening is to help Carl get some peace and sleep. The grandfather offers to stay with him during the night, which Carl finds reassuring. The parents agree that he will not need to attend high school the next day, and it is decided that the professionals will return the following day to see how the situation has progressed. Carl nods wearily.

At times, members of a person's social network or other involved actors may be more concerned about the situation than the person themselves. In such cases, the person who is the focus of concern may decline to participate in a meeting. A dialogical meeting can nevertheless be held with members of the social network or professionals alone, with the aim of acknowledging and alleviating their worry and jointly exploring constructive ways of responding to the situation.

In some instances, meetings may be arranged in the person's home or another familiar setting, allowing the individual to decide for themselves whether and how to participate. People often choose to be present initially in a limited way—for example, by listening from another room—and may later join the conversation more actively.

Because the focus of care is the situation rather than an individual "patient," addressing distress and concern is meaningful even when it is primarily experienced by those close to the person. Working in this way can also indirectly support the person at the center of concern, as changes in the surrounding relational configuration may open up new possibilities for understanding, support, and agency.

Sometimes the dialogue brings up emotionally difficult themes or topics that may not be advisable to address immediately in a joint setting. These may include situations involving domestic violence or sexual abuse. In such circumstances, facilitators may gently steer the discussion toward other topics, collaboratively make an action plan for how to proceed, and continue the conversation later in separate constellations. Nevertheless, the emergence of such themes is important, as it helps guide the direction of care and may relate to issues that have long been part of a person's everyday life without anyone having addressed them.

In most cases, the difficulties faced by people seeking help are reactive to current life challenges and relatively mild, making it easy to enter into dialogue in the ways described above, and enabling the next steps of the care process to be collaboratively defined during the first meeting. At other times, entering into dialogue may itself empower the network's agency—people become more curious about one another, their communication improves, and the effect carries over immediately into their everyday life, since they are already in contact with one another outside the meeting. In some situations, however, several sessions and a more clearly structured plan are needed (see Section 4.5).

4.4.5 Concluding the Dialogue

A minimum of one hour is reserved for each meeting. Toward the end of the meeting, the facilitators begin orienting participants toward closure: they summarize the discussion, ensure that the most important matters have been expressed, and collaboratively formulate a plan for next steps with all involved. Finally, they may ask clarifying questions about participants' well-being or functioning, if these have not already emerged during the dialogue.

Tip: Save routine questions about symptoms, sleep, functioning, substance use, and suicidality until the end. Entering into dialogue often becomes difficult if the facilitator begins the meeting with closed, routine questions. If you decide in advance to ask them only during the final 10–20 minutes, genuine dialogue proceeds more naturally—and you will often notice that many of the topics you intended to ask about arise spontaneously in the conversation. If something still remains unclear, there is still time to ask about it at the end.

Dialogue typically generates a considerable amount of clinically relevant information that traditional assessment methods fail to capture. At the end of the meeting, the facilitators may summarize this information and reflect on how it might guide the next steps in the helping process. The basic principle is that key interpretations and decisions are made during the meeting, not outside it. This reduces the risk that professionals develop interpretations or plans separately from the dialogue—interpretations that may not be grounded in what emerged in the meeting and could inadvertently steer the process in the wrong direction or consume resources unnecessarily. It also keeps decision-making transparent and fosters trust. In addition, extra work outside of meetings decreases, and the tone of discussion remains more respectful and polyphonic than in informal conversations, for example, in the office or in the team meetings.

Compared to working alone, immediate reflective discussion and the use of co-facilitation or team facilitation also reduce the need for additional "venting." This lightens the emotional load on facilitators and helps them remain open to diverse perspectives and treatment ideas. As a result, facilitators often have more capacity to meet a greater number of people in the course of a workday.

Another foundation for trust and a sense of safety is that the same facilitators continue to oversee the helping process for as long as needed. For this reason, facilitators provide their contact information to all participants and explain that they may be contacted directly between meetings—or alternatively through the service coordinator—if questions arise or if the plan needs to be modified.

Example of Concluding the Dialogue—Carl's Crisis (Continued)

At the end of the meeting, Matt and Jane review what has been discussed. They emphasize that the most important thing right now is that Carl can rest and that someone is nearby to help him feel safe. Carl says he feels most secure with his grandfather, and the plan sounds good to him.

Matt and Jane remind the family that if any concerns arise during the evening or night, they can contact the service coordinator directly. They also give contact details to Carl and tell him that he may call himself if he becomes frightened. In addition, it is agreed that they will return the following day to continue the conversation from where it left off.

They then call the physician while the family listens, briefly summarize the situation, and agree that the doctor will issue a short sick leave certificate and write a precautionary prescription for a sleep medication in case Carl is unable to sleep. Carl is told that he does not have to take it—the choice is his. It is agreed that the grandfather can administer the medication if needed, as this feels safer to Carl.

Finally, they ensure that the plan feels sufficiently good to everyone involved and that it is safe to rely on for the night. Matt and Jane also make sure that everyone has their direct contact information as well as the service coordinator's number, which can also be used during the night.

Matt and Jane leave the family home. They exchange a few words about the situation—how nice it was that Carl joined the meeting in the end, and that they hope the night goes smoothly. After that, they shift to talking about their own plans for the evening after work and no longer speculate about Carl or the family's situation. Matt offers to write up the documentation from the visit so that Jane has time to take her child to their hobby.

4.5 After the Meeting

4.5.1 Dialogue Is Enough

A holistic system differs from a reductionist system in that the practical course of care is built case by case around the needs of the specific situation and person seeking help, rather than around group-level treatment guidelines or a predetermined service menu. In practice, a dialogical network meeting may therefore lead to very different solutions regardless of the presenting problems.

One guiding principle is to remain in open dialogue for as long as it is safe to do so, and to anchor the helping process as closely as possible in the person's real living environment and everyday events. For this reason, resource-intensive treatments and approaches that pathologize individual problems—such as standardized therapy packages, medication as a default, or hospitalization—are not offered as first-line interventions. Instead, the initial aim is to proceed with one meeting at a time and observe how the situation develops through dialogue.

For many people, a single dialogical meeting, either alone or with others, is sufficient in itself. When a dialogical space is established, people often feel genuinely met and heard with their concerns and begin to reflect on their own situation and each other's circumstances in a more reciprocal way. Through a network orientation, the effects transfer more directly into daily life, helping to open up relational difficulties or activate everyday resources so that no further help is required. Often, simply knowing that another meeting can easily be arranged reduces the need for follow-up contacts.

If the situation appears to be clarified during the first few dialogical meetings and people feel they are managing well, it can be agreed that they will contact the facilitators if a new meeting is needed. Alternatively, a follow-up meeting may be scheduled for a later time if people wish to monitor the situation and feel that this arrangement provides a sense of safety. A physician may be consulted when necessary—for example, to determine whether a short sick leave would be helpful. The dialogue may also give rise to the idea that it would be beneficial to invite additional people to participate, such as colleagues, family members, or friends. In such cases, meetings are arranged flexibly according to the schedule that suits them best.

Example of Planning the Continuation of Care—Carl's Crisis (Continued)

Matt and Jane return the following day as agreed. The mother appears visibly relieved. She reports that Carl eventually agreed to take the sleep medication and slept well into the morning. According to her, Carl is still a bit groggy, but otherwise he seems much more like himself.

They sit down again at the table in the same places as before. The family recounts how the evening went: Carl had been frightened at times but could be calmed with conversation. Carl himself says that he slept for the first time in a long while and that the voices did not disturb him in the same way. He especially appreciated that his grandfather stayed the night.

Jane asks how yesterday's discussion felt. Carl replies that it felt all right—he has never been able to talk to anyone about the syndicate in this way before. He explains that he came across it a few weeks ago on social media. Jane repeats what Carl has said and invites him to tell more. The others also show interest.

Carl describes the syndicate and how it has made his life difficult recently. The father tries to say that such a syndicate does not exist. This causes Carl to become agitated for a moment, and he begins arguing with his father. Nurse Matt reflects what he has heard and remarks that the topic is clearly difficult. He adds that, in addition to the syndicate, he would also be interested to hear what else has been going on in Carl's life lately. Carl says that school has been hard recently. He also mentions something he would not like to talk about in front of the others. Matt asks whether he might feel comfortable talking about it privately. Matt and Carl then go to Carl's room to talk, while the others continue reviewing the events of the previous evening and the current situation.

In the private conversation, Carl explains that a few weeks earlier he had been messaging with a girl. When he sent her a message, he heard the bullies mocking him. Carl suspected that the syndicate was somehow behind the bullies' voices. Matt repeats Carl's words, but Carl does not respond to the reflection. They sit quietly for a moment, and then Matt summarizes what was said earlier—how Carl had messaged the girl—and says he would be interested to hear more about her. Carl begins to talk, and Matt follows along, summarizing and asking clarifying questions.

Carl and Matt return to the others. Matt says that the conversation felt meaningful to him and that he believes it would be important to continue it with Carl. Carl nods. It is agreed that Matt and Carl will meet again privately later in the week at the outpatient clinic. It is also agreed that the same group will meet with the physician the following week to review how things are progressing and whether the sick leave needs to be extended. The family is encouraged to make contact at any time if concerns or questions arise before then. Matt and Jane summarize the content of the meeting and the plan and ensure that the family feels able to manage until the next appointment.

4.5.2 When Other Services Are Needed

Dialogue often reveals that people might also benefit from other types of services. In such cases, they are not simply referred elsewhere—unless they already have an existing direct contact through which they can arrange an appointment themselves. Instead, the facilitators organize a new dialogical network meeting and invite, as needed, professionals from the relevant services.

If people receive more appropriate help elsewhere and feel that they no longer require dialogical network meetings or, for example, symptom-relieving psychiatric care, the focus of the helping process can gradually be shifted. It can also be agreed that professionals from other services may contact the facilitators when necessary to arrange new network meetings, particularly if they are unable to provide the planned support on their own.

Example of Support from Other Services—Carl's Crisis (Continued)

Matt and Jane return the following week as agreed. A physician also attends the meeting. Between the meetings, Matt has met with Carl privately several times, and together they have explored the situation in more depth. In these discussions, it has emerged, among other things, that Carl feels excluded at high school and has fallen behind in several courses to the point that he no longer knows what to do. He also feels a strong romantic interest in a girl but does not dare approach her. He says he has tried a few times, but the anxiety became unbearable: he froze, unable to speak, and panic rose in him. Sending her a message led to overwhelming shame, and he has been unable to sleep since.

At the beginning of the meeting, Matt, Jane, and the physician first ask how the family has been and what they feel would be most important to begin with. The family reports that Carl has calmed down and no longer talks as much about the syndicate. The father reflects that he himself has not been as quick to argue against it. The mother says that Carl has slept the past few nights without medication, and Carl appears noticeably more alert during the meeting. Jane reflects this observation to Matt, who notes that Carl had already seemed much brighter during their private meeting. Matt says he thinks it would be important to share something about their conversations and asks Carl whether he would like to say anything about them. Carl nods and says it would be good if Matt shared. Matt checks whether there is any topic Carl would prefer not to discuss, but Carl indicates no such concerns.

Matt briefly summarizes the situation and asks the family how it sounds to them. They say they had not realized how difficult school had been for Carl, as he has always done well before. Matt asks Carl how this sounds to him, and Carl says he had been nervous about how his parents would react.

Jane asks the family for permission for her, Matt, and the physician to reflect aloud for a moment on what they have heard. The facilitators discuss what has emerged in the meeting, how important it is that Carl and Matt have been able to talk, and how good it is that the family now knows more about the situation. Jane notes that she found herself wondering how Carl could be supported in returning to school, and also in not having to manage everything alone. Matt and the physician say they have been thinking the same, and the physician suggests that someone at the school might be able to help. Jane says she had been thinking similarly and suggests that the matter should also be discussed with Carl. The practitioners turn to the family and invite their thoughts.

Carl says it sounded like the practitioners genuinely want to help, but he is doubtful that anyone can really help because of the syndicate. The parents reflect that there may be support available at the school. Matt reflects that although Carl is somewhat doubtful, it may still be important to try. He also notes that the parents have raised the idea of involving a school staff member. He asks Carl whether it would be acceptable if someone from the school joined the conversation. Carl replies that he does not mind either way.

At the end of the meeting, it is agreed that Matt will contact the school to arrange a joint meeting. He steps out to make the call while the others sort out practical matters. It is decided that the physician will extend the sick leave until the next meeting, and the family is encouraged to make contact with any concerns in the meantime. Matt returns and reports that the school is available for a meeting the following week. He asks whether everyone would be comfortable meeting at the school.

The following week at the school, Jane and Matt first outline the situation in very general terms and ask Carl to clarify as needed. They then say that they have been wondering what thoughts the school counselor might have, and whether the school could provide support to help Carl return.

The counselor outlines the practical support options available: for example, extra tutoring in subjects where Carl has fallen behind; the possibility of completing assignments more flexibly and in smaller parts; and a designated staff member whom Carl could turn to during the school day. The counselor also suggests that Carl could return to school gradually—attending a few lessons at first and increasing attendance over time. She also mentions that the school has a peer support group for students with social anxiety, which Carl could join if he wishes.

Jane and Matt ask Carl and his parents how this sounds and what they feel would be feasible. The discussion continues by exploring how the support could be put into practice and how collaboration between the school, the family, and the care team should proceed. It is agreed that the school may contact the facilitators directly if challenges arise or if the plan needs further refinement.

In many situations, however, it is beneficial for the facilitators to retain overall responsibility for the helping process, inviting more specialized expertise and competencies into the network meetings only when needed. This helps keep the process more goal-oriented and coherent, allowing additional support to be tailored more precisely to the person's actual needs. Additional expertise may come, for example, from social services or occupational health services. More examples are provided in Table 4.3.

In practice, a holistic system enables situations to be viewed and supported comprehensively, at both the social and individual levels. This may include, in addition to traditional mental healthcare and social services, other dimensions of well-being such as nutrition, lifestyle, daily routines, relationships, spirituality, or existential concerns—depending on what is meaningful for the people involved. The guiding principle is a flexible, experimental approach: small changes are "pushed" and tested from

Table 4.3 Situational indicators guiding continued support and planning

Indicators suggesting a need for continued support	*Possible directions of care following the establishment of a dialogical space*	*Who could be invited to participate*
Situation has stabilized; person feels able to cope	Monitoring and everyday support without intensive treatment	Family members, close friends
Some issues unresolved but no acute risk	Follow-up meeting with the same network	Additional people who may bring helpful perspectives
Need for multidisciplinary support; multiple overlapping concerns	Expanded network meeting	Social services, physician, therapist, teacher, employer, community actors
Somatic concerns, sleep problems, nutritional issues, possible physical illness	Medical assessment and treatment and/or lifestyle support	Physician, nurse, dietitian, physical trainer, health and lifestyle professionals
Loss of meaning, identity confusion, existential distress, cultural dislocation, marginalization, language barriers	Meaning-oriented support; culturally sensitive coordination	Trusted others, counselors or therapists, peer support, cultural mediators or interpreters, community or faith-based resources
Persistent symptoms, recurrent crises, relationship difficulties, need to process past experiences	Psychotherapeutic or other structured therapeutic work	Psychotherapist, occupational or arts therapist, physician
Financial difficulties, unemployment, housing instability	Social or financial support	Social worker, debt counselor, housing services, employment services
Concerns at work or school (absences, overload, bullying, performance pressure)	Support directed at the work or study environment	Employer, occupational health services, union representative, teacher, school counselor
Relationship problems (conflict, violence, separation crisis, loneliness)	Relationship-focused support and mediation options	Close others, family worker, couples therapist, family therapist, mediator, support groups, peer support
Acute risk of violence, psychosis, danger to self or others	Immediate crisis intervention in the safest setting	Physician, inpatient staff, emergency services, police/official assistance

different angles to see what reduces the distress and worry related to the situation. In this way, support is built on people's own experiences and everyday contexts, rather than on predetermined care pathways.

4.5.3 When Ongoing Psychiatric Care Is Needed

If the situation remains unresolved—if participants disagree about the plan or continue to feel unable to manage—the next dialogical meeting is arranged as soon as possible. If needed, the constellation of the meeting is adjusted, and/or additional individual, supportive, and more structured meetings are held to build trust and ensure safety. This process continues until all involved feel sufficiently safe and a shared understanding has emerged, providing a basis for planning more structured treatment process. During this phase, necessary somatic examinations and health checks are also arranged to rule out other contributing factors.

The first circumstance in which immediate medication or hospitalization may be required is when the person behaves so threateningly or is so confused that meaningful contact cannot be established via dialogue, and they pose a danger to themselves or others. Situations in which a person has not slept for an extended period often also require urgent medical intervention.

In other cases, symptom-focused interventions are primarily offered when the situation does not improve despite the dialogical meetings. In practice, this need may become apparent after only a few meetings, or later on if the person's condition worsens or the situation does not progress. In such situations, some may benefit from longer term psychotherapy, others from medication, and some may require hospital care. The key principle is to act according to the current situation and need, while keeping interpretations open so that the contextual nature of psychological difficulties remains visible, and the problem is not overly pathologized as an individual internal disorder. Plans are actively re-evaluated and can be adjusted at any time if people's situations or needs change. The general guideline is to keep the helping process as simple and manageable as possible, allowing different strategies to be tried calmly and minimizing unnecessary overlapping work.

If the situation does not progress, deteriorates, or if people again require help, they may contact either the facilitators directly or the service coordinator to reorganize the process and arrange new dialogical meetings. The system then returns to the open-dialogue phase. Figure 4.2 illustrates a flow of helping process for responding different situations, outlining pathways from immediate network meetings to intensive support, hospitalization, or dialogical follow-up depending on safety and change over time.

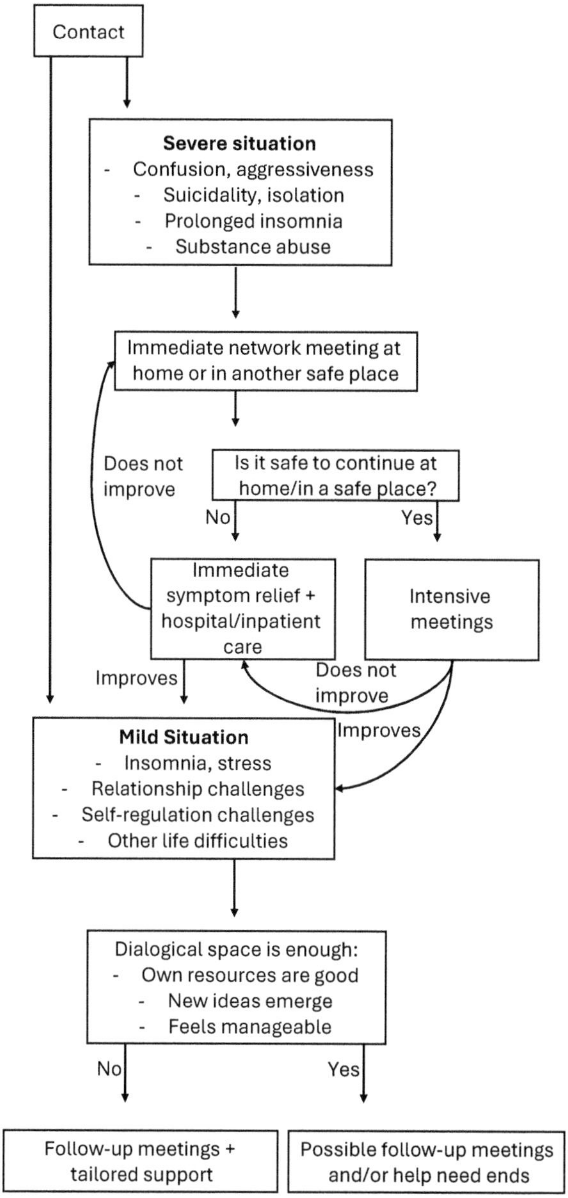

Figure 4.2 Pathway for responding to severe and mild situations.

Example of Continued Psychiatric Care—Carl's Crisis (Continued)

Carl's situation gradually begins to improve. He slowly returns to school and feels he is catching up with his studies. He has been meeting regularly with Matt, and they have been discussing the issues that have been troubling him. Carl no longer talks much about the syndicate, and Matt has not felt it necessary to bring it up. Instead, their conversations focus on other matters: anxiety, social relationships, returning to school, and the feelings connected to these.

Matt and Jane have visited the family a few times each month, exploring the situation from different perspectives. Over time, Carl begins to feel that the syndicate has left him alone. He reflects—almost with a hint of humor—on how he ever even came up with such an idea. He tells them he has made new friends in a group and gained confidence in social situations. The frequency of meetings is reduced, and eventually they agree that Carl and the family can get in touch again if needed.

About a year later, Carl calls Matt in distress. He says the bullies' voices have returned, and he can't sleep. Matt reassures him and asks him to tell more. Carl explains he recently tried to ask a girl out but was rejected. Matt reflects aloud that the experience must have felt painful and that it sounds like it may have stirred up some older feelings again. He suggests they meet already that afternoon at the clinic.

Carl comes to the appointment. This time Matt offers coffee. Talking feels relieving to Carl, but already the following night he calls the emergency line: he still cannot sleep, and the voices are telling him to harm himself. The service coordinator asks whether Carl could come to the hospital for one night to rest. Carl arrives with his parents. The coordinator also invites a doctor, and together they briefly go through the current situation and what has happened.

Carl explains he met with Matt earlier in the day and that the voices subsided for a while but returned in the evening. His parents tell the coordinator and doctor how similar situations have been handled in the past. They agree that Carl will stay for one night in the hospital and receive a sleep-supporting medication. Carl falls asleep almost immediately.

The next day Matt, a staff member from the inpatient ward, Carl, and the family meet. They go through how the situation developed. Matt asks each person to share how they see the situation, what feelings it evokes, and how the issues raised in the conversation sound to them. Carl says he already feels better and the voices have quieted. He thinks he is able to manage at home. His parents also feel the situation is safe enough—after all, they have managed through even more difficult phases before.

They agree that Carl will go home and receive a sick leave note for the rest of the week. They also agree that Matt will visit the family during the week and update the doctor afterward regarding the need to extend sick leave. Carl is given a few nights' worth of sleep-supporting medication to take home.

When Matt visits the family, everyone feels the situation has calmed, and Carl has not needed the medication. Matt and Carl schedule a follow-up meeting for the next week to go through the situation. They meet a few more times, after which they agree that Carl can get in touch again whenever needed.

4.6 When a Dialogical Space Cannot Be Reached

It is not always possible to establish a dialogical space, even when all the steps described above are followed. Sometimes a person's condition or circumstances are such that a meaningful connection cannot be formed despite various attempts. At times, people cannot be properly reached, and at other times, they may become provoked by the offer of help. In some situations, a family member may be worried without sufficient grounds, and treatment is not considered necessary. In other cases, the conversation simply does not progress for a variety of reasons: someone may remain silent, others may talk excessively, and someone might leave the situation abruptly, slamming the door behind them.

Example of an Unsuccessful Dialogue—Bob, Who Had Barricaded Himself at Home

The service coordinator receives a call from a person who reports that his friend, Bob, has barricaded himself inside his apartment. The coordinator asks clarifying questions: what their relationship is like and what the friend thinks may have happened. The friend explains that during their last meeting Bob spoke in strange ways that sounded delusional. He had not dared to challenge Bob, as Bob is impulsive and easily angered. Together, they conclude that it would be good to try to reach Bob and arrange a meeting. The friend does not want to take part himself because he fears Bob's reaction. They agree that the service coordinator will try to make contact.

Bob does not answer the calls. The coordinator checks the staff schedule and sees that Matt and Jane have time to visit Bob's apartment.

Matt and Jane go to knock on the door, but Bob does not open. A nauseating smell seeps from inside. Matt and Jane become concerned. When nothing is heard, they request assistance from the police. The police and ambulance arrive, and the door is opened with a master key. It is agreed that the officers will remain at the doorway so that Bob does not become startled by their presence.

Bob is found lying naked on the floor, muttering to himself. Jane stays a little farther back while Matt crouches beside him, introduces himself, and asks how Bob is doing. Bob does not respond. Jane finds some clothing and hands it to Matt, who gently asks whether he may help Bob get dressed. Bob suddenly lashes out, pulls away, and backs into a corner.

Matt tries to talk to him and establish contact, but Bob does not respond. A police officer intervenes in a firmer tone, which makes Bob shout. Matt tries to calm him, reflecting aloud that Bob seems frightened and that their intention is to help. After 5 minutes, no progress has been made, and Bob appears even more agitated. He begins to mutter threateningly. It is decided that Bob will be transported to the emergency department.

When the police help Bob to his feet, he starts swinging his arms and tries to retreat to the corner again. The officers eventually guide him into the patrol car and transport him to the emergency department, where he is admitted to the psychiatric ward for observation.

Matt and Jane agree that Jane will accompany Bob to the hospital, as Matt has another appointment. At the hospital, they sit down and review the events. Jane explains how the situation unfolded and that Bob is clearly frightened by something. She reflects that Bob is likely even more confused and scared now after being brought in against his will. She wonders how they might convey to him that they do not want to harm him, that he is safe, and that they are trying to help. Bob does not respond. He scans the room anxiously and occasionally shouts threats. Toward the end of the meeting, Bob attempts to strike the doctor, and he is secluded and medicated against his will.

The next day, Bob is calmer and more responsive. Jane visits him in the seclusion room together with a ward nurse. Bob says he remembers Jane from the previous day. He explains that his neighbors have installed cameras in his apartment and mock him whenever he does anything. He also suspects they have tried to poison him.

Jane repeats parts of what Bob says and notes that he clearly seemed frightened the day before and must still be distressed. She tells him that in the hospital he is safe and that there is no immediate threat. Jane turns to the ward nurse and says that Bob seems calm at the moment and asks whether he could go to the ward for lunch. The nurse agrees, and they decide to end the seclusion. Jane accompanies Bob to lunch and asks him light questions—who he is, what his life is like. Bob answers cautiously. Jane and Bob agree to meet again the next day.

It is important to note, however, that situations such as those described above are very common precisely in a reductionistic mental health system. By actively striving toward a *dialogical space*, it is often possible to increase the likelihood that such difficulties do not arise in the first place. This will not always succeed, but the foundation of a holistic system is to *increase the probability of success* by prioritizing high-quality encounters and, through them, fostering collaborative relationships. Such relationships are themselves a form of effective mental health care, while simultaneously providing a stronger foundation for more delineated or reductionist treatments and for sustaining engagement with care. Dialogical space may also emerge later, even if it is not possible initially.

The guiding principle is that every new interaction is an opportunity for dialogue. It should also be emphasized that a successful dialogical relationship does not depend on fluent or skilled verbal conversation, but rather on the embodied experience of being encountered and heard, and of feeling sufficiently safe for new perspectives and shared thinking to become possible. Thus, instead of "good" conversation, the aim is to strengthen the *embodied and emotional sense of safety and collaboration* in the situation, so that participants begin to feel more at ease and the worry or distress they experience starts to subside. This is seen as an intrinsic therapeutic goal, because it is precisely worry and distress that typically serve as indicators for interpreting a situation as a mental health disorder.

If the worry persists and does not begin to ease, or if strong confrontation develops between workers and participants, the constellation of meetings may be adjusted and/or an external facilitator invited to help navigate the situation. In such cases, an outside professional joins the meeting to reflect on the process and to support the re-emergence of a dialogical space by reassessing the helping process. The basic methodology of reflective practice can be applied, for example, by having the external facilitator temporarily guide the discussion and invite all participants to reflect on the process as if the workers themselves were service users, with an equal capacity to articulate their thoughts, experiences, and feelings about what is unfolding.

This is often helpful, as strained or unfavorable interaction can affect professionals as well: interpersonal chemistry may not work, and the style of working may inadvertently shift toward a more authoritarian stance, which in turn can provoke further resistance among participants. An external facilitator can observe the situation with greater distance and help restore a dialogical tone of the meeting, which often opens up new understanding and supports the development of an updated, more functional plan.

4.7 Summary of Dialogical Space

Holistic and dialogical practice is grounded in the idea that understanding and addressing unfavorable situations occurs most effectively through reciprocal and polyphonic encounters that can be arranged flexibly and promptly in settings where people feel safe when seeking help. Rather than beginning with diagnosis or predefined methods, helping starts from the service user's lived experience and the perspectives of their close social network. Through dialogical methods such as open-ended questioning, reflective listening, repetitions, and attending to participants' utterances, these voices are brought into relation with one another, allowing a shared understanding of the situation to emerge. When joint dialogue is difficult to establish, trust is built through flexibility in the different composition of participants and by emphasizing emotional safety, enabling the process to be tailored to the needs of those involved. This process itself optimizes common therapeutic factors across contexts: being heard, feeling included, and engaging in joint reflection enhance agency and create space for flexible, simple, and context-sensitive responses to everyday challenges.

Diagnostic categories and predefined interventions may be used, but only insofar as they genuinely support the situation at hand. In this respect, the holistic framework differs from reductionistic approaches that emphasize symptom classification and standardized treatment protocols. Within a holistic framework, the primary aim is to create a space for genuine encounter and the emergence of shared meaning, from which the care pathway is shaped on a case-by-case basis. When the care process becomes stalled or difficulties arise, new dialogical spaces can be promptly created by reorganizing the process—bringing together all relevant participants and actively fostering reciprocal, reflective, and curious dialogue to restore shared meaning.

Beyond increased personalization of care and the optimization of common therapeutic factors, this type of approach has been associated with the strengthening of social capital, mutual trust, and support within the general population (Aaltonen et al., 2011). Strengthened social capital and community support can provide emotional containment and everyday coping resources, increasing individuals' capacity to manage distress and helping to prevent situations from escalating to a level that would be interpreted as a psychiatric.

The contrast between holistic and reductionistic frameworks becomes particularly evident in routine clinical situations, as illustrated in Table 4.4.

Table 4.4 Examples of how similar situations may be approached within holistic and reductionist frameworks

Situation	*Holistic framework*	*Reductionist framework*
A young person reports anxiety and insomnia	A joint meeting is arranged with the family and teacher. Everyone shares their perspective, and practical everyday adjustments are agreed upon together.	Symptoms are recorded; a diagnostic suspicion is made (e.g., anxiety disorder); medication is initiated or the person is referred to an evidence-based therapy.
A person hears voices	A network meeting is held where the voices are explored as experiences with multiple possible meanings. Safety, participation, and shared understanding are strengthened.	Voices are interpreted as symptoms of a psychotic disorder. A diagnosis is made and neuroleptic medication is initiated.
An unemployed adult becomes depressed	The impact of unemployment on daily life and self-esteem is discussed. Solutions are sought collaboratively with close others and the broader support network.	Depressive symptoms are assessed, and if diagnostic criteria are met, treatment is started according to clinical guidelines (e.g., medication, psychotherapy).
A young person withdraws from social relationships	Family and network members meet together. The meaning of withdrawal is explored, and efforts focus on strengthening participation and trust.	Withdrawal is interpreted as a symptom of depression, social anxiety, or a prodromal symptom. Treatment is initiated based on the interpretation and diagnosis.

(*Continued*)

Table 4.4 (Continued)

Situation	*Holistic framework*	*Reductionist framework*
A parent is worried about a child's restlessness at school	Parents, teacher, and child meet together. Restlessness is viewed from different perspectives, and practical adjustments are agreed upon.	ADHD assessments and questionnaires are conducted; the child is referred to child psychiatry and possibly to medication.
An older adult feels lonely and low in mood	Life situation and social relationships are explored. Practical everyday solutions are sought together (e.g., activities, community involvement).	Symptoms are interpreted as depression. Antidepressant medication and referral to psychotherapy are initiated.
A student experiences panic attacks during lectures	The student, an academic advisor, and a close person discuss the meaning of the experiences. Coping strategies and study-related support are identified together.	Panic attacks are diagnosed as panic disorder. SSRI medication and CBT are initiated.
A family is in crisis due to a young person's substance use	The whole family meets together. The meanings of substance use and the family's concerns and hopes are discussed openly.	The young person is referred to substance-use services. Treatment focuses on reducing the individual's use; further assessment and therapy are offered if the young person commits to abstinence.
An employee feels burnt out	The employee, supervisor, and occupational health services meet. Workload and possible adjustments are discussed collaboratively.	Burnout is recorded as a depressive disorder to enable sick leave; treatment is provided in occupational health services according to guidelines.
A child has nightmares following parents' divorce	The family meets to discuss the child's experiences. Fears are taken seriously, and daily routines are adjusted to increase safety and predictability.	Nightmares are interpreted as symptoms of anxiety or a sleep disorder. The child is referred to further assessment and behavioral therapy.

References

Aaltonen, J., Seikkula, J., & Lehtinen, K. (2011). The comprehensive open-dialogue approach in Western Lapland: I. The incidence of non-affective psychosis and prodromal states. *Psychosis: Psychological, Social and Integrative Approaches, 3*(3), 179–191. https://doi.org/10.1080/17522439.2011.601750

Bergström, T., Kurtti, M., Duthie, A., Valtanen, K., & Seikkula, J. (2025). Open dialogue. In O. Smoliak, E. Tseliou, T. Strong, S. Bava, & P. Muntigl (Eds.), *The Routledge international handbook of postmodern therapies* (pp. 174–185). Routledge. https://doi.org/10.4324/9781003376231-14

World Health Organization. (2021). *Guidance on community mental health services: Promoting person-centred and rights-based approaches.* World Health Organization. https://creativecommons.org/licenses/by-nc-sa/3.0/igo/

Chapter 5

Special Topics

The next chapters turn from the core event of the holistic system—the dialogical space—to a set of practical questions that often determine whether a service model remains genuinely holistic in everyday work. In the previous chapters, the argument has been that many difficulties currently operationalized as psychiatric or mental health disorders are best understood as emergent, context-bound situations, and that effective help therefore begins with building a shared understanding in dialogue.

Yet real systems are shaped not only by ideals but by administrative requirements, risk considerations, regulatory frameworks, professional boundaries, and training traditions. Special topics such as diagnosis-making, medication use, hospitalization, and role distribution are precisely the points where a model's underlying ontology becomes visible: either the system continues to organize care around the evolving situation as a whole, or it quietly slides back toward reductionist defaults in which problems are defined early, allocated to specialized pathways, and treated according to prespecified categories.

The aim of this chapter is, therefore, to show how the dialogical foundation can be protected and operationalized when the work becomes difficult, urgent, or institutionally constrained. Rather than treating diagnoses, medications, wards, or professional hierarchies as separate "modules" that override the dialogical process, these topics are approached as design challenges: how can a system meet legitimate needs for safety, coordination, documentation, and relief of acute distress while still keeping the person's lived situation—and the network's shared understanding—at the center? Each section examines one such pressure point and outlines principles for responding in a way that preserves flexibility, reduces reification and coercion, and supports continuity across settings.

Note that the term "symptom" is used in this chapter to facilitate communication across disciplines, institutions, and regulatory frameworks, to ensure a shared point of reference among reductionist frameworks. From the perspective of the holistic framework, however, a more

DOI: 10.4324/9781003777939-8

appropriate vocabulary would refer instead to experiences, distress, or situational difficulties—terms that better capture the contextual and relational nature of what is being addressed.

5.1 Diagnoses

Because, in the holistic system, support is organized *case by case*—guided by the shared understanding that emerges in the dialogical process rather than by diagnosis-specific, group-level treatment guidelines—making a psychiatric diagnosis at the outset of care is not necessary. Descriptive diagnoses can nevertheless be used when they are helpful in the given situation.

Today, people may also identify themselves as meeting certain diagnostic criteria, as these have become widely embedded in popular culture, including through social media. Many such criteria describe general and easily relatable psychosocial difficulties or human traits. Because psychiatric diagnoses have long been used as tools to reduce stigma, some diagnoses have become socially acceptable—and even guilt-relieving—ways of framing particular characteristics or life challenges, even though they are, by definition, *descriptive* rather than explanatory (Bergström, 2023).

For a holistic helping system, the crucial issue is the position from which a diagnosis is offered. If, for example, psychiatric professionals assign a diagnosis at the very beginning of care, dialogical engagement and the case-specific tailoring of the process become more difficult, as both the problem and its solution become predefined. By contrast, if a person themselves reports that they believe they meet the criteria for a particular diagnosis, this does not in itself hinder open dialogue or the construction of a shared understanding of their overall situation. On the contrary, it can serve as a fruitful starting point for exploring what meaning the diagnosis holds for them, what it captures, what they actually hope for from services, and how they would like others to relate to them and to their difficulties.

Example of Self-Diagnosis—Abigail, Who Wonders About Having a Diagnosis

Abigail calls the service coordinator. She explains that she continually struggles in her professional work: managing her calendar is difficult, she forgets meetings, misplaces items, and often leaves agreed-upon tasks unfinished. She says that she has looked into the matter and noticed that her symptoms resemble those of ADHD. Abigail wonders whether she could undergo an assessment.

Service coordinator Sam listens, asks clarifying questions, and reflects back what Abigail has said: that Abigail has recognized many ADHD diagnostic criteria that seem to describe her. Sam also asks whether, besides a formal assessment, there might be other ways to help. Abigail says that she naturally hopes for relief from her difficulties and has wondered whether medication might help, and, therefore, she needs correct diagnosis.

Sam and Abigail agree that she could come in for a meeting to think things through together. Sam asks whether Abigail would like anyone else to join the session. Abigail reflects that her difficulties also burden her partner, and arguments occur frequently, but she does not want to trouble them. Sam encourages her to consider inviting the partner, especially if Abigail feels that the difficulties affect the relationship. Abigail says she will think about it and suggests that a meeting within the next month might be good. Sam checks the schedule and sees that nurse Anna and psychologist Jane would be available the following week.

Abigail arrives at the meeting with her partner. She begins listing the symptoms she has noticed. Anna and Jane listen, ask follow-up questions, and invite the partner's perspective. The partner explains that Abigail's forgetfulness itself is not troubling, but they do recognize that the couple argues a lot.

Anna and Jane ask whether they might reflect together for a moment, while Abigail and her partner simply listen. Jane says that Abigail appears to be facing several challenges and has wondered whether they match ADHD. Jane adds that she is curious what ADHD means *to* Abigail, and what feelings the diagnosis evokes for her. Anna continues that she was thinking along similar lines and that she also sensed strongly that Abigail feels inadequate—especially at work. She asks Jane whether she sensed something similar. Jane confirms this, noting that she felt it particularly when Abigail talked about work pressure and her sense of not managing. She says that she is wondering what "not managing" means for Abigail in practice and what might help. She also wonders whether she heard echoes of the same theme when the couple talked about their relationship. Anna nods and says that she had a similar impression and would be very interested to hear what Abigail and her partner think of their reflections.

Anna and Jane turn back to the couple. Abigail, now tearful, begins to speak about her feelings of inadequacy: she has always felt inferior, that she does not manage well, and that she is somehow abnormal. Anna reflects her words and asks the partner what they think. The partner says, surprised, that they had not known any of this—they have always seen Abigail as exceptionally confident. Even in arguments, the partner often feels cornered and has no choice but to defend themselves.

Abigail begins crying more. Jane says that hearing Abigail's experience was moving and that it evoked a strong feeling in her as well. Anna agrees, asks gently how Abigail is feeling now, and hands her a tissue.

Abigail says that she feels guilty mainly because of the arguments. Anna reflects this and links it to Abigail's earlier description of feeling inadequate. Abigail nods and says that she does not want to treat her partner badly. Anna reflects her words again and asks the partner whether this brings up any thoughts. The partner answers that they generally do not feel Abigail treats them badly—quite the opposite.

Jane adds that, listening to the conversation, she had a strong sense that Abigail carries a deep feeling of inferiority and insufficiency, which may color many situations—but that this is only her own impression, and she would very much like to hear Abigail's view. Abigail, now calmer, begins describing how she has experienced this feeling throughout her life and how she believes it affects both her work and her relationship.

By the end of the conversation, Abigail looks noticeably relieved. The couple says they found the session helpful and would like to continue the discussion. They agree to meet again with the same team the following week.

Although diagnoses are not necessary for arranging help within a holistic system—and especially in the early stages of a care process, it is often advisable to avoid them—they can nevertheless be used when needed, for example, in the following situations:

1 When long-term treatment is required and clearer differential diagnostic information is needed to support, for instance, medication planning.
2 In the context of sick-leave certificates, disability pensions, medication reimbursement, or any other situation requiring communication with actors outside the mental health system.

Even in these cases, it is not meaningful to pursue excessive precision in psychiatric diagnosis, as diagnostic validity and discriminant capacity are inherently weak. In most situations, it would be sufficient to use only *high-level diagnostic codes* that help clinicians broadly identify whether certain symptom-focused treatments might be useful or harmful, and what kinds of supportive measures a person might need. As is already common practice, coding can be based on the *quality of symptoms*, which is usually straightforward to determine during the initial sessions. Additional specifiers describing symptom severity and duration could be added. These would help justify urgency and immediate interventions in situations that have become prolonged or require rapid symptom relief, and the same coding system could support justification for different types of social or occupational supports.

From the perspective of a more comprehensive, holistic system, one might also question whether traditional disease categories and terms are needed at all, or whether diagnostic codes or general symptom descriptions would suffice. Such an approach would reduce the problem of reification—whereby people come to explain their life difficulties through diagnostic labels that often carry self-fulfilling, inaccurate, and othering stereotypes.

Using diagnostic codes primarily for administrative purposes would not, in practice, differ greatly from the systems already in place in many countries, where service in-take, psychiatric sick-leave, or disability decisions are based on a psychiatric diagnosis that itself is grounded in the clinician's description of the person's current situation. What would differ is that the practice would become more transparent and reduce the pressure to pathologies a person's characteristics with disease concepts. This could, in turn, decrease situations in which a psychiatric diagnosis becomes the *prerequisite* for accessing necessary support, forcing individuals' difficulties to be framed as a medical disorder—often diverting care and rehabilitation in directions that are not useful for resolving the actual situation.

When the situation does not need to be explained away through a diagnosis, attention can shift to concrete life circumstances, environmental factors, strain, relationships, and working conditions—factors that are often directly modifiable and that typically provide a more accurate explanation for the difficulties at hand.

Example of Using Diagnoses—Abigail, Who Is Considering a Diagnosis (continued)

As the meetings progress, Abigail begins to be more compassionate toward herself. The couple argues less, and Abigail feels she is coping better at work. She still struggles, however, with tasks that require sustained concentration, and she becomes easily exhausted.

With Abigail's permission, psychologist Jane arranges a network meeting together with occupational health services and Abigail's employer to review the situation. Jane and Abigail visit Abigail's workplace. The desired adjustments to Abigail's workload cannot be implemented in the way they had hoped, and the accumulation of tasks increases her exhaustion. It is agreed that the physician will issue a short sick-leave certificate to allow time to identify what support may be helpful and to determine how best to proceed. In the medical report, the doctor uses a high-level diagnostic code, but instead of the word *mood disorder*, the report uses the same descriptive language that has been used in conversations with Abigail.

Abigail is still wondering about an ADHD diagnosis, and she and Jane agree to proceed with psychological testing. The assessment indicates mild vulnerabilities in attentional functioning. Abigail and Jane decide that they should meet once more together with the physician.

Jane, Abigail, and the doctor meet to discuss the situation from several perspectives. They review that the employer cannot make the necessary adjustments to Abigail's workload and that the strain at work is affecting her overall well-being. Abigail says that she would still like to try medication used for treating attention-related difficulties. Based on the discussion, background information, and the psychologist's assessment, the physician prescribes a trial of stimulant medication. On the prescription, the doctor uses a high-level diagnostic code, but in practice, Jane and the doctor discuss the medication with Abigail simply as something she may temporarily use in specific work situations that require a certain kind of focused attention. They also explore other ways to strengthen attention and concentration over time so that Abigail could manage her work without medication in the future.

Abigail tries the medication and feels that it helps her manage some of her tasks more effectively. She gains small experiences of success, and her overall capacity begins to recover. The medication, however, also causes side effects: reduced appetite and an occasional sense of feeling "stuck." They discuss this together with the physician and agree to try further task adjustments in the workplace so that Abigail might cope without the medication.

Jane and Abigail continue meeting with the employer. They systematically review the situation and eventually agree that Abigail's tasks will be temporarily adapted to better match her abilities. Deadlines become more flexible, and she is given more room to manage her workload.

After these adjustments, Abigail manages without medication and feels that this also strengthens her self-esteem. Both her well-being and work performance begin to improve.

A final meeting is held with occupational health services and the employer to summarize the process. The employer is satisfied with Abigail's performance, and it is agreed that she will continue to have more influence over how she organizes her work.

Later, Abigail meets with Jane and Anna together with her partner. They revisit the earlier conversations: what initially emerged in the sessions and where the feelings of inadequacy may have originated. Abigail explains how she has experienced these feelings since childhood—how her parents were demanding, how school valued performance, and how her siblings always seemed to do better, while she was more restless and less interested in schoolwork.

The group meets a few more times to work through the themes that emerged in the dialogue and to consolidate the process. The treatment is then concluded as agreed. Abigail is encouraged to get in touch at a low threshold if she feels the need for further support in the future.

A practice in which diagnoses are used primarily to *describe* a situation rather than to define presumed underlying mechanisms corresponds closely to the original purpose of modern psychiatric classification: to facilitate communication between professionals, support the coordination of care, and organize services. In this sense, descriptive diagnostics—precisely because it does not reduce difficulties to predetermined causal entities—is indeed compatible with a holistic system.

Table 5.1 illustrates a model aligned with a holistic framework by organizing a person's current experiences into broad, descriptive categories corresponding to contemporary high-level diagnostic groupings. The urgency of care is indicated by a separate urgency code reflecting the need for psychiatric symptom relief. In addition, the table outlines potential add-on interventions that may be used alongside a dialogical, needs-adapted process when acute or prolonged distress requires additional support.

The purpose of the table is not to explain problems through disease mechanisms but to offer a practical example of how to describe a situation, support the coordination of care, and assess when medication, crisis support, or other forms of assistance are warranted. The table is, therefore, indicative rather than prescriptive: it is intended to demonstrate how different situations can already be described with existing higher-level diagnostic categories in ways that are more consistent with a holistic framework.

Table 5.1 Example of indicative symptom clusters and needs-based add-on interventions within a holistic framework

Experience cluster (aligned with major contemporary diagnostic groupings)	*Urgency of psychiatric symptom relief (specifier)*	*Possible add-on interventions (alongside the dialogical process)*
Psychosis (confusion, hallucinations, loss of shared reality, difficult interaction, "unusual" behavior)	**Low:** contact possible, supportive network adequate, shared sense of coping	Monitoring, needs-based support
	High: no contact, aggression/confusion, insufficient support network, shared concern, previous withdrawal symptoms/relapses after stopping neuroleptics	Needs-based crisis care; initiation of neuroleptic medication or return to a previous dose; cautious dose reduction if there is a history of withdrawal-related symptoms
Mania (restlessness, disinhibited behavior, grandiosity, loss of control, severe insomnia)	**Low:** contact intact, able to self-regulate, support network functional	Monitoring, needs-based support
	High: loss of contact, risk-taking behavior, aggression/impulsivity, shared concern	Needs-based crisis care, mood stabilizer initiation/adjustment; short-term neuroleptics or sedatives if needed; SSRIs with high caution; close monitoring
Mood difficulties (low mood, impaired functioning, hopelessness, despair)	**Low:** first contact, support network functioning, sense of coping	Monitoring, needs-based support
	High: acute suicidality, collapse of functioning, prolonged episode, shared concern	Needs-based crisis care, initiation or intensification of antidepressant medication; return to previous dose if indicated; for severe/prolonged cases: ECT/psychedelic/ketamine evaluation, long-term psychotherapy

(*Continued*)

Table 5.1 (Continued)

Experience cluster (aligned with major contemporary diagnostic groupings)	*Urgency of psychiatric symptom relief (specifier)*	*Possible add-on interventions (alongside the dialogical process)*
Anxiety- and compulsion-related difficulties (persistent fear or anxiety, panic reactions, avoidance, intrusive thoughts, and compulsive coping behaviors)	**Low:** support network functioning, shared experience of coping	Monitoring, needs-based support
	High: acute suicidality, collapse of functioning, prolonged difficulties, concern about coping	Needs-based crisis care, short-term medication; breathing and calming techniques; exposure-based therapies, long-term psychotherapy
Difficulties in executive functioning and social interaction (concentration, daily functioning, social overload)	**Low:** first contact, support network functioning, sense of coping	Monitoring, needs-based support
	High: significant decline in functioning	Environmental/ routine adjustments; occupational therapy; stimulant medication if indicated; social skills support, long-term psychotherapy

Note: Across all experience clusters, the presence of significant substance use should be understood as an indicator for increased treatment intensity and closer support, regardless of the specific presentation. Similarly, experiences of trauma should be actively explored and taken into account in all situations, as they may shape both current difficulties and responses to care, independently of category.

In a fully holistic system, the codes supporting service organization could describe situations and related needs with greater precision. In line with the logic of Figure 3.3, an adverse situation could function as a basic Code 1, prompting an initial dialogical meeting, represented by solid arrows, on the basis that someone is experiencing distress or concern. If the situation becomes prolonged or requires more acute support, Code 2, illustrated by dotted arrows, could be used together with a subcode indicating whether—based on shared understanding in dialogue—support should be directed primarily toward individual factors (e.g., psychotherapy), toward social contexts (e.g., family or environmental support), or both.

For longer-term support needs, Code 3, represented by dash–dotted arrows, and corresponding subcodes could indicate the level at which challenges primarily arise and the type of assistance most likely to prevent adverse situations from recurring. This approach acknowledges that some individuals experience enduring difficulties that, within a given cultural or societal context, place them at heightened risk of unfavorable situations—such as permanent disability, vulnerability to rebound psychosis, homelessness, poverty, or the absence of a supportive network. Situation-level diagnostics would thus make it possible to target long-term or structural factors more effectively and to strengthen preventive efforts.

Within such situational diagnostics, psychotropic medication could be guided by subcodes classified according to typical symptom-focused indications similarly as in Table 5.1, such as psychosis, mania, elevated mood/anxiety, lowered mood/depression, insomnia, difficulties with executive functioning, or—if symptoms do not clearly fit—mixed or unspecified presentations. Additional codes, alongside urgency, could also indicate caution with medication, for instance, when dosing needs to be adjusted slowly because of previous relapses during dose reduction. In this way, situational diagnostics and associated subcodes would immediately convey what the situation involves and how medication might be planned without presupposing hidden causal mechanisms or relying on classic disease entities at all.

5.2 Medication

In holistic framework, psychotropic medication is typically approached with caution, including an emphasis on the lowest effective dose and a primary focus on situations involving risk of harm to oneself or others, prolonged insomnia, or circumstances in which the situation does not otherwise begin to improve. From holistic perspective, there are several reasons for adopting a cautious approach to psychopharmacology.

First, in a low-threshold system, many people enter services whose situations may, from a reductionist perspective, be interpreted as mental disorders, even though their "symptoms" are likely to resolve spontaneously or after only a few meetings—without the need for long-term medication. If symptomatic medication were automatically initiated for everyone, overmedication would quickly become a systemic problem. For the same reason, diagnostic labeling is best avoided in the early stages of the support process.

Second, psychotropic medication poses multiple challenges, which is why avoiding unnecessary long-term treatment should be a systemic priority. Although medication may appear lightweight and easily scalable—and is often simpler to initiate than other interventions—it is, for following reasons, *resource-intensive*:

1. Slow therapeutic response and monitoring:
   Most psychotropic medications require weeks or months before their effects can be meaningfully evaluated. This prolongs treatment even in situations that might otherwise resolve after a few sessions or with other forms of support.
2. Complexity of tapering:
   Gradual dose reduction after long-term use is often difficult, and rapid tapering can trigger withdrawal effects that complicate or prolong care.
3. Challenges of long-term use:
   The brain may adapt to medication over time, diminishing its effectiveness and increasing the need for dose escalation and more intensive monitoring (e.g., Li, 2016; Targum, 2014). This heightens the risk of adverse effects and increases strain on the system. For example, in the case of neuroleptic medication, one proposed mechanism is dopaminergic sensitization: prolonged dopamine receptor blockade may lead the brain to compensate by increasing receptor sensitivity, which can reduce therapeutic effects over time and increase vulnerability to withdrawal symptoms (Seeman, 2011; Horowitz et al., 2021).

Especially long-term psychotropic medication is associated with numerous side effects and complications that can manifest across different parts of the service system and consume substantial resources. Despite this, long-term treatment remains common and is often justified on the grounds that it prevents relapse. However, evidence for the long-term benefit–risk ratio of psychotropic medication, even in the treatment of people diagnosed with schizophrenia and other psychoses, remains limited and in many respects inconsistent (e.g., Correll et al., 2018; Vinkers et al., 2024).

In the treatment of people diagnosed with schizophrenia, much of the evidence supporting long-term neuroleptic use derives from registry studies in which periods without medication are associated with higher rates of relapse and mortality (e.g., Tiihonen et al., 2017; Taipale et al., 2020). However, such designs, in which individuals serve as their own controls, cannot definitively establish medication efficacy, because medication-free periods may also reflect poorer adherence, adverse effects, or withdrawal phenomena—particularly when medication is discontinued without adequate support and gradual tapering, as is likely the case in naturalistic samples. In this context, withdrawal-related symptoms may also be misinterpreted as manifestations of the underlying disorder, thereby reinforcing the rationale for continued long-term treatment.

When evaluating all people diagnosed with psychosis from the first onset, long-term studies suggest that greater cumulative exposure to neuroleptic medication is associated with poorer long-term outcomes (e.g., Bergström et al., 2018, 2020; Bergström & Gauffin, 2023; Harrow & Jobe, 2018; Joukamaa et al., 2006; Moilanen et al., 2013). However, these findings are similarly subject to confounding by indication, as individuals with more severe or persistent symptoms are more likely to receive higher doses and longer treatment durations. Although these studies have included statistical adjustment for confounders, this limitation cannot be fully addressed in observational designs and can only be reliably controlled through randomized studies.

One randomized controlled trial (RCT) found that gradual dose reduction after first-episode psychosis was associated with better functional outcomes at a seven-year follow-up (Wunderink et al., 2013). A recent replication showed that although tapering increased relapse risk in the short term, relapse itself did not adversely affect long-term prognosis (Moncrieff et al., 2023; 2025), and most participants were able to reduce medication without major difficulties. At the individual level, experiences of tapering were generally positive, not only because of reduced side effects but also because the process enhanced a sense of agency and strengthened the therapeutic relationship (Morant et al., 2023). Within a holistic system of care, such effects are regarded as intrinsically valuable components of effectiveness, alongside changes in symptoms.

Several assumptions that have historically been used to justify long-term medication use in the treatment of psychosis—such as the view of people diagnosed with schizophrenia as having a uniformly progressive illness, or the idea that psychosis is inherently neurotoxic—have not received consistent empirical support (e.g., Rund, 2014; Zipursky et al., 2013). This is understandable, since psychiatric diagnoses are descriptive constructs based on heterogeneous symptom patterns and life trajectories and, therefore, do not permit straightforward causal inferences about medication effects or outcomes. For example, people diagnosed with schizophrenia may show higher relapse risk during medication reduction, but this largely reflects the severity and recurrence of symptoms on which the diagnosis itself is based, rather than the presence of a distinct latent disease entity. In this sense, the diagnosis functions primarily as a descriptive marker of elevated risk inferred from previous clinical presentation and longitudinal course, rather than as a causal explanation.

While dose reduction or discontinuation is associated with increased relapse risk at the group level, longitudinal studies also indicate that many individuals diagnosed with psychosis experience good long-term outcomes with minimal medication or none at all (Bergström et al., 2020; Bergström & Gauffin, 2023; Harrow & Jobe, 2018). It is also well established that responses to psychotropic medication vary substantially between individuals, independently of diagnostic category (e.g., Maj et al., 2020; 2021). These findings highlight the limits of reductionist, group-average knowledge: aggregated effects may obscure substantial individual variation in treatment response, recovery trajectories, and the role of medication over time (Speyer & Roe, 2024).

For these reasons, psychiatry has increasingly emphasized *personalized* psychopharmacology. Medication should not be evaluated solely on diagnosis or population-level evidence but in relation to each person's subjective experience, goals, and tolerance for risk (Maj et al., 2020; 2021). In practice, this means attending to which effects the person finds meaningful and what trade-offs they are prepared to make regarding both discontinuation and maintenance.

At the same time, a more holistic and pluralistic understanding of medication effects has emerged (Aftab & Stein, 2022). Rather than viewing effects as linear—assuming that a specific neurobiological change automatically produces a specific psychological outcome—psychotropic medications are seen as acting through interconnected mechanisms: neurobiological processes, psychological factors, expectations, meanings, environmental influences, social interactions, and lived experience. This account better fits the often nonspecific and individually variable effects of medication: the same drug may help one person and hinder another, regardless of diagnosis, depending on context.

This pluralistic view aligns well with the holistic framework, in which care is tailored to each situation and its emergent properties. Medication is not initiated or continued automatically but considered within a broader process aimed first at strengthening safety and stability through other means. A selective approach avoids the risks of default maintenance treatment, such as continuing medication "just in case" without systematic reevaluation. At the same time, medication can be initiated rapidly when needed, as the holistic system lacks redundant assessment steps, referrals, or waiting lists that usually delay acute support.

While the holistic system recognizes that both acute and maintenance psychotropic medication is sometimes necessary, it is not understood—consistent with the pluralistic view—as a targeted intervention acting on a specific disease mechanism. This does not diminish its value: for example, prolonged insomnia associated with severe distress can endanger functioning and heighten risk, making short-term sedative medication essential. Likewise, reducing overwhelming anxiety or confusion may be necessary before any other form of support becomes possible.

Example of Medication Use—Kate, Who Struggles With Anxiety

Kate calls the service coordinator and explains that she can no longer leave her home without having a panic attack. The coordinator asks more questions: in what situations the attacks occur, how long they have been happening. Kate describes her situation. Together they consider what might help and whether Kate has anyone who could support her. Kate sounds desperate but mentions that she does have one close friend. She says she doesn't want to burden her. The coordinator gently encourages her to share what is going on and to let the friend decide for herself whether she wants to help.

The coordinator and Kate agree that the situation sounds distressing enough that it would be good to meet soon. Since the evening is already late, they decide to try to arrange a meeting for the next day. Kate feels that she can manage until then.

The following day, facilitators Matt and Jane visit Kate at her home. Kate's friend Laura is also present. Kate explains her situation, and Laura says that she has indeed noticed that Kate has been struggling for a long time. The facilitators follow the conversation, helping Kate and Laura explore the situation from different angles. Kate recognizes some events that could explain why things have become particularly difficult right now. Laura promises to support her, and they agree to meet again.

At the next meeting, Kate is visibly anxious. She is sweating and shaking, unable to sit still. She explains that she tried going outside, but the panic attacks intensified, and she no longer dares to leave her apartment. Even staying at home feels unbearable. Kate reports that she has not been sleeping and feels unable to continue. She also shares that she has begun to have thoughts of ending her life.

Matt and Jane reflect together and share with Kate that her distress appears so overwhelming that medication might be worth considering as additional support. They ask what she thinks, and she agrees. At the same time, the facilitators focus on grounding—talking about everyday matters, guiding her breathing, and using their calm presence to help her feel safer in the moment.

One of the facilitators calls the on-duty physician, summarizes the situation, and puts the phone on speaker so that Kate and both facilitators can discuss options together with the doctor. They agree to start short-term medication to ease the acute anxiety and support sleep, as well as a small-dosage longer-acting medication intended to reduce anxiety over time. Laura agrees to pick up the medication for Kate. Another meeting is scheduled, and Kate is assured that she can reach out at any time if her distress intensifies or if she notices side effects.

Kate manages through the weekend, but leaving home remains difficult. Matt and Jane reflect that medication effects typically emerge with delay, and meanwhile it may be helpful to explore ways of soothing herself. They check for side effects—Kate has not noticed any. As the conversation progresses, they decide to try going for a walk together. During the walk, the facilitators ensure that Kate feels safe, chat casually, and regularly ask how she is doing. A couple of days later, they manage a slightly longer walk.

Jane and Matt begin arranging regular meetings in which Kate gradually exposes herself to difficult situations. At times, they meet also with Laura and with Kate's parents, with whom she has had strained relationships for years. They discuss what originally triggered the difficulties, what emotions are involved, and what Kate is currently experiencing. Gradually, she becomes more capable of coping, and the anxiety episodes become less intense. Her relationship with her parents also improves as long-standing tensions come to the surface and are talked through.

Little by little, Kate is able to visit the outpatient clinic independently to meet Jane and the physician. They decide to begin tapering the medication slowly.

During the tapering process, distress occasionally intensifies. When this happens, the pace of dose reduction is slowed, and time is allowed for the situation to stabilize before proceeding further. At times, Jane and Kate meet weekly, at other times less often, depending on need.

After a year, the medication has been discontinued entirely. Kate still experiences anxiety at times but feels able to manage it. She continues to meet Jane occasionally, and they eventually conclude the treatment by mutual agreement—leaving open the option for Kate to contact Jane again whenever needed.

5.2.1 Medication Management from a Drug-Centered Perspective

As mentioned above, in a holistic system, the effects of psychotropic medication are understood pluralistically—that is, as generic, symptom-relieving influences rather than targeted corrections of presumed underlying pathologies. Thus, psychiatric medications can be understood as influencing mental states primarily by acting on general brain functions through neurotransmitter systems (Moncrieff, 2018). From this drug-centered perspective, their clinically relevant effects can be viewed as alterations in experience, emotion, and behavior—effects that cut across diagnostic categories. In this sense, medication can sometimes support a broader therapeutic process by reducing or reshaping distressing experiences, in a way that may make it easier to address the personal, relational, and contextual factors that contribute to ongoing difficulties. This is broadly analogous to the role of analgesics in pain management: they can help relieve suffering and enable engagement with recovery and rehabilitation, even though symptomatic relief does not, by itself, specify or resolve underlying causes.

If a situation calls for longer-term pharmacological support, a holistic system aims to keep medication as simple as possible, drawing on established principles of medication management of psychotropics (e.g., Bergström et al., 2022; Isohanni et al., 2021) to optimize the individual benefit–risk ratio and minimize the risks associated with long-term use. These principles include:

1 Open and honest information-sharing, in which potential benefits, harms, uncertainties, and withdrawal risks are explained in clear and accessible terms.
2 Strengthening the therapeutic relationship and shared understanding, so that medication decisions are made collaboratively in light of the person's own goals, values, and concerns.
3 The "low-dose principle," meaning that medication is initiated at a low dose, which is generally better tolerated and may support adherence to care, and is increased gradually only as needed, based on individual response and tolerance.
4 Regular review, ensuring that the usefulness and appropriateness of medication are repeatedly assessed rather than continued automatically on the basis of diagnosis or routine.
5 Ongoing evaluation of necessity, considering whether the medication is still needed, or whether the dose could be reduced or the treatment discontinued.
6 Slow, planned tapering if medication is reduced, minimizing withdrawal risks, and ensuring that the person can proceed at a manageable pace.

One of the major challenges in a reductionist framework—where medication is initiated based on diagnosis and often continued mechanically—is precisely the risks associated with long-term use and polypharmacy, which have been linked to increased mortality and adverse drug effects compared to simpler regimens (Parabiaghi et al., 2024). For adverse effects, many service users are also reluctant to remain on medication (Vinkers et al., 2024).

Rapid or abrupt discontinuation, in turn, increases the likelihood of withdrawal symptoms and raises the probability that medication must be restarted, sometimes at a higher dose than before. This dynamic may strain the therapeutic relationship and initiate a vicious cycle in which treatment becomes increasingly coercive.

A holistic system seeks to prevent such cycles through case-based, transparent, and collaborative medication guidance. Crucially, the person is informed openly about the potential benefits and challenges of both initiating and discontinuing medication, and treatment is planned together based on the person's own aims and preferences.

Because individuals may disagree about their diagnosis or the necessity of medication, one effective approach is to describe medications in terms of their actual, generic effects, rather than presenting them as essential treatments for an assumed disease mechanism. People often find it easier to understand—and to accept—that a medication may help with severe distress or agitation than to accept that it "treats schizophrenia" or another abstract, latent disorder. This framing is also more accurate than the conventional practice of justifying treatment necessity with reference to hypothesized underlying diseases that cannot be empirically demonstrated and are not predicted by contemporary theories of psychopathology.

Table 5.2 illustrates how such a shift in explanatory language—from disorder-centered explanations to concrete descriptions of medication effects—can itself enhance trust, support engagement with treatment, and reduce the risk of becoming caught in cycles of repeated hospitalization.

In addition to selective initiation, a second central principle of a holistic support process is the aim to keep medication at the minimum effective dose. In practice, this requires well-controlled dose-reduction strategies. If medication is started at a high dose—for example, to calm acute confusion or severe agitation—it becomes important to subsequently reduce the dose in a planned manner and identify the level at which the person can function in the given situation. Ideally, this process may reveal that medication is no longer needed at all.

Particularly when medication has been used long-term, a sufficiently prolonged and gradual taper may be crucial, with the option of returning to a previously effective dose if necessary (Vinkers et al., 2024). In the case of long-term neuroleptic treatment, it has been suggested that dose reduction should occur over months or even years, depending on the starting dose, with each step involving a decrease of roughly one quarter to one half of the previous dose. This corresponds to approximately a 5–10 percentage-point decrease in dopamine D_2 blockade (Horowitz et al., 2021).

A phase-based approach is often recommended, for example, with intervals of three to six months between reductions, and progressively smaller dose decrements as the dose gets lower. The pace is adjusted to the individual: some may prefer even slower reductions—such as 10%

Table 5.2 Medication decisions within holistic and reductionist care systems

Holistic system	*Reductionist system*
Mike arrives at the hospital in a confused state after abruptly discontinuing his neuroleptic medication. He is told that the confusion and sleeplessness may be related to the rapid discontinuation, and that restarting the medication could help him feel more settled. At the same time, staff emphasize that if Mike wishes to taper the medication later, it will be important to plan this carefully together. Mika agrees to this plan and restarts the medication. He is informed that the medication may ease distress and improve sleep—factors that could support his recovery from a difficult life situation—but that medication alone is not a sufficient treatment and can cause troubling side effects, especially at higher doses. Mike is also told that although rapid discontinuation carries a risk of symptom return, many people eventually manage without medication or with only a small dose. The shared goal from the outset is, therefore, to find the lowest helpful dose, which will later be easier to reduce. Mike and the treatment team jointly create a plan for how the medication will be optimized and how it can best support him in this situation.	Mike arrives at the hospital in a confused state after abruptly discontinuing his neuroleptic medication. The medication is restarted against his wishes. Once Mike's symptoms begin to stabilize, he is offered psychoeducation focused on improving adherence to treatment. He is told that he has a psychotic disorder, that this is a brain disease caused by a disturbance in the dopamine system, and that he must adhere to at least two years of maintenance medication to prevent relapse and avoid long-term brain deterioration. Mike tries to explain that he does not feel he has a disease, that he believes his difficulties stem from other issues, and that the medication causes side effects that reduce his quality of life. His account is interpreted as a lack of insight. Mike becomes agitated, and the medication dose is increased. After discharge, Mike stops taking the medication, leading to severe withdrawal symptoms and the reinitiation of involuntary treatment.

or less of the previous dose—and a return to a prior dose should always remain an option (Horowitz et al., 2021). It has also been proposed that the final steps before discontinuation of neuroleptics should consist of *very small* doses—sometimes as little as 1/40 of a typical therapeutic dose—to minimize the sudden drop in D_2 blockade that may otherwise trigger psychosis-like withdrawal phenomena (Horowitz et al., 2021).

A holistic system could use such strategies to help distinguish who can manage without medication, who benefits from dose reduction, and who requires long-term maintenance at a stable dose. It is important to note, however, that these strategies have not yet been extensively tested in large

RCTs and are likely applicable only to a subset of service users. Nonetheless, recent years have seen the development of more comprehensive guidance both for neuroleptic medication tapering (e.g., Horowitz et al., 2021) and for optimizing psychotropic prescribing more broadly (e.g., Horowitz & Taylor, 2024). These approaches are compatible with the holistic framework.

5.2.2 *Psychotropic Medication Use in a Holistic System: Compatibility with Regulatory Frameworks*

At first glance, a holistic framework—where medications are used primarily according to their effects on symptoms, rather than according to a diagnosis—may appear to conflict with usual clinical guidelines or regulatory standards, which often require that medication be tied to a specific disease-based indication. In many countries, such indications are justified on grounds of patient safety, making a formal diagnosis a prerequisite for initiating treatment.

In practice, however, psychotropic drugs are already used broadly across diagnostic boundaries on a symptomatic basis, even if this is not always explicit. Diagnostic categories in everyday clinical work are often—implicitly or explicitly—adjusted to fit medication decisions. Sometimes, a diagnosis is assigned *primarily* to permit the use of a desired medication, rather than the other way around. Off-label prescribing is also widespread because psychotropic medications have generic, state-altering effects rather than specific disorder-correcting mechanisms.

It is also crucial to recognize that the evidence base for regulatory approval—RCT data on efficacy and safety—is itself based on symptom change, not on the correction of a disease mechanism. Psychiatric RCTs do not and cannot establish effects on specific underlying disorders, because such disorders cannot currently be empirically verified. In this respect, a drug-centered approach is consistent with the scientific foundations of psychopharmacology and closely reflects actual clinical practice. A holistic system would make this reality more transparent and, therefore, more amenable to regulation, safety monitoring, and accountable prescribing.

Diagnostic categories and formal indications can still be used—as administrative anchors—to justify medication when needed, as outlined in Section 5.1.

5.3 Hospital Care and Need for Continuous Support

If a person poses an acute risk to themselves or others, or if the situation does not improve through dialogical space, psychiatric inpatient care can be used when necessary. In a holistic system, inpatient units should operate within the same framework and aim from the outset to facilitate dialogical encounters with the person and their network within the ward environment. The threshold for admission is kept deliberately low so that hospital care can begin without a referral or detailed pre-assessments whenever the responsible clinicians, together with the network, deem it necessary. The primary goal of inpatient care in a holistic system is not prolonged containment or symptom suppression, but the restoration of safety, stabilization of the situation, and the reestablishment of dialogical contact in a way that enables a timely return to community-based support.

In addition to a low threshold for admission, a holistic system can be expected to reduce the need for involuntary treatment more broadly, because the ethos is one of rapid, network-involving response and a style of interaction that carries a lower risk of escalation or provocation than a more reductionistic system. If a person must nevertheless be brought to hospital against their will, organizing dialogical meetings and building a collaborative relationship can be particularly challenging in the early stages of inpatient care. Precisely, in such situations, it becomes essential to try to establish trust through flexible means—for example, by offering different formats for conversation and creating space to share the difficult experiences that involuntary admission and coercive interventions often evoke.

If seclusion is required, it should be kept as brief as possible, and the person should be given the opportunity to return to the ward whenever it is safe for them and others. In these circumstances, symptom-relieving medication may be appropriate. Because seclusion and forced medication are extremely difficult for both service users and staff, all parties should be offered the opportunity to process these events afterward. Team-based work and shared responsibility are especially important on inpatient units so that individual staff members do not become overburdened and so that a climate of fear—which increases the risk of authoritarian practices, escalations, and involuntary care—does not take hold.

Care on the ward is integrated as quickly as possible with the person's real life and everyday context. For this reason, from the very beginning and with the person's consent, the unit aims to invite those relatives and professionals whose involvement would be important for improving the situation. Ideally, facilitators from outpatient care would join these meetings from the start of the inpatient stay. Home visits, trial periods outside the ward, and other means of testing everyday routines are used flexibly in order to minimize the risk of institutionalization.

If these trials show that the person can manage at home and their network has no significant concerns, discharge can occur flexibly. In a holistic system, inpatient staff may continue working together with outpatient facilitators for a period after discharge—particularly when a strong therapeutic relationship has been formed during the admission or when there is concern that the person may struggle at home and face a risk of rapid readmission. Otherwise, the outpatient facilitators continue working according to the principles described earlier. If needed, a new hospital admission can be arranged with a low threshold, and the facilitators will resume organizing dialogical meetings on the ward together with inpatient staff to reorganize the process.

Example of Inpatient Care—Bob, Who Had Barricaded Himself at Home (continued)

Bob, facilitator Jane, and the ward nurse meet daily on the inpatient unit. Gradually, Bob begins to talk more about himself. It becomes clear that he has no family and that he has struggled with a severe alcohol problem for many years. Jane asks about everyday matters: how Bob spends his days and who, if anyone, is part of his social circle. Bob mentions the same friend who had previously contacted services out of concern. Bob is open to the idea of his friend visiting him on the ward.

A joint meeting is arranged with the friend. The friend explains that he has been worried about Bob but feels Bob already looks somewhat better. Bob agrees—he says that he had been awake for days and suspects he may have used substances unknown to him, though he has little recollection of the preceding weeks. Although his condition has improved, the physician expresses concern and reflects that it would be important for Bob to stay in hospital a little longer so that his overall health can be assessed more thoroughly. Additional toxicology tests could also be taken, even though nothing notable appeared at admission. Bob does not object.

Bob's general condition continues to improve. In one of the meetings, Jane reflects that it might be helpful to invite someone from addiction services, who could bring additional perspectives on how Bob might best be supported going forward. Bob is initially skeptical but eventually agrees.

A meeting is held with Jane, Bob, the ward nurse, and a clinician from addiction services. Jane and the nurse reflect on Bob's situation. Bob is asked how this sounds to him. He remains somewhat reserved toward the new clinician but slowly begins to talk more. The addiction clinician also shares what the conversation evokes for him and what thoughts he has about Bob's situation. It is agreed that they will meet again in the same composition and invite Bob's friend to join as well.

At the next meeting, Bob feels that he can now trust the addiction clinician more. A social worker joins some of the subsequent meetings to help clarify Bob's financial situation, income, and the condition of his apartment. Meetings gradually begin to take place in Bob's home, and eventually he is able to spend nights there. His friend attends several of the meetings and supports Bob with practical matters.

Occasionally, Bob experiences increasingly intense and frightening states while at home, and in those moments he returns to the hospital for a few days to rest. Over the years, however, these experiences become less frequent. His psychiatric contacts are gradually reduced, and his neuroleptic medication is slowly tapered. Discontinuation leads to temporary insomnia and a brief intensification of distress. When Bob returns to the hospital, he is given a slightly higher dose for a short period, which quickly stabilizes the situation. He can then return to the lower dose, after which tapering proceeds even in more cautious steps.

Over time, Bob develops a strong relationship with addiction services and begins attending their groups. With the social worker's support, he finds a vocational training program and gains new goals in life. His psychiatric contact is slowly phased out, and eventually it is agreed that Bob—or a clinician from addiction services—can get in touch whenever needed to reorganize support.

A holistic system can also centralize specialized assessments and interventions that require a hospital environment, such as forensic psychiatric evaluations, electroconvulsive therapy, ketamine treatment, and, in the future, potentially psychedelic-assisted therapies. These interventions are used selectively and situationally, primarily when other approaches have not provided sufficient relief, or when symptoms are so severe (e.g., catatonia or profound depression) that establishing a functional connection is not otherwise possible.

Ideally, the option for short-term overnight stays would be integrated into outpatient-oriented services, with low-threshold access, continuous staffing, and a more home-like environment, rather than relying solely on formal inpatient admissions in hospital settings. Such flexible arrangements could help stabilize acute situations while maintaining continuity of care, reducing the need for prolonged hospitalization and excessive medication use, and keeping care as close as possible to the person's everyday community context.

Some individuals require long-term support to maintain stability, safety, and everyday functioning in the context of enduring vulnerabilities or limited resources. Existing models of supported accommodation could be further developed in a holistic direction by drawing on community-based approaches such as the Soteria model, thereby creating living environments that are more homelike and grounded in practices consistent with the holistic framework. Such units can also provide opportunities for peer support and for carefully structured medication-reduction strategies. The Soteria model is discussed in more detail in Chapter 10.

Example of Soteria-House Support—Homeless Alex

Susan contacts services because she is worried about her brother, Alex, who has a long history of life stressors, periods of homelessness, and substance use. Recently, Alex has appeared increasingly confused and distressed. He has attempted to contact Susan repeatedly and has also come into contact with the police. Susan feels unsure how to help and calls a facilitator for advice.

A network meeting is arranged promptly at a shelter where Alex had previously been staying. Alex is currently missing, but a dialogical conversation takes place with Susan and the shelter staff. Together, they reflect on Alex's recent behavior, how he may be experiencing the situation, and where he might currently be found. Based on this shared reflection, the facilitator and Susan are able to locate Alex. He is in poor physical and mental condition and is unable to engage in sustained conversation. Given the severity of the situation, it is agreed that Alex requires hospital care. To ensure a safe transfer to hospital, they decide together to initiate an official referral, which also enables transportation, even though Alex does not explicitly oppose hospitalization.

In the hospital, new meetings are arranged promptly with Alex and Susan. Medical assessment is initiated, including somatic examinations and necessary treatment. Small-dose psychotropic medication is also started to address acute confusion, distress, and sleep disturbance. Over the following weeks, Alex's condition improves, but he is still homeless and remains somewhat confused and vulnerable, suggesting a need for longer-term supportive care.

After discharge, Alex is brought to a Soteria house by his sister and the familiar facilitators. The house is run mainly by former service users. Upon arrival, he is welcomed by two staff members who spend time sitting with him in the common area. Rather than conducting formal assessments, staff ask how Alex is feeling, what feels most difficult at the moment, and what helps him feel even slightly safer. Alex says that he feels overwhelmed and frightened about his future.

During the first days, staff remain closely present in everyday situations—sharing meals, engaging in casual conversation, and spending quiet time together. Alex often paces and speaks anxiously about his fears. Staff listen attentively, reflect back what they hear, and avoid challenging or interpreting his experiences. They acknowledge that the situation feels frightening and emphasize that now he is safe and not alone.

Medication is discussed openly but not intensified immediately. Staff explain that some people find medication helpful for calming intense distress or improving sleep, while others prefer to see whether a supportive environment is sufficient. Alex expresses a wish to try managing with minimal medication for now. The focus is, therefore, on rest, establishing a gentle daily rhythm and reducing environmental stimulation.

Over the following days, Alex begins to sleep for longer periods. His fears persist, but he becomes less agitated and more able to talk about what he is experiencing. In conversations, Alex starts connecting his distress to life events and disappointments, including a relationship breakup, long-term substance abuse, and ongoing insecurity related to housing and work. Staff listen and reflect without drawing conclusions, allowing Alex to make sense of his experiences at his own pace.

As weeks pass, Alex becomes increasingly engaged in everyday activities, such as cooking, walking outside, and spending time with other residents. Susan visits regularly, and joint conversations help rebuild trust and clarify how she can support Alex without becoming overburdened. Medication remains at a low dose and is gradually reduced as Alex's sense of stability improves.

Network meetings are arranged with Soteria staff, Susan, and a familiar facilitator. Social workers are also invited, and with their support, Alex is able to secure his own apartment.

Over time, Alex begins spending nights at his own home while continuing to visit the Soteria house during the day. Together with the staff and his sister, he plans a gradual transition back to independent living, with the shared understanding that he can return to the house or increase contact if distress intensifies.

The same facilitators continue working with Alex, gradually inviting vocational support services into the meetings to support his return to work. At times, Alex's distress intensifies. On a few occasions, he spends nights at the familiar Soteria house, which helps him regain a sense of safety.

By the end of the process, Alex reports that he still occasionally experiences "unusual" thoughts and fears but feels capable of living with them and of seeking support when needed. Eventually, he settles into his new job, establishes new relationships, and reports a high level of satisfaction with his life.

5.4 Professional Roles

Because the holistic system reallocates resources from other tasks toward the facilitation of dialogical spaces, this inevitably reshapes professional roles. In practice, professionals—regardless of their original discipline—would need training in the kind of *generic relational work* described earlier, which optimizes the common therapeutic factors in virtually all clinical encounters and, therefore, enhances the effectiveness of the holistic system as a whole.

Such relational work would be supported, for example, by certain practices familiar from psychotherapy: building a working alliance, adopting an explorative stance, and forming an individual, contextual understanding of a person's current situation. From the perspective of a holistic system, teamwork and co-facilitation are also essential so that the process remains polyphonic from the outset and responsibility is shared among workers. This enables them to meet people more calmly and safely, without pressure to produce rapid solutions, interpretations, or decisions.

A core competency shared across all professions is the ability to create and sustain a dialogical space; however, a holistic system also requires more specialized roles through which such work can be anchored in clearly defined tasks, grounded in a shared understanding. Below, the potential implications for different professional groups are outlined.

5.4.1 Nurses

The most substantial changes would concern nurses. Their work would shift from assessment duties, routine checkups, and standardized interventions toward more psychotherapeutically and network-oriented tasks, emphasizing service navigation and the facilitation of dialogical spaces. This would strengthen continuity of care, support more goal-oriented, dialogically informed work, and make it possible to establish a strong alliance and a nuanced understanding of the service user's situation early in the process. Nurses' professional identity would gradually rely less on traditional nursing roles and more on expertise in holistic practice.

5.4.2 *Physicians*

Physicians could retain responsibility for care processes, but as other professionals receive additional training, practical responsibility for day-to-day work could be distributed more broadly, shifting the physician's role toward need-adapted consultation. If legal responsibility for care continues to rest with the physician, it is crucial to ensure that this responsibility remains reasonable, especially in settings where other staff have not yet been adequately trained in holistic framework.

Ideally, legal responsibility would be shared more widely between organizations and networks, increasing their decision-making power and ensuring that service users are informed transparently about potential risks and harms of different practices—including long-term maintenance treatment, hospitalization, and involuntary interventions.

Such shared responsibility directly reduces the risk of authoritarian care, because decision-making no longer depends on the risk-aversion of a single profession but on collective judgment. At the same time, it can improve patient safety and reduce escalation, as jointly informed decisions support more careful consideration of when intensive interventions such as medication or hospital care are genuinely needed. Shared responsibility also reduces individual workers' burden and improves well-being at work, which in turn strengthens relationships and lowers the risk of fear- or overload-driven mechanical responses.

It also reduces the tendency to default to standardized, risk-avoidant practices—for example, continuing long-term medication or hospitalization "just in case" because an individual clinician fears legal or other negative consequences.

When the definition of problems and responsibility is shared, physicians' time can be freed from routine assessments and administrative tasks and redirected toward more direct clinical work. In milder situations, responsibility can be assumed by other professionals and the social network, allowing medical resources to be focused from the outset on more complex or acute cases that are most likely to benefit from medical expertise and interventions. Physicians may then participate in network meetings as co-facilitators, particularly when medical documentation, diagnostic clarification, or immediate symptom relief is required. Increased availability and closer collaboration within teams also enable more careful monitoring and long-term optimization of medication, thereby supporting the development of safer and more deliberate deprescribing practices.

5.4.3 Psychologists and Psychotherapists

Psychologists could conduct more targeted assessments—for example, of cognitive capacities, learning abilities, emotional functioning, and personality—using established methods. However, such assessments would likely be needed less frequently, and when they are carried out, they could be more hypothesis-driven, since dialogical work already generates rich information to guide tailored support. This more focused approach would improve the psychometric validity of psychological assessments and free psychologists' time for facilitating dialogical meetings.

Both psychologists and psychotherapists generally have, through their training, capacities for the kind of understanding and interaction needed to create and maintain dialogical space. Their expertise can be particularly valuable when dialogical work becomes challenging or when longer-term individual psychotherapy is needed.

5.4.4 Social Workers

Social workers typically possess strong competence in contextual thinking and network coordination. They could play a central role particularly when multiple agencies or actors need to be involved, when flexible forms of support must be organized, and when work must be coordinated externally—for example, concerning benefits, housing, or financial matters.

5.4.5 Occupational, Physiotherapy, and Other Therapeutic Professions

Many therapists already have training that aligns well with a holistic orientation. A holistic system would enable broader and more flexible use of their expertise—not only in supporting daily functioning and strengthening the connection between body and mind, but also in providing individualized guidance on lifestyle-related factors such as sleep, physical activity, nutrition, and everyday routines. Working closely with individuals and their networks, these professionals can help translate shared goals into concrete, embodied practices that enhance agency, resilience, and self-regulation in daily life. More broadly, their involvement supports a shift from symptom-focused interventions toward practical, situation-based support that promotes sustainable well-being.

5.4.6 Experts by Experience

Experts by experience often have an intuitive affinity with a holistic framework, as they do not need to unlearn reductionist practices or rigid professional boundaries. Their active involvement in care processes and in the facilitation of dialogical spaces can increase authenticity and strengthen trust, safety, and flexibility. Experiential perspectives can also challenge taken-for-granted professional assumptions and bring attention to aspects of situations that may otherwise remain invisible within formal service logics.

At the same time, it is crucial to recognize that a holistic framework does not automatically resolve questions of power, representation, or epistemic authority. When a holistic system is implemented through existing institutions, those institutions continue to define, evaluate, and legitimize experiential knowledge and its practical use. If the system adopts a selective or skeptical stance toward certain experiential concepts or narratives, it may already be implicitly ranking forms of lived experience—thereby reproducing patterns of epistemic exclusion that do not fundamentally differ from those found in reductionist systems.

Related questions also concern the boundaries of participation: to what extent professionals may draw on their own lived experience, where such boundaries are drawn, how responsibilities are allocated, and how experiential contributions are recognized, compensated, and sustained over time. One challenge arises from the fact that holistic systems already blur existing professional boundaries, redefining the roles of expertise, education, and other formal requirements.

In this sense, holistic framework does not provide ready-made answers to these power-related issues. Their value lies rather in making such tensions more visible and discussable. By shifting the focus away from discipline-specific problem definitions toward complex situations as shared objects of concern, a holistic framework can create more favorable conditions for genuinely pluralistic forms of knowledge to be applied to phenomena that are currently operationalized as psychiatric disorders.

It is also important to acknowledge that holistic frameworks may differ from existing forms of lived experience work, which in many countries have been organized around specific diagnostic groups. In a holistic system, experiential roles would, therefore, need to be grounded in different foundations. One option is to base experiential expertise on familiarity with the use of holistic services—knowledge of their structures, relational dynamics, strengths, and development needs—rather than on identification with particular diagnoses.

At the same time, such a redefinition inevitably represents a normative, top-down epistemic stance. By specifying what counts as relevant experiential expertise, the system itself begins to delimit, value, and organize lived experience in particular ways. This risks reproducing the very problems outlined above: if certain experiential concepts or forms of articulation are treated with skepticism or excluded, experiential knowledge is implicitly ranked, and the system may cease to be genuinely open to divergent perspectives. In this sense, attempts to reframe experiential roles reveal a fundamental paradox. If no shared foundations are articulated, reductionist frameworks are likely to regain dominance by default; yet if such foundations are defined too rigidly, the openness required for pluralistic engagement is undermined.

From a dialogical perspective, this tension cannot be resolved through fixed role definitions alone. Rather, it must be continuously negotiated in practice. A core task for both experiential experts and other professionals is, therefore, to prioritize the creation and maintenance of dialogical space in which multiple perspectives can emerge, interact, and transform dynamically. In this way, dialogism functions not as a solution that eliminates epistemic tensions but as a balancing principle that keeps them visible, contestable, and productively in play.

As a result, experts by experience should have access to the same training opportunities in holistic approaches as other professionals. This supports abovementioned polyphony and enhances the overall quality of services. Training access should also be reflected in appropriate compensation and opportunities for career development. Although the absence of a regulated healthcare title may legally restrict certain tasks in some countries, experiential experts can participate as equal partners in the facilitation of dialogical processes, as this work relies on relational, communicative, and reflective skills that are not profession-specific. They may also contribute in administrative, managerial, and service research and development roles, where experiential and practice-grounded perspectives can meaningfully inform the design, evaluation, and ongoing transformation of services.

5.5 Training

To ensure that all workers—regardless of professional background—have the skills needed to facilitate dialogical encounters, additional training is required. A key challenge in the early stages is that many professionals must first *unlearn* reductionist thinking and working habits. For this reason, training must be closely integrated with everyday practice—through, for example, direct supervision in clinical work—so that learning occurs within ordinary encounters.

For the holistic system to function responsively and flexibly, it is essential that workers come to know and trust one another and share a common understanding of the aims of care. Differences of opinion must be possible without anyone's perspective being dismissed or minimized. Training, therefore, needs to provide a forum where workers can get to know each other and gradually develop a genuine culture of teamwork. Alongside theoretical content, training emphasizes practical exercises that build the interactional skills required to facilitate dialogical meetings.

Although training can support the development of a holistic system, the holistic framework itself is not a single method, nor is it tied to specific, bounded training packages in the way many psychotherapeutic schools are. Rather, it functions as an organizational and practice-level framework—much as reductionism currently does. In the existing system, many practitioners already work in relatively holistic ways but are required to operate within reductionist structures and procedures.

If the underlying ontology of the system shifts toward a holistic orientation, it becomes possible to reach a critical mass in which teams begin to operate holistically "by default" in everyday situations. In such a context, practitioners with more reductionist orientations will also need to adapt to the holistic framework, just as holistically oriented practitioners are currently required to adapt to reductionist practices. Their specialized expertise, however, remains valuable and can be meaningfully integrated in situations that call for more narrowly defined or technical knowledge.

Holistic practice is supported by the fact that its core principles are largely intuitive and grounded in ordinary relational capacities. These principles rely primarily on the reorganization of resources and the creation of conditions for collaborative team functioning, rather than on technically complex methods. Nonetheless, it is likely that a certain critical mass of competence and familiarity must be built before holistic ways of working scale more broadly. For this reason, some form of predefined training and orientation pathway is needed. The role of training within the broader reorganization of the service system is discussed in more detail in Section 6.3 of Chapter 6.

References

Aftab, A., & Stein, D. J. (2022). Psychopharmacology and explanatory pluralism. *JAMA Psychiatry*, *79*(6), 522–523. https://doi.org/10.1001/jamapsychiatry.2022.0470

Bergström, T. (2023). From treatment of mental disorders to the treatment of difficult life situations: A hypothesis and rationale. *Medical Hypotheses, 176*, 111099. https://doi.org/10.1016/j.mehy.2023.111099

Bergström, T., & Gauffin, T. (2023). The association of antipsychotic postponement with 5-year outcomes of adolescent first-episode psychosis. *Schizophrenia Bulletin Open*, *4*(1), sgad032. https://doi.org/10.1093/schizbullopen/sgad032

Bergström, T., Hulkko, A., Hartikainen, S., Koponen, H., Lieslehto, J., Jääskeläinen, E., & Isohanni, M. (2022). Psykoosilääkehoidon ohjaus voi tehostaa skitsofrenian hoitoa. *Duodecim, 138*(9), 787–793. https://www.duodecimlehti.fi/duo16810

Bergström, T., Seikkula, J., Alakare, B., Mäki, P., Köngäs-Saviaro, P., Taskila, J. J., Tolvanen, A., & Aaltonen, J. (2018). The family-oriented Open Dialogue approach in the treatment of first-episode psychosis: Nineteen-year outcomes. *Psychiatry Research, 270*, 168–175. https://doi.org/10.1016/j.psychres.2018.09.039

Bergström, T., Taskila, J. J., Alakare, B., Köngäs-Saviaro, P., Miettunen, J., & Seikkula, J. (2020). Five-year cumulative exposure to neuroleptic medication after first-episode psychosis and its association with 19-year outcomes. *Schizophrenia Bulletin Open, 1*(1), sgaa050. https://doi.org/10.1093/schizbullopen/sgaa050

Correll, C. U., Rubio, J. M., & Kane, J. M. (2018). What is the risk–benefit ratio of long-term neuroleptic treatment in people with schizophrenia? *World Psychiatry, 18*, 149–160.

Harrow, M., & Jobe, T. H. (2018). Long-term neuroleptic treatment of schizophrenia: Does it help or hurt over a 20-year period? *World Psychiatry : Official Journal of the World Psychiatric Association (WPA), 17*(2), 162–163. https://doi.org/10.1002/wps.20518

Horowitz, M. A., Jauhar, S., Natesan, S., Murray, R. M., & Taylor, D. (2021). A method for tapering neuroleptic treatment that may minimize the risk of relapse. *Schizophrenia Bulletin, 47*(4), 1116–1129. https://doi.org/10.1093/schbul/sbab017.

Horowitz, M., & Taylor, D. M. (2024). *The Maudsley deprescribing guidelines: Antidepressants, benzodiazepines, gabapentinoids and Z-drugs*. John Wiley & Sons.

Isohanni, M., Jääskeläinen, E., Miller, B. J., Hulkko, A., Tiihonen, J., Möller, H.-J., Hartikainen, S., Huhtaniska, S., & Lieslehto, J. (2021). Medication management of antipsychotic treatment in schizophrenia—A narrative review. *Human Psychopharmacology: Clinical and Experimental, 36*(2), e2765. https://doi.org/10.1002/hup.2765

Joukamaa, M., Heliövaara, M., Knekt, P., Aromaa, A., Raitasalo, R., & Lehtinen, V. (2006). Schizophrenia, neuroleptic medication and mortality. *The British Journal of Psychiatry: The Journal of Mental Science, 188*, 122–127. https://doi.org/10.1192/bjp.188.2.122

Li, M. (2016). Neuroleptic-induced sensitization and tolerance: Behavioral characteristics, developmental impacts, and neurobiological mechanisms. *Journal of Psychopharmacology (Oxford, England), 30*(8), 749–770. https://doi.org/10.1177/0269881116654697

Maj, M., Stein, D. J., Parker, G., Zimmerman, M., Fava, G. A., De Hert, M., Demyttenaere, K., McIntyre, R. S., Widiger, T., & Wittchen, H. U. (2020). The clinical characterization of the adult patient with depression aimed at personalization of management. *World Psychiatry: Official Journal of the World Psychiatric Association (WPA), 19*(3), 269–293. https://doi.org/10.1002/wps.20771

Maj, M., van Os, J., De Hert, M., Gaebel, W., Galderisi, S., Green, M. F., Guloksuz, S., Harvey, P. D., Jones, P. B., Malaspina, D., McGorry, P., Miettunen, J., Murray, R. M., Nuechterlein, K. H., Peralta, V., Thornicroft, G., van Winkel, R., & Ventura, J. (2021). The clinical characterization of the patient with primary psychosis aimed at personalization of management. *World Psychiatry: Official Journal of the World Psychiatric Association (WPA), 20*(1), 4–33. https://doi.org/10.1002/wps.20809

Moilanen, J., Haapea, M., Miettunen, J., Jääskeläinen, E., Veijola, J., Isohanni, M., & Koponen, H. (2013). Characteristics of subjects with schizophrenia spectrum disorder with and without neuroleptic medication - a 10-year follow-up of the

Northern Finland 1966 Birth Cohort study. *European Psychiatry: the Journal of the Association of European Psychiatrists*, *28*(1), 53–58. https://doi.org/10.1016/j.eurpsy.2011.06.009

Moncrieff, J. (2018). Research on a "drug-centred" approach to psychiatric drug treatment: Assessing the impact of mental and behavioural alterations produced by psychiatric drugs. *Epidemiology and Psychiatric Sciences, 27*(2), 133–140. https://doi.org/10.1017/S2045796017000555

Moncrieff, J., Cooper, R. E., Stockmann, T., Amendola, S., Hengartner, M. P., & Horowitz, M. A. (2023). The serotonin theory of depression: A systematic umbrella review of the evidence. *Molecular Psychiatry*, *28*(8), 3243–3256. https://doi.org/10.1038/s41380-022-01661-0

Moncrieff, J., Crellin, N., Stansfeld, J., Cooper, R., Marston, L., Freemantle, N., Lewis, G., Hunter, R., Johnson, S., Barnes, T., Morant, N., Pinfold, V., Smith, R., Kent, L., Darton, K., Long, M., Horowitz, M., Horne, R., Vickerstaff, V., Jha, M., ... & Priebe, S. (2023). Neuroleptic dose reduction and discontinuation versus maintenance treatment in people with schizophrenia and other recurrent psychotic disorders in England (the RADAR trial): An open, parallel-group, randomised controlled trial. *The Lancet. Psychiatry*, *10*(11), 848–859. https://doi.org/10.1016/S2215-0366(23)00258-4

Moncrieff, J., Pillai, E., Marston, L., Lewis, G., Barnes, T. R. E., Johnson, S., & Priebe, S. (2025). The association between relapse and the outcome of schizophrenia and recurrent psychotic disorders. *The British Journal of Psychiatry: The Journal of Mental Science*, *227*(4), 673–679. https://doi.org/10.1192/bjp.2024.304

Morant, N., Long, M., Jayacodi, S., Cooper, R., Akther-Robertson, J., Stansfeld, J., Horowitz, M., Priebe, S., & Moncrieff, J. (2023). Experiences of reduction and discontinuation of neuroleptics: A qualitative investigation within the RADAR trial. *EClinicalMedicine*, *64*, 102135. https://doi.org/10.1016/j.eclinm.2023.102135

Parabiaghi, A., Monzio Compagnoni, M., D'Avanzo, B., Caggiu, G., Galbussera, A. A., Tettamanti, M., Fortino, I., & Barbato, A. (2024). Association of antipsychotic polypharmacy and two-year all-cause mortality: A population-based cohort study of 33,221 Italian continuous users. *Journal of Clinical Medicine*, *13*(7), 2073. https://doi.org/10.3390/jcm13072073

Rund, B. R. (2014). Does active psychosis cause neurobiological pathology? A critical review of the neurotoxicity hypothesis. *Psychological Medicine*, *44*(8), 1577–1590. https://doi.org/10.1017/S0033291713002341

Seeman, P. (2011). All roads to schizophrenia lead to dopamine supersensitivity and elevated dopamine D2(high) receptors. *CNS Neuroscience & Therapeutics*, *17*(2), 118–132. https://doi.org/10.1111/j.1755-5949.2010.00162.x

Speyer, H., & Roe, D. (2024). Implications of the RADAR trial: The dignity of risk taking. *The Lancet. Psychiatry*, *11*(1), 10. https://doi.org/10.1016/S2215-0366(23)00368-1

Taipale, H., Tanskanen, A., Mehtälä, J., Vattulainen, P., Correll, C. U., & Tiihonen, J. (2020). 20-year follow-up study of physical morbidity and mortality in relationship to neuroleptic treatment in a nationwide cohort of 62,250 patients with schizophrenia (FIN20). *World Psychiatry: Official Journal of the World Psychiatric Association (WPA)*, *19*(1), 61–68. https://doi.org/10.1002/wps.20699

Targum, S. D. (2014). Identification and treatment of antidepressant tachyphylaxis. *Innovations in Clinical Neuroscience*, *11*(3–4), 24–28.

Tiihonen, J., Mittendorfer-Rutz, E., Majak, M., Mehtälä, J., Hoti, F., Jedenius, E., Enkusson, D., Leval, A., Sermon, J., Tanskanen, A., & Taipale, H. (2017). Real-world effectiveness of neuroleptic treatments in a nationwide cohort of 29 823 patients with Schizophrenia. *JAMA Psychiatry*, *74*(7), 686–693.

Vinkers, C. H., Kupka, R. W., Penninx, B. W., Ruhé, H. G., van Gaalen, J. M., van Haaren, P. C. F., Schellekens, A. F. A., Jauhar, S., Ramos-Quiroga, J. A., Vieta, E., Tiihonen, J., Veldman, S. E., Veling, W., Vis, R., de Wit, L. E., & Luykx, J. J. (2024). Discontinuation of psychotropic medication: A synthesis of evidence across medication classes. *Molecular Psychiatry*, *29*(8), 2575–2586. https://doi.org/10.1038/s41380-024-02445-4

Wunderink, L., Nieboer, R. M., Wiersma, D., et al. (2013). Recovery in remitted first-episode psychosis at 7 years of follow-up of an early dose reduction/discontinuation or maintenance treatment strategy. *JAMA Psychiatry*, *70*, 913–920.

Zipursky, R. B., Reilly, T. J., & Murray, R. M. (2013). The myth of schizophrenia as a progressive brain disease. *Schizophrenia Bulletin*, *39*(6), 1363–1372. https://doi.org/10.1093/schbul/sbs135

Chapter 6

Reorganizing Mental Health System

The previous chapters have outlined the conceptual foundations of holistic psychiatry, examined how challenges currently operationalized as mental health disorders or problems can be understood within this framework, and clarified how holism reshapes the primary aims of support. They have also described dialogical space as the core context through which unfavorable situations can begin to reorganize.

At the level of individual encounters, dialogical work provides the conditions for shared understanding, agency, and context-sensitive support. Yet for such encounters to occur consistently—and to have durable effects beyond single meetings—the surrounding service system must be organized in ways that actively support them. Without structural alignment, dialogical practice risks remaining an exception within a predominantly reductionist system, vulnerable to being overridden by diagnostic gatekeeping, fragmented responsibilities, and institutional routines.

This chapter shifts the focus from clinical interaction to system-level design. It examines how mental health services can be reorganized so that dialogical spaces are not dependent on individual practitioners' commitment or skill but become the system's default mode of operation. This chapter addresses questions of organizational structure, resource allocation, workforce competencies, financing, leadership, and legislation, showing how each of these dimensions can either constrain or enable a holistic system. The central argument is that a more holistic system does not primarily require new methods or substantial additional resources, but a reorientation of existing structures around responsibility, continuity, and the facilitation of dialogical encounters as the system's organizing principle.

6.1 Foundations for Systemic Reorganization

A primary goal of service reorganization is to increase the likelihood of creating dialogical spaces in which unfavorable situations can be addressed

DOI: 10.4324/9781003777939-9

when people request help. This likelihood can be strengthened by designing services that directly support the key dimensions of dialogical space:

- **Space in Time:** First contact should occur when people request it, and sufficient time should be allocated for the meetings. This requires centralized service coordination that allows immediate access without pre-assessments or referrals.
- **Physical Space:** Meetings should take place in environments where people feel safe and comfortable. This is supported by mobilizing teams and maintaining flexibility in the choice of meeting location.
- **Social Space:** All individuals who play a meaningful role in unfavorable situations should be invited into the process. Workers should encourage those requesting help to reflect on who might contribute to joint meetings, and this inclusive approach should be maintained throughout all phases of care.
- **Discursive Space:** Conversations should be polyphonic, enabling the creation of shared understanding about what is happening and what might help. Such dialogue simultaneously builds trust and strengthens relationships. At the same time, it is important to recognize that professionals inevitably occupy a position of authority and power within the encounter, whether this is made explicit or not. Because professional language and institutional roles can easily shape and dominate the process, workers need to acknowledge this asymmetry consciously. They can support a genuinely dialogical space by following people's lead, creating room for different perspectives, avoiding pathologizing language, and adopting a stance of curiosity—opening space through wondering and asking new questions.
- **Mental Space:** There should be openness and readiness for change, especially at the moment when people reach out for help and may be more receptive to new perspectives. Workers should tolerate uncertainty, keep an open mind about possible solutions, and be prepared to meet each new situation in a case-by-case manner.

At best, a dialogical space creates a shared, safe, and open setting where everyone involved can better express their perspectives, listen to one another, and gradually build a mutual understanding of the situation. It often immediately reduces fragmentation, lowers anxiety, and interrupts crisis-maintaining feedback loops by slowing the interaction, validating experience, and widening the range of possible meanings. In doing so, it often allows the unfavorable situation itself to reorganize; relationships stabilize, agency increases, and concrete next steps become clearer and easier to agree on.

If the situation is prolonged or severe, the mutual understanding created in the dialogical space can be used immediately to guide more reductionist support—case-by-case, proportionally and without losing holistic orientation.

To guarantee dialogical space and ensure that the necessary structures for care coordination and case-by-case support are properly established, a holistic service system requires a clearly designated body to oversee its development and maintenance. In principle, this could sit within social services or a comparable sector; however, in many Western countries, psychiatry and mental health system is the most feasible institutional home.

First, psychiatry holds significant definitional power over what counts as mental health and mental disorder. If it continues to operate within a reductionist framework, the development of a truly holistic system becomes almost impossible, as difficulties and solutions would remain conceptualized in one-directional, illness-centered terms. At the same time, psychiatric and mental health services provide an organizational base from which holistic care can be coordinated purposefully and coherently, and—when necessary—can ensure access to acute symptom relief.

Second, psychiatry and wider mental health services already possess substantial resources in many countries. If these resources are reorganized differently, a more holistic system could be implemented without major increases in funding or legislative reform. When a holistic framework is adopted, resources naturally begin to redistribute toward maintaining it: help can be provided without elaborate diagnostic or administrative predefinitions, reducing the need for specialized units, gatekeeping, referral pathways, and sequential assessments. This frees up capacity previously tied to overlapping evaluation procedures and allows services to focus on immediate encounters. It also eliminates queues for initial assessments, thereby reducing delays, preventing deterioration, and likely diminishing overall demand as more people feel adequately met and supported at the point of contact.

Third, a holistic system actively enhances the agency of individuals and their networks from the outset, thereby decreasing reliance on professional intervention. Because family members and other significant actors are invited to participate from the beginning, support processes move more quickly into the context of everyday life. This reduces the need to populate professionals' calendars with pre-scheduled interventions and creates flexibility, allowing workers to respond swiftly when needs are most acute.

Fourth, because care in a holistic system is tailored around an individual's specific situation, there is less need to move people between different professionals and units. This cuts down on redundant work and enables more rapid experimentation with concrete, situation-specific forms of help.

It also allows for smoother integration of other services and specialized expertise, supporting more efficient distribution and targeting of resources.

Fifth, a holistic system is more permissive toward private- and third-sector or different forms of community-based support that are not traditionally framed as medical treatments but that may genuinely help individuals—such as lifestyle services, hobbies, and social groups. The holistic stance also acknowledges that some people may benefit from complementary or alternative practices. At the same time, it minimizes the problematic aspects of such practices, which often arise from reductionist claims about unverified mechanisms. Within a holistic framework, no such mechanistic explanations are required: effects are assumed to emerge on multiple levels regardless of method, enabling more constructive dialogue and reducing unnecessary polarization.

Sixth, selective and minimal psychopharmacology is likely to shorten overall treatment duration, as fewer resources must be devoted to medication initiation, follow-up, and tapering. In the longer term, this reduces overall service use by preventing medication-related complications, which often burden both psychiatric and general medical services.

Seventh, a holistic system improves the ability to take overall responsibility for care. One team remains responsible for the entire process regardless of the type of difficulty. In reductionist systems, services are siloed and workers often manage only one phase of care, making it difficult to maintain a coherent overview. Responsibility is frequently shifted from one provider to another, and workers may develop a misleading picture of what people actually benefit from, as they see only narrow slices of situations and its consequences. This can lead to over- or underestimation of specific interventions and limit the extent to which care is aligned with individuals' broader life situations.

By contrast, when responsibility remains with a single team, practitioners gain a more complete understanding of each person's trajectory. Care is no longer experienced as a series of disconnected interventions but as a continuous process that evolves with the needs of the individual and their network. Seeing the long-term effects of care helps practitioners refine their judgment and make more informed, less assumption-driven decisions. This strengthens shared professional thinking and enables resources to be directed flexibly toward what is genuinely helpful. Moreover, carrying full responsibility creates an incentive for practitioners to support individuals in reorganizing their daily lives and networks in ways that reduce service dependence and minimize relapse risk.

In sum, when support is organized around a single responsible team and services revolve primarily around dialogical spaces, the system begins to *self-correct*. Resources are gradually freed from processes and structures that are no longer necessary and redirected toward immediate, relationship-centered encounters. Overlapping assessments and diagnostic gatekeeping diminish, easing the burden on specialized and inpatient services and reducing long-term service demand. Because the model simultaneously strengthens the agency of individuals and their networks, much of the meaningful change occurs in everyday environments, enhancing the resilience of close relationships and broader communities and further reducing pressure on formal services.

6.2 Reorganization and Resources

Figure 6.1 illustrates a stereotypical reductionist service system in which care is divided into primary and specialized tiers. Primary services handle mild difficulties, while specialized services manage more severe, complex, or chronic problems. In many countries, access to mental health services is routed through primary care, which aims to triage individuals so that, for example, "mild mood symptoms" are treated within primary services or their mental health equivalents.

Primary units assess the nature of the problem, may initiate medication, and monitor progress. They can refer individuals onward to more specialized workers if the difficulties appear linked to financial strain, social issues, or functional impairments requiring occupational therapy. Some primary units offer evidence-based interventions for specific disorders, such as brief cognitive-behavioral treatments. If difficulties are judged not to fall within mental health, individuals may be discharged or redirected back to other primary care units. Referrals to private or third-sector services may also be issued.

When difficulties are more severe or prolonged, individuals may be referred to specialized and secondary-level services. Most countries have some form of intake or crisis clinic responsible for initial specialist assessment and differential diagnosis. Acute or life-threatening crises may lead directly to hospital admission. From hospital, individuals may be referred either back to primary services or into specialized units depending on diagnostic conclusions.

Within specialist care, diagnosis determines onward referral to disorder-specific teams offering highly specialized, evidence-based treatments. Diagnostics continue, and follow-up reviews are performed similarly to primary services. If, during treatment, a person's presentation appears inconsistent with the unit's profile, they may be redirected to another unit or back to intake. If a crisis emerges, they may again be sent to crisis services or hospital. When long-term support is needed, various maintenance services—supported housing, long-term medication monitoring, or group programs—may be offered. In many countries, such maintenance work is eventually transferred back to primary services or other sectors.

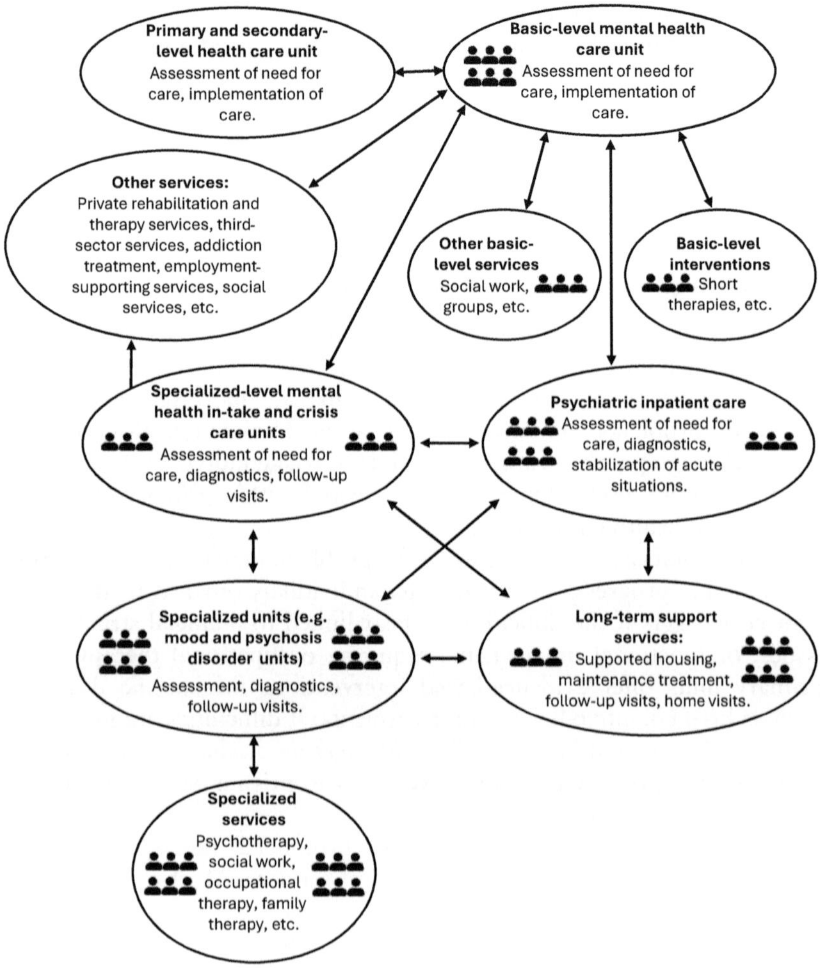

Figure 6.1 Stereotypical care pathways and resourcing in a reductionistic system

The arrows in Figure 6.1 show the multitude of directions in which a person may be moved within a reductionist system. Even this complex illustration is a simplification: most systems involve substantially more tiers, units, and parallel processes. The figure's 60 human icons represent the distribution of resources: the majority are concentrated in intake, assessment, and inpatient units responsible for diagnostic allocation, as well as in specialized units offering disorder-specific interventions.

Because reductionist systems encourage specialization, a large number of different actors become involved, and overall responsibility is easily fragmented. Many services are delivered more or less automatically when certain criteria are met, irrespective of whether they address the individual's actual needs. This leads to long waiting times, difficulty accessing care, and inefficiencies, as interventions may not align with real-life situations. Resource shortages increase the risk that the implicit goal of assessment becomes workload management—shuffling individuals between units—rather than meaningful support.

The fundamental contrast with a holistic system lies in its centralization of responsibility. In a holistic system, a single team or unit is responsible for the entire process from beginning to end. The structural separation between primary and specialist care is dissolved, as is the logic of disorder-specific service lines. Most staff resources are pooled into the coordination of holistic, dialogical work. Rather than being referred from one service to another, individuals remain with their team, and additional actors are invited into the process as needed. This creates a strong incentive for workers to tailor support in ways that help people function in their everyday settings. The threshold for initiating prolonged or intensive interventions—such as medication or hospitalization—therefore rises, and attention shifts to concrete, transferable solutions.

Figure 6.2 illustrates how this reorganization reshapes care pathways and resource allocation. As dialogical work becomes the system's core activity and responsibility remains with one team, resources formerly tied to intake and assessment are redirected into this work. Because long-term hospitalization and certain specialized interventions are expected to decrease, resources from these areas can also be newly allocated to dialogical practice. The figure demonstrates that a holistic system does not necessarily require significant additional funding after implementation; rather, it re-orients existing, currently fragmented staff resources toward a unified purpose.

In holistic system, individuals are not routinely sent elsewhere. At key transitional moments, other services may be invited into joint meetings. This maintains shared understanding across sectors and secures continuity, eliminating the need to repeatedly restart the relationship with new workers. Besides coordinating work and resources, this structure strengthens the working alliance—a core common factor in mental health outcomes.

6.2.1 Resource Configuration and Capacity Planning

The optimal level of staffing for a holistic mental health unit centered on the facilitation of dialogical encounters cannot be defined with precision. Resource needs vary according to cultural and societal factors, population size, socioeconomic conditions, degree of urbanization, the availability of private- and third-sector services, and the strength of primary care infrastructure.

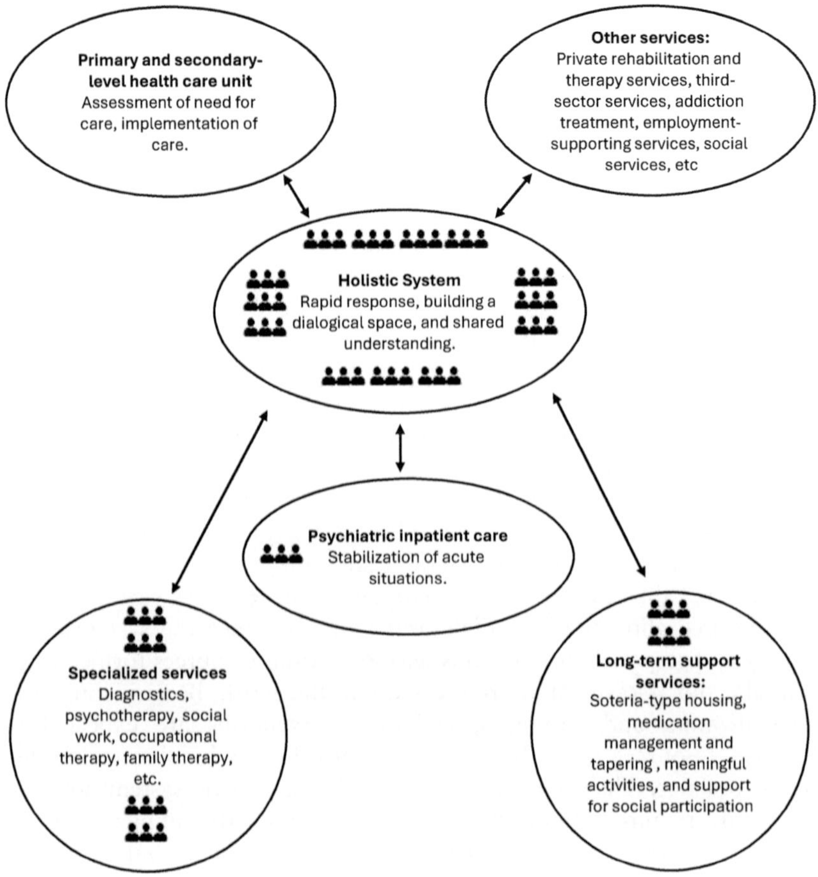

Figure 6.2 Holistic System

As an illustrative benchmark, in the Open Dialogue system in Western Lapland, the minimum staffing required to coordinate network-oriented dialogical care has historically been approximately 60–80 staff per 100,000 inhabitants, depending on the time period and method of calculation (e.g., Bergström et al., 2025; 2026). Of these, around 5–10 per 100,000 were physicians, 20–30 per 100,000 specialized professionals (psychologists, social workers, occupational therapists), and the remainder nurses. An additional 20–40 staff per 100,000 were allocated more heavily toward psychiatric inpatient and other specialized services, partly overlapping with the same workforce and characterized by flexible movement between tasks according to system and service user needs. In the Trieste community mental health service—another example of a comprehensive and holistic, whole-service approach to mental health care described in more detail in Chapter 10—the Department of Mental Health employed approximately

87–90 staff per 100,000 population, excluding general hospital staff and NGO-provided support services (Mezzina, 2014).

Although the workforce of a holistic system can be organized administratively under a single unit whose primary task is the facilitation of dialogical spaces, in practice, it is necessary to distribute these resources into smaller, locally embedded community-based sub-units. Local units serve their own catchment area, are easier to manage administratively, and operate closer to the everyday contexts of service users. Smaller teams also strengthen team cohesion, familiarity, and the interpersonal trust within teams essential for a model grounded in shared responsibility. While the optimal population size for each community unit depends on local factors, based on the above examples, a catchment area of roughly 30,000–60,000 inhabitants is likely to provide favorable team sizes and manageable coordination of care pathways.

Despite important organizational, cultural, and rural–urban differences, the Open Dialogue system in Western Lapland and the Trieste community mental health service in Italy operate whole mental health systems with broadly similar staffing intensities—on the order of approximately 80–100 staff per 100,000 population—suggesting that comprehensive, community-based models of care may require comparable levels of human resources. However, it is important to emphasize that these figures are illustrative and primarily drawn from experiments and practical experiences in high-income Western countries, where service systems are generally well resourced and where care pathways are administratively and financially streamlined—even if resource use is not always optimal. In settings where psychiatric and mental health systems are underdeveloped or under-resourced, building a holistic system may require additional investment. This may present challenges in low- and middle-income countries where the service infrastructure and workforce capacity may be insufficient to establish a holistic system solely by reallocating existing resources.

At the same time, many such countries possess strong traditions of community-based and participatory forms of care, which can be implemented without large financial investment. Even in these contexts, however, it is essential to strengthen core competencies among the workforce and, where necessary, develop legal and regulatory frameworks that safeguard human rights and ensure that practitioners are equipped to engage with the full spectrum of human experience without resorting to authoritarian or discriminatory practices.

6.3 Strengthening Core Competencies in the Workforce

Within a holistic system, contextual and relational ways of working become the foundational mode of care. This requires a workforce trained not merely in technical procedures but also in the facilitation of dialogical encounters. In practice, such training can be delivered through peer-based, work-integrated learning, whereby staff members train one another as part of their everyday practice. This approach reduces the dependence on multiple "top-down" method-specific trainings that, in reality, practitioners may find difficult to adopt systematically or apply consistently. Moreover, training becomes productive work in itself: training sessions and supervision directly support care delivery while simultaneously ensuring quality monitoring. Peer training and modeling, however, presuppose that a core group of staff first develop a sufficiently strong grounding in the holistic framework.

Training needs can largely be met using existing continuing education and supervision resources, provided these are reprioritized. A generic, system-wide training program has a clear rationale: it scales a unified and common approach to helping—regardless of the specific presenting issue—more effectively than a collection of discrete method- or disorder-specific trainings. Additional efficiencies arise when a subgroup of staff train first and subsequently train their colleagues alongside routine work. This model can be implemented at regular intervals. Over the longer term, it would be most effective to integrate training in the holistic framework into basic health and social care curricula, thereby eliminating the need to "unlearn" older models early in one's career and allowing the holistic orientation to be internalized organically through co-working and team-based practice without the need for additional training programs.

Despite the emphasis on generic competencies and the optimization of common helping factors across mental health care, a holistic system still requires more specialized and sharply defined expertise. Such expertise is most naturally cultivated on top of a general holistic foundation, which equips workers with strong baseline capacities to sustain high-quality therapeutic interaction, to remain responsive within complex interpersonal dynamics, and to tailor psychotherapeutic and psychosocial methods on a case-by-case basis. By foregrounding relational attunement and situational judgment, this foundation reduces the risk of mechanically applying psychosocial techniques in ways that may diminish their effectiveness and instead supports practitioners in shaping interventions to the specific needs of the person, the relational context, and the competencies they already possess.

Specialized skills can also be supported through collaboration with private or third-sector providers, to whom service users may be referred depending on the overall structure, availability, and funding models of the service system—provided that the need for such referral is first jointly identified within the dialogical process. This allows specialized services, often developed under reductionist assumptions, to be deployed more precisely in response to actual needs, reducing fragmentation and unnecessary duplication of work. And because the holistic framework relies heavily on interactional practices commonly used in psychotherapy, certain specialist interventions—such as individual and longer term psychotherapy—could also be provided in-house, enabling specialists to work more closely with the core treatment network. This, in turn, allows psychotherapeutic work to be tailored more fluidly to the unfolding situation and need.

6.4 Financing Structures and Incentive Alignment to Reduce Medicalization

A central challenge in developing a holistic system is that, in many countries, the financing of mental health services is organized according to the logic of reductionist service production. In practice, funding streams are highly fragmented, and both insurance-based and publicly funded systems typically require that individuals be classified as suffering from a diagnosable disorder that warrants a particular treatment. This structural reliance on diagnosis reinforces medicalization: access to services and benefits becomes contingent on reducing a person's difficulties to a mental disorder category. In some countries, healthcare funding is even directly tied to diagnostic rates, interpreted as indicators of morbidity and thus of the need for additional resources.

Despite these structural constraints, the development of a holistic system can begin within existing financing frameworks, by drawing on the use of diagnostic codes and related administrative criteria in the manner outlined earlier. The same coding logic can be used to justify eligibility for various social benefits. Because these codes can be derived directly from current diagnostic classifications—using, for example, higher order diagnostic groupings—progress toward a holistic system need not initially require major structural or legislative reform. What matters most is the *practical meaning* attached to these codes: whether they are treated as entities that explain problems or as administrative tools that justify access to services and specific forms of support.

In the longer term, however, it would be beneficial to develop financing models not tied to disease constructs but rather to a person's current situation and collaboratively assessed needs. In fact, such an approach is not far removed from current practice: descriptive diagnostic categories are already used administratively to secure treatments and benefits. Within a holistic system, the explicitly descriptive and administrative nature of diagnostics would make the actual problems and their contextual roots more transparent, without reframing them as something they are not. This would help align funding more precisely with real needs, thereby improving cost-effectiveness. For example, work-related stress would be less likely to be reframed as a depressive disorder requiring long-term pharmacotherapy if the focus of care were the identified stressors and the person's current capacity to respond to them.

Another major challenge is that in many countries' mental health providers—both public and private—are funded according to service volume. Under such models, providers have few financial incentives to develop holistic services whose explicit aim is to support people in ways that reduce their need for professional help. While reducing long-term service use is socially beneficial, it may create economic disadvantages for providers if revenue is tied to utilization rates.

In future, a more holistic framework could be supported, for example, through outcome-based financing, where the primary metric is not service volume but the person's own evaluation of how well they were helped—combined with a reduced need for services. If utilization falls below an expected benchmark and the person reports satisfaction with the support received, a portion of the cost savings could be reimbursed to the provider. Expected utilization benchmarks for the development of the situation can be modeled using administrative data through machine learning or other multivariate methods, as described in more detail in Chapter 9. However, such models introduce many risks for providers, funders, and service users alike and would require small-scale pilot studies and further investigation before wider implementation.

Regardless of the precise financing model, a holistic system is likely to be more cost-effective than a reductionist, institution-heavy system in which large shares of resources are consumed by specialized units, diagnostic gatekeeping, repeated assessments, and overlapping interventions. Over time, a holistic framework may reduce pressure on the mental health system as a whole by shifting focus away from viewing difficulties primarily as individual disorders. This reduces medicalization, overtreatment, and the othering stigma that diagnostic labels can perpetuate, while improving service responsiveness and enabling communities to support individuals more effectively. Resources can then be distributed more flexibly across other sectors—such as social services or employment supports—according to actual need.

To maintain a holistic system, at minimum the financing model must allow for consistent facilitation of dialogical encounters and the flexible allocation of services according to the shared understanding developed within them. In many countries, this could be accomplished with modest adjustments to existing structures—through better prioritization of resources, strengthening population-based core funding, consolidating financing streams, or allowing greater discretionary scope in service provision beyond diagnosis-linked reimbursement rules. In practice, this would most likely require a population-based global budget model with integrated regional responsibility for mental health care. A regional team or service network would receive a stable per-capita budget and retain responsibility for coordinating support across the full continuum of care.

In some contexts, progress toward a holistic system may also be supported through hybrid models, in which many preventive, community-based, or low-threshold supports are funded by non-profit organizations, foundations, or local communities. Under such arrangements, the public sector would finance dialogical facilitation and institutional psychiatric care such as hospitalization, while community actors would provide complementary support that integrates seamlessly into the helping process. This reduces pressure on specialized, infrastructure-heavy services and enables care to be embedded more naturally in everyday environments without extensive bureaucracy or major organizational expansion.

A key difficulty, however, is that most existing holistic systems or pilots have been heavily publicly funded, which is not feasible everywhere. In many countries, health and social care financing is multi-channeled, scarce, regionally uneven, or dependent on market-based actors. In such settings, holistic integration cannot be achieved simply by changing practices or reallocating resources. Countries without robust public funding for mental health care may need to rely on mixed sources—insurance, project-based funding, private actors, or community-driven solutions. Here, the development of a holistic system requires careful design of alternative financing arrangements to ensure that services are cohesive rather than fragmented or dependent on ephemeral funding streams.

Across all financing environments, the core logic remains the same: when attention shifts from diagnostic categories to people's real situations and the dialogical work centered on them, overlapping assessments and gatekeeping diminish, access becomes faster, and resources begin to flow toward where they are most useful. Over time, this may reduce the overall burden on the mental health system, regardless of whether funding is primarily public, insurance-based, hybrid, or community-driven. A holistic orientation allows systems to remain functional and cost-effective even under constrained resource conditions—provided that its basic principles are preserved and that service development is guided by long-term planning.

6.5 A Leadership Perspective

Beyond structural, professional, and financial considerations, a decisive factor in developing a holistic system is how services are led in practice (e.g., Gauffin et al., 2025). In the reductionist framework, services are organized around predefined directives and diagnosis-based care pathways, with leadership flowing top-down. This model prioritizes clarity of procedure, unidirectional control, and linear cause–effect reasoning. Its central aims are predictability, controllability, and risk minimization—features well suited to closed systems such as industrial production, where processes, problems, and solutions can be specified in advance.

Holistic leadership, by contrast, rests on a different logic and aligns more naturally with open, complex systems in which processes cannot be fully defined beforehand (e.g., Stacey, 2011). Mental health services are a paradigmatic example of such systems (e.g., Gauffin et al., 2025): challenges are multilayered and ambiguous, and solutions emerge through multilevel interaction, contextual understanding, and iterative, exploratory work. In these environments, organizing principles are best understood as emergent and continuously evolving—albeit within intentional boundary conditions defined by the organization. Consequently, leadership becomes less vertical and more horizontal: instead of directing from the top, it enables self-organization from the bottom up within a shared framework.

In this sense, the leader within a holistic system resembles a facilitator of network dialogue. Their central task is to create orienting structures, goals, and boundary conditions that enable teams to organize themselves toward these aims. As a result, teams hold greater responsibility and decision-making autonomy in case-by-case service coordination. Leadership becomes less about prescribing details and more about maintaining the integrity and coherence of the whole.

In practical terms, the key responsibility of a leader in a holistic system is to ensure that staff hold a sufficiently shared understanding of the system's purpose—namely, the case-specific facilitation of dialogical encounters—and that they have the structures, competencies, and working conditions required to enact this purpose. Traditional top-down leadership remains necessary only in specific circumstances that require immediate, decisive action.

Adopting a holistic framework also transforms how service organization is designed. As administrative structures become lighter and more coherent, leadership becomes distributed across smaller and more manageable units embedded closer to everyday work. This proximity strengthens leaders' substantive understanding, increases team cohesion, and ideally enables leaders to participate—at least partially—in frontline activity, preserving insight into what teams actually need. Reducing hierarchical layers simultaneously streamlines governance and frees resources from administrative overhead, allowing them to be redirected toward functions that more directly support holistic practice.

Structural adjustments alone, however, are insufficient. Leadership can also be used deliberately to foster the adoption of holistic thinking. Yet if this is attempted too broadly or too forcefully in contexts where holistic principles are not yet widely understood, there is a substantial risk that the effort will be interpreted through a reductionist lens. In such cases, the change becomes reabsorbed into the existing paradigm: new guidelines are created, additional care pathways are designed, detailed process maps are drafted, and administrative oversight increases. Such top-down, mechanistic reform may appear structural but does not alter the underlying logic of service delivery.

By contrast, if the holistic framework is clearly articulated as a long-term direction and small-scale pilots are initiated in areas where service coordination and holistic practices are already partially established, leadership can act as a catalyst for consolidation and broader cultural transformation. This requires leaders to define the overall direction while giving teams latitude to organize their work in response to the situations they encounter. Implementation is strengthened through shared discussions, low-hierarchy structures, situational decision-making authority, and continuing professional education that supports the methodological skills needed for dialogical facilitation. Leadership, in other words, does not direct the content of care; it builds the infrastructure in which holistic work can unfold and where solutions emerge from context rather than from pre-specified protocols.

When leadership, resource organization, and everyday clinical practice all begin to reflect the same logic, the system can gradually transform into a holistic one without extensive top-down control. At that point, the holistic system is no longer a reform imposed from above but becomes the organization's operating culture—just as reductionism functions now.

6.6 A Legislative Perspective

Although in many countries mental health systems can already be steered toward a more holistic orientation within existing legal frameworks—through strategic leadership, enhanced workforce competence, and shifts in organizational structures and resource allocation—legislative reforms can play an important role in supporting and sustaining a holistic system.

Internationally, laws governing mental health care are often incomplete, outdated, or inconsistently applied, thereby reinforcing a reductionist logic that medicalizes life problems as psychiatric disorders (WHO, 2021). Such frameworks not only narrow the scope of care but also expose individuals to direct human rights violations, including discrimination, undue restriction, and coercion. For these reasons, international bodies have emphasized the need to update mental health legislation so that it aligns with human rights principles and supports a shift toward participatory, community-based, non-coercive services (Pūras, 2017; WHO, 2023).

Legislation thus functions both as an enabler and a removal of constraints: it defines minimum standards for service content and quality, ensures equality before the law, and directs systems toward community-embedded support and dialogical practice. The following is based on WHO (2023) guidance on rights-based mental health legislation.

6.6.1 *Decision-Making Capacity and Supported Autonomy*

A first key issue concerns legal capacity. In reductionist systems, it is common for a person's decision-making authority to be curtailed on the basis of diagnosis, symptom expression, or perceived "riskiness," even when the situation would allow for strengthened autonomy through supported decision-making. A holistic system requires that the person's will and preferences remain the foundation of care—even during crises or when functional capacity is temporarily diminished. Legislation should therefore establish a clear presumption of full legal capacity, with any transfer of decision-making power restricted to narrowly defined, exceptional circumstances. In place of substituted decision-making, the system must build structures for supported decision-making, in which individuals receive help clarifying their own wishes without losing control to others.

6.6.2 *Minimizing Coercion and Promoting Voluntary Engagement*

A second legal question concerns the use of coercion. Reductionist systems rest on the assumption that well-being or public safety can at times be ensured only through restrictive measures. In practice, this has normalized involuntary medication, involuntary hospitalization, seclusion, restraint, and other forms of coercion—interventions that often undermine trust, heighten fear, complicate care, and paradoxically increase the likelihood of further coercion (WHO, 2023).

A holistic system is built upon voluntariness and collaboration. For this to be realized, legislation must clearly emphasize that coercion is not the default and that systems are obliged to develop non-coercive crisis responses and support mechanisms. This does not preclude responding to acute crises; rather, it requires that responses focus on presence, listening, relational safety, de-escalation, and network-based support rather than restrictive interventions.

6.6.3 *Service Accessibility and the Removal of Diagnostic Gatekeeping*

A third legislative dimension concerns accessibility. In many countries, diagnostic or tier-based service pathways are legally anchored in eligibility criteria that determine who receives which form of care. These structures divert resources toward gatekeeping and the administrative processing of criteria, often resulting in the movement of individuals between multiple providers before help begins.

In a holistic system, the request for help itself constitutes a sufficient indication for a dialogical meeting; no diagnostic certainty is required to begin support. To enable this, legislation must allow access to services without diagnosis-based eligibility and must ensure that services can be delivered flexibly—in homes, communities, and everyday environments—without heavy administrative prerequisites. The law should support flexible use of services, rather than binding them to rigid structures, methods or predetermined care pathways.

6.6.4 *Quality, Inclusiveness, and the Role of Social Networks*

A fourth issue concerns quality and inclusiveness. A holistic system recognizes that individuals are embedded within social networks that can be active participants in care. Legislation must therefore guarantee opportunities for meaningful involvement of family members, close others, and other relevant network participants, without requiring them to hold specific legal roles or delegated authority. The aim is not to transfer decision-making power to relatives but to establish authentically collaborative care. At the same time, the law can mandate culturally and socially accessible services—including language support, mobile teams, or community-based modalities—which are basic prerequisites for holistic work.

6.6.5 *Oversight, Accountability, and Cross-Sector Coordination*

A fifth legislative focus concerns the monitoring and development of the system. The transformation implied by a holistic framework is profound: it shifts the balance of authority away from professional control toward shared decision-making and partnership. Since much of the necessary support lies outside health care itself (housing, income support, employment, education, family and child services, the legal system), the law must require cross-sector coordination, information-sharing, and joint initiatives so that support can take place in real-life contexts. Holistic care also requires transparent and independent oversight, tracking issues such as the use of coercion, service accessibility, equality, and people's lived experiences. Legislation may require the systematic collection and publication of such data, enabling the system to evaluate and correct itself.

Legislation can also help ensure that legal responsibility does not fall disproportionately on a single professional or discipline. In reductionist systems, liability for decisions may rest with an individual psychiatrist, which can lead to overly cautious, risk-averse practices. In a holistic system, care is delivered through collaborative, network-based processes; imposing individualized legal responsibility is therefore inappropriate. Responsibility should instead reflect the genuinely shared nature of decision-making.

6.6.6 *The Limits and Risks of Legal Reform*

The types of legislative changes described above can be difficult to implement if practice remains grounded in a reductionist logic. For example, WHO (2023) recommends prohibiting all forms of involuntary treatment—a goal that may be challenging in systems where coercion is currently routine. If the law were to suddenly prohibit involuntary measures in such contexts, there is a risk that coercive practices might migrate into unregulated "grey zones," or that individuals might no longer receive support but instead be subjected to other forms of social control, such as criminal justice measures.

For these reasons, priority should be given to strengthening the holistic system itself, as such systems can be expected to reduce the need for coercive interventions. This expectation aligns with empirical findings showing limited evidence for the effectiveness of coercive measures—such as involuntary hospitalization or seclusion—in preventing harm or dangerous situations (e.g., Corderoy et al., 2024; Nyttingnes et al., 2023; WHO, 2023). Research similarly provides little or mixed support for compulsory outpatient treatment in countries where it has been implemented (Kisely et al., 2017; 2025, Kocher & Swartz, 2025; WHO, 2023).

In a holistic system, problematic cycles can be prevented by reversing the sequence: by offering immediate, participatory, real-life support that reduces escalation and thereby the likelihood of coercion. Table 6.1 illustrates how a holistic service model, by altering the underlying production logic of care, can itself minimize the need for involuntary interventions.

6.7 Summary of Service Reorganization

The core premise of a holistic system is a shift away from structures in which care is organized around diagnoses, gatekeeping functions, and hierarchically tiered levels of treatment. Instead, support is organized around the person's current situation, their social networks, and the concrete needs arising in everyday life. Reorganization begins with the principle that one team assumes full responsibility for the process from start to finish, coordinating dialogical spaces at the outset and at key transition points. Based on the understanding generated in these dialogues, the team facilitates the practical helping process in a case-specific manner, drawing on more reductionist forms of specialized expertise whenever needed. This reduces the need to move people from one service to another, diminishes duplicative

Table 6.1 Illustrative comparison of how holistic and reductionist service logics shape pathways toward or away from coercion

Holistic system	*Reductionistic system*
Rapid response—the aim is to reach the person immediately and with a low threshold	**Assessment**—decisions are made clinic-centered and often without involving the person's network
Dialogue—a shared understanding of the situation is built together with the person and their network	**Diagnosis**—the situation is interpreted primarily through the lens of illness
Support in the person's own environment—help is provided where the difficulties actually emerge	**Hospitalization criteria**—focus is on risk avoidance and on whether the person meets the threshold for inpatient care
Building change—support focuses on everyday life, relationships, concrete factors, and the systematic building of trust	**Transport to another unit**—moving the person breaks everyday connections and existing therapeutic relationships
The situation calms—an inclusive approach reduces conflict and the risk of escalation	**Resistance**—separation and involuntary transfers increase fear and conflict
Situations leading to coercion do not emerge—both formal coercion and "coercion in the dark" decrease	**Coercion**—the chain easily results in involuntary treatment

assessment work, and shortens delays in receiving help—thereby reducing the overall burden on the entire service system.

A holistic system does not inherently require major additional resources; rather, it requires reallocation. Because care is no longer dependent on diagnoses or complex referral chains, much of the current assessment and gatekeeping work becomes unnecessary. The same applies to specialized units: once care is structured around dialogical encounters and personalized real-life support, siloed service structures lose their relevance, allowing a significant proportion of the workforce to be redirected toward immediate encounters with those seeking help.

The functioning of such a system depends on a workforce sharing a foundational competence in dialogical practice. This competence can be strengthened through supervision and training integrated directly into everyday clinical work. At the same time, the system can retain and utilize specialized expertise but does so by integrating it into the holistic helping process through flexible dialogical structures, with the same team maintaining responsibility for the overall process.

A holistic system also requires a different way of understanding financing and incentives. Whereas reductionist systems link funding to predefined diagnoses and service utilization, a holistic system emphasizes needs-based support, where success is defined not by the volume of care delivered but by whether the support is no longer needed and people feel genuinely helped. Over time, a well-functioning holistic system is more cost-effective, as it is likely to reduce overtreatment, medicalization, and duplicative processes, as well as the need for high-intensity interventions such as long-term institutional care and long-term medication.

Leadership also assumes a different form in a holistic system. Rather than governing from the top-down micro-management, leadership primarily involves creating the direction and enabling conditions that allow teams to work autonomously in accordance with the system's aims.

Legislation forms the system's invisible backbone. In many countries, existing mental health laws are built upon a reductionist logic that directly supports involuntary interventions, diagnostic gatekeeping, and individualized medicalization. A holistic system instead requires the protection of legal capacity, a move away from the primacy of coercion, and the enabling of flexible, community-based, participatory forms of support. The role of legislation is to ensure that care occurs in the context of the person's will, everyday environment, and networks, and that the system operates equitably, collaboratively, and in accordance with human rights.

When these structural, financial, professional, and legal components align, a holistic system begins to self-correct: gatekeeping diminishes, flexibility and learning increase, the need for coercion declines, and resources become directed precisely where they are most useful. A holistic system is not a method but a reorganization of mental health care such that people, their networks, and their everyday contexts constitute the primary frame of reference for practice.

References

Bergström, T., Kurtti, M., Duthie, A., Valtanen, K., & Seikkula, J. (2025). Open dialogue. In O. Smoliak, E. Tseliou, T. Strong, S. Bava, & P. Muntigl (Eds.), *The Routledge international handbook of postmodern therapies* (pp. 174–185). Routledge. https://doi.org/10.4324/9781003376231-14

Bergström, T., Miettunen, J., Partanen, K., Yrjänheikki, V., Rantamaa, K., Hietasaari, T., Öfverberg, E., Gauffin, T., & Petäjäniemi, J. (2026). After the open dialogue: A within-area comparison of treatment, experiences, and outcomes in western Lapland 20 years after service fragmentation. *Community Mental Health Journal*, Early online. https://doi.org/10.1007/s10597-026-01591-z

Corderoy, A., Kisely, S., Zirnsak, T., & Ryan, C. J. (2024). The benefits and harms of inpatient involuntary psychiatric treatment: A scoping review. *Psychiatry, Psychology, and Law: An Interdisciplinary Journal of the Australian and New Zealand Association of Psychiatry, Psychology and Law*, *32*(5), 734–781. https://doi.org/10.1080/13218719.2024.2346734

Gauffin, T., Bergström, T., & Patja, K. (2025, November 20). Strategic management of the regional mental health service systems. *Hallinnon ja kuntatutkimuksen tiedepäivät 2025*. (p. 27).

Kisely, S., Bull, C., & Gill, N. (2025). A systematic review and meta-analysis of the effect of community treatment orders on aggression or criminal behaviour in people with a mental illness. *Epidemiology and Psychiatric Sciences*, *34*, e12. https://doi.org/10.1017/S2045796025000058

Kisely, S., Campbell, L. A., & O'Reilly, R. (2017). Compulsory community and involuntary outpatient treatment for people with severe mental disorders. *Cochrane Database of Systematic Reviews*, *3*, CD004408. https://doi.org/10.1002/14651858.CD004408.pub5

Kocher, S., & Swartz, M. (2025). Assisted outpatient treatment: Are court-ordered antipsychotic medications effective?. *CNS Spectrums*, *30*(1), e17. https://doi.org/10.1017/S1092852925000045

Mezzina, R. (2014). Community mental health care in Trieste and beyond: An "Open Door-No Restraint" system of care for recovery and citizenship. *Journal of Nervous and Mental Disease, 202,* 440–445. https://doi.org/10.1097/nmd.0000000000000142

Nyttingnes, O., Benth, J. Š., Hofstad, T., & Rugkåsa, J. (2023). The relationship between area levels of involuntary psychiatric care and patient outcomes: A longitudinal national register study from Norway. *BMC Psychiatry*, *23*(1), 112. https://doi.org/10.1186/s12888-023-04584-4

Pūras, D. (2017). *Report of the Special Rapporteur on the right of everyone to the enjoyment of the highest attainable standard of physical and mental health* (A/HRC/35/21). Yhdistyneet kansakunnat Human Rights Council. https://undocs.org/A/HRC/35/21

Stacey, R. D. (2011). *Strategic management and organisational dynamics: The challenge of complexity* (6th ed.). Pearson.

World Health Organization. (2021). *Guidance on community mental health services: Promoting person-centred and rights-based approaches*. World Health Organization. https://creativecommons.org/licenses/by-nc-sa/3.0/igo/

World Health Organization (2023). *Mental health, human rights and legislation: Guidance and practice*. World Health Organization. https://www.who.int/publications/i/item/9789240080737

Chapter 7

Challenges of the Holistic Framework

The preceding chapters have outlined how a holistic framework can reorganize mental health care around dialogical spaces, shared responsibility, and context-sensitive support. This chapter turns to the practical, conceptual, and institutional challenges that arise when such a framework is introduced into systems long shaped by reductionist assumptions. Rather than treating these challenges as peripheral obstacles, this chapter examines them as structural tensions inherent in any attempt to transform the epistemological, professional, and organizational foundations of psychiatry and mental health services.

This chapter begins by exploring tensions between reductionist and holistic modes of understanding, focusing on professional identity, expertise, leadership, and authority. It then examines divergent perspectives on problem definition and service demand, including the social appeal of diagnosis, medicalization, and concerns about access and resource use. Subsequent sections address the cognitive and philosophical complexity of holistic thinking, practical risks related to implementation and equity, and common concerns regarding safety, medication use, and psychiatry's medical role. This chapter concludes by synthesizing these challenges and outlining conditions under which a transition toward a holistic system can proceed responsibly—acknowledging uncertainty, ethical complexity, and political constraints while clarifying why such a transition remains both necessary and feasible.

7.1 Tensions between Reductionism and Holism

At present, the holistic framework differs markedly from both the general population's intuitive ways of understanding mental distress and the conceptual orientation embedded in the basic training of most health professionals. For practitioners in high-status expert roles in particular, shifting toward a more holistic mode of working requires a substantial transformation of professional identity—a process that may be burdensome and elicit resistance.

DOI: 10.4324/9781003777939-10

These same professionals are often key subject-matter experts or occupy leadership positions that significantly shape the development of the entire service system. As a result, new practices are typically adapted to fit the prevailing reductionist framework, which can obscure or dilute the holistic perspective, especially if it is perceived as threatening one's professional status or role.

The coexistence of divergent epistemological and practical orientations can generate tensions both within services and across sectors. In the absence of shared concepts and values, collaboration becomes more difficult, and the effectiveness of care may suffer. From a reductionist perspective, holistic practices may appear overly loose, vague, or even unsafe, particularly if they are perceived as diminishing the use of "evidence-based" interventions. Conversely, from a holistic standpoint, reductionist practices may seem overly individualized, authoritarian, or unnecessarily narrow in scope. Even when the benefits of a holistic system are acknowledged, the prevailing reductionist model may still feel safer and more manageable, offering clear roles, criteria, and procedural certainty. This does not mean that the model is the most effective way to organize services, but rather that system-level change appears risky in contexts already characterized by excessive workload and structural complexity. Transitioning to a holistic framework may therefore seem unrealistic precisely when services are most strained.

Tensions are amplified by the fact that psychiatric expertise is reconceptualized within a holistic system. Rather than diminishing professional competence, the shift reorients it away from the authority of individual experts and toward shared, polyphonic decision-making. Expertise becomes less a function of professional status and more a matter of how each practitioner participates in constructing situational understanding. In effect, the holistic system democratizes professional roles, strengthens the collective agency of teams, and reduces hierarchical dynamics so that decisions rest on distributed expertise rather than the authority of a single discipline. While this can reduce pressure on individual clinicians and improve well-being at work, it may also provoke uncertainty among those accustomed to strong professional identity markers or clear procedural guidelines.

Democratizing professional roles does not eliminate the need for specialized knowledge; rather, it reshapes how such knowledge is used. Physicians remain responsible for medical expertise, nurses for continuity of care and practical organization, psychologists and psychotherapists for psychological phenomena and relational processes, and social workers for navigating bureaucratic systems and mobilizing external actors. In a holistic system, these competencies are not ranked hierarchically but are integrated into dialogical helping processes such that each profession's expertise complements the others more effectively. Responsibility thereby shifts toward interdisciplinary teams, increasing transparency in decision-making and reducing the legal and professional risks borne by individual practitioners.

However, if workers perceive their roles as becoming blurred or threatened, various defensive reactions may emerge—such as reasserting professional boundaries or creating new specialized tasks to reinforce one's status. Such tendencies run counter to the principles of a holistic system and can reintroduce siloed divisions of labor. Minimizing these risks requires a carefully managed and gradual development process anchored as close to frontline practice as possible. The focus must remain on strengthening collective team agency and maintaining clear, shared role definitions aligned with the system's aims.

For this reason, it is essential that responsibility for the holistic system and its leadership is assigned to a clearly defined body that carries the mandate to articulate the care philosophy and overall division of labor. When principles and roles are transparent and widely understood, practitioners are more likely to experience their work as coherent and meaningful, and the holistic framework becomes not a threat but an opportunity. This also ensures that helping practices remain purpose-driven and that every professional—regardless of discipline—occupies a meaningful place within the shared, holistic helping process.

A central challenge in developing a holistic system is that resistance may be strongest among the leadership levels whose support is necessary for implementation. This stems from the fact that a holistic system substantially simplifies service structures, immediately reducing the need for multilayered administration. As decision-making shifts from hierarchical structures toward team-based and distributed expertise, traditional managerial roles lose much of their existing power and control functions. At the same time, the meaning of leadership changes: rather than administrative oversight, it becomes a facilitative practice grounded in supporting dialogue and team agency. For many leaders, this can feel unfamiliar and destabilizing to established professional identity.

It is therefore understandable that such systemic change elicits uncertainty, particularly among those whose authority is tied to the current structures. Yet leadership does not lose relevance within a holistic system—quite the opposite. Its focus shifts toward creating the culture, trust, and enabling conditions necessary for holistic work to flourish. Successful transformation therefore requires that leaders are offered a clear role as architects of the new system, as well as support in adopting a facilitative, rather than directive, leadership model.

7.2 Divergent Perspectives on Problem Definition and Service Demand

Beyond the resistance that may arise among practitioners and organizational leaders, tensions can also emerge in relation to service users themselves. First, people often seek simple, rapid solutions to their difficulties—solutions that a holistic system may not be able to offer as quickly. Although the aim of active listening and collaborative problem-solving is to create an experience of immediate support, the process may nevertheless feel slower when compared with traditional models in which help is channeled directly through an expert, commonly in the form of a diagnosis or medication.

In addition, in many countries people are accustomed to relying on specific experts and expecting unidirectional interpretations of their problems—for example, receiving a diagnosis. Even though a psychiatric diagnosis does not, in principle, explain the origins or meaning of a person's difficulties, it can still provide a sense of structure and of being understood. A diagnosis may also alleviate guilt, particularly in individualistic Western societies where personal struggles are often attributed to individual responsibility and interpreted as signs of weakness or failure. At times, people may even feel dismissed if certain forms of distress are not attributed to a medical disorder.

As noted earlier, efforts to reduce stigma have long sought to normalize diagnostic labels rather than to deepen public understanding of the underlying phenomena these labels describe (e.g., Read et al., 2006). As a result, some diagnoses have become socially accepted ways of describing a wide range of human traits and life challenges. For many, a diagnosis has become part of their identity and, importantly, a prerequisite for accessing essential services and supports.

It is crucial, however, to recognize that the widespread appeal of diagnoses is largely a response to a lack of viable alternatives. Societal stigma still persists toward individuals whose functioning does not align with cultural norms and expectations. Social media has likely intensified these pressures by both amplifying public judgment and shaping increasingly narrow behavioral norms. In such a climate, a medical diagnosis may be the only socially sanctioned explanation for reduced functioning or psychological distress. This dynamic contributes to a narrowing of what counts as "normal," fueling diagnostic inflation as increasingly common human experiences are framed as medical disorders, thereby reducing the specificity and clinical utility of diagnostic categories.

Although a diagnosis may be meaningful for many and provide a vocabulary through which to articulate their experiences, relying on diagnostic categories as tools for identity formation can present challenges. Diagnoses are unavoidably culturally grounded and derived from consensus classifications created by experts within a particular sociocultural and historical context. They therefore reflect the views of a relatively narrow demographic group (high-status medical professionals) concerning what should be considered normal or abnormal. When individuals come to define themselves through such categories, diagnoses can unintentionally reinforce stereotypes and rigid assumptions and may generate conflict—for example, when diagnostic criteria are not met or when classification systems change.

More broadly, the idea that a person's experiences are taken seriously only after they are medicalized as a disorder can be understood as a by-product of reductionist thinking. From a holistic perspective, suffering, distress, and non-normative traits are real and worthy of attention in their own right. People can and should be supported without requiring that their experiences first be reframed as medical abnormalities.

A complication, however, is that contemporary service systems often require the medicalization of personal characteristics in order for individuals to access needed support. This dynamic has expanded the remit of mental health expertise into an increasingly broad range of human experiences. In turn, this has contributed to the internalization of diagnostic identities and increased pressure on services. When service systems become overloaded, timely help becomes more difficult to obtain—thereby prolonging and intensifying the need for support.

In this context, the transition toward a more holistic system can appear risky. If waiting lists and referral processes were abruptly removed, it is feared that demand would become unmanageable. Consequently, even an inefficient yet predictable system may be viewed as the "lesser evil," despite its role in perpetuating chronicity. Politically and financially, it is often considered safer to expand existing resources within the current model than to restructure the architecture of services so that existing resources would be used differently—and potentially more efficiently—without requiring additional investment.

Thus, a central concern involves relaxing entry criteria for services, which is feared to result in unpredictable increases in service use and thus in resource demands. Yet it is important to note that under existing systems, people already expend considerable effort attempting to enter care, and these attempts themselves consume substantial resources that could instead be directed toward immediate, meaningful encounters. For example, triage, assessment, and referral processes consume a large proportion of mental health service capacity, even though they are intended to control demand.

Over the longer term, the broader adoption of a holistic system may actually reduce overall system burden precisely because it does not individualize problems. It may lessen feelings of guilt, increase recognition of the situational nature of distress, and soften socially constructed "mental health problem" categories and the stigma attached to them. At the same time, it may strengthen personal agency and enhance the capacity of communities to support their members in difficult situations without relying as heavily on specialized services or professional intervention.

Some concern relates also to the possibility that, without predefined treatment packages or tightly structured service pathways, people might use services excessively or remain in care "by choice." It is important, however, to recognize that people do not seek mental health services for their own sake or remain in them without reason. Services provide—or are expected to provide—something that is missing from a person's life: relief from distress, companionship in the face of loneliness, reassurance that potential illness will not go unnoticed, or—in some systems—a necessary prerequisite for financial support. For many, real alternatives do not exist, and service use becomes obligatory: refusal or disengagement can lead to coercive interventions.

A holistic system reduces these dynamics by moving care into people's everyday environments and by mapping out their actual needs while activating existing social networks. In this way, the service system is less likely to become the central organizing structure around which a person's life is built, and everyday life is more readily anchored in other meaningful contexts. This also frees resources for those who genuinely require longer term forms of support.

7.3 The Complexity and Challenges of Holistic Thinking

The holistic framework runs counter to a fundamental human tendency: the inclination to simplify, compartmentalize, and categorize phenomena into readily digestible parts. Adopting such a framework often requires a deliberate shift in both mindset and professional habit, which can be cognitively and emotionally demanding. For this reason, holistic thinking may be experienced as complex, ambiguous, or even threatening. This sense of complexity becomes pronounced when one attempts to approach holism from within a reductionist framework—particularly if the implicit aim is to formulate generalizable models by mapping linear causal relationships among multiple factors. Under such an approach, the number of potential variations appears endless.

Holism is also accompanied by a set of philosophical considerations. Emergence—the idea that wholes possess properties not reducible to their constituent parts—is frequently invoked as a placeholder concept in instances where a phenomenon is not yet sufficiently understood. It is often assumed that, as science advances, increasingly precise causal mechanisms will ultimately reveal how complex phenomena can be broken down into their elementary components. Under such a view, the core premise of holism may appear merely as an admission of ignorance: an acknowledgment that we do not yet understand how the interaction of parts generates the whole.

Even if this were the case, emergence can still function as a useful heuristic when phenomena do not in practice reduce to discrete, isolable components. In clinical work this is particularly salient: a person's state cannot be inferred from group-level definitions or symptom profiles, nor can causal relationships be meaningfully derived from diagnostic classifications.

Despite its apparent complexity, the holistic system paradoxically renders the mental health service structure considerably simpler. Its foundation is not the exhaustive mapping of causal chains, but rather a shift of focus from individual elements to the whole. A holistic system therefore emphasizes the generic, common factors of mental health care, reducing the need for practitioners to master multiple theories or specialized treatment models. This lessens cognitive burden: practitioners are not required to interpret experiences as evidence of some underlying entity or continually evaluate which specific method is "correct" for a given situation. What matters more is to follow the person and their social network, help them explore their circumstances from different perspectives, and co-construct a shared understanding of how their situation might be addressed concretely.

Holistic practice also distributes expertise more broadly across different actors, enabling more comprehensive forms of support and reducing the tendency to reframe diverse life phenomena as psychiatric disorders. At best, this can strengthen community capacity, guide policy and services toward supporting broader determinants of well-being, and reduce the likelihood that individuals are funneled unnecessarily into mental health care. Such a shift in thinking, however, is gradual, and holistic approaches must inevitably coexist with more reductionist ones for a considerable period. This coexistence brings a range of practical challenges, as efforts to work holistically encounter institutional structures, expectations, and habits still shaped by reductionist logics.

7.4 Practical Challenges of Governing Situations in Reductionist Systems

The contemporary public healthcare system is largely organized according to a reductionist logic. This same principle underpins many mental health development initiatives and the strategies that guide them, ranging from national policy frameworks to project-based reforms and local managerial practices.

As discussed above, the development of a holistic system is, in many countries, at least partly feasible within existing structures. Doing so, however, requires active leadership support and forms of governance aligned with the dynamics of complex systems—most notably leadership grounded in dialogical interaction. The challenge is that, from the perspective of policymakers, senior managers, and funders, reductionist systems tend to appear clearer and easier to control, as problems and the interventions designed to address them are predefined. A holistic system, by contrast, requires more open architecture and a broader distribution of responsibility across frontline workers, service users, and their networks. For many—leaders, staff, and service users alike—this shift can initially feel uncertain or even alarming. For this reason, the development of a holistic system must emphasize the centrality of team-based work and shared overall responsibility, ensuring that no individual is left to carry responsibility alone.

Keeping definitions and care pathways more open inevitably raises a number of practical and ethical concerns. A common worry is that care may become overly dependent on the personal preferences of individual practitioners, thereby generating inequities. I.e., when shared rules are not tightly standardized, the course of care may depend more on which staff members happen to be involved and on how initial encounters are structured.

Some development projects have, for example, found that increasing responsiveness and comprehensiveness improved care for people with milder difficulties but not for those with more severe problems (Iyer et al., 2025). Although such projects did not follow the holistic framework presented in this book, the observation highlights important questions about prioritization and the allocation of support. When needs are defined largely through negotiation, the process may favor not only certain practitioner preferences but also those service users who are better able to articulate their needs or insist on specific forms of care. Furthermore, when work becomes concentrated around the initial and transitional phases of care, individuals requiring long-term support may receive less attention—including those for whom accessing and organizing care is already difficult.

These challenges, however, are not insurmountable. As noted earlier, increasing responsiveness and broader holistic thinking across the population may, over time, reduce the number of people with "mild" difficulties seeking formal mental health services. When support becomes more accessible through other routes, and when communities gain greater resilience and tolerance for diversity and life challenges, problems are less readily pathologized as individual disorders, and communities gradually strengthen their own capacity to support members in everyday contexts. In addition, rapid responsiveness allows for more accurate assessment and planning based on a richer, mutually constructed understanding of a person's current circumstances. This enables services to be organized more precisely according to actual need, preserving resources for those who require more substantial support.

The flexibility inherent in a holistic system—compared to reductionist models—also makes it possible to modify care processes quickly when interventions prove ineffective or harmful. This, however, requires adequate staff training and structures that support individualized planning. One risk is that only a subset of staff may be trained in the holistic framework, while much of the system continues to operate according to the older logic. In practice, this makes implementation challenging: holistic functioning requires broad adoption, reaching a critical mass of practitioners who share the conceptual foundation. Such systemic change is often perceived as risky and too labor-intensive.

A key practical challenge—both organizationally and financially—is determining how a holistic system should be operationalized and measured in a way that allows controlled implementation. Because flexibility and contextual responsiveness are at the core of the holistic framework, overly rigid operationalization risks transforming the system into a categorized and inflexible one—the very opposite of its intended logic. Development efforts, definitions, and indicators should therefore be grounded in the principles of open, complex systems, such as self-organization, adaptability, and the acceptance of a degree of unpredictability. The aim is not to construct a strict regulatory framework but to establish direction and broad operational boundaries within which services can organically reorganize toward holistic practice when certain preconditions are met. Such thinking fits poorly within existing reductionist structures, managerial models, and measurement systems, which are not well designed to support or pilot such approaches.

Another challenge of operationalization concerns the proposed ontology in which mental health problems are understood as unfavorable situations rather than individual disorders. This inevitably raises ethical and practical questions: Who determines when a situation is unfavorable? From whose perspective? And on what grounds?

In most cases, the origin of concern—and thus the definition of the unfavorable situation—is relatively clear: someone feels they, or another person, can no longer cope, manage, or feel well. The alleviation of this concern is itself a meaningful indicator that the situation is improving. In such cases, the request for help is sufficient justification for arranging an initial dialogical meeting, and legally the "patient" is the individual whose situation is the source of concern. In practice, mental health services already operate largely in this manner.

However, there are many situations in which it is unclear whose "problem" the situation is. For example, a person experiencing mania may view their state positively—even as empowering—because it may heighten perceived creativity, performance, or opportunity. At the same time, the situation may be immediately unfavorable for relatives and care providers—and later likely for the individual themselves. In such conflicting scenarios, the goal is to seek compromise and balance: preventing escalation while strengthening the agency of the individual and their network so the situation remains tolerable for as many people as possible, for as long as possible, and is less likely to deteriorate.

There are, however, situations—such as violence or abuse—where compromise is impossible without worsening the situation for one party.

Here, a human-rights-based approach becomes the guiding principle: assessment and action must revolve around protecting fundamental rights, prioritizing those in vulnerable positions, who in such cases hold the legal status of the patient. WHO (2021; 2023) likewise emphasizes that human rights should be the primary organizing principle of the system, and their importance becomes especially salient in ethically ambiguous situations. *This principle provides the holistic system with a foundation that minimizes ethical risks arising from operationalization.*

It is also important to recognize that, within a holistic system, situations are understood primarily as processes—not as categorical entities comparable to disease classes acting as underlying causes. Many conflicted or unfavorable situations begin to shift already in the early phases of the process as the circumstances are reframed, allowing ethical questions to be resolved more readily as the situation evolves.

For example, in cases of intra-family violence or abuse, the process can be staged so that the rights and safety of the victim are secured first. This may involve decentralizing the support process through separate meetings and immediate changes in living arrangements so that the original situation begins to transform. Once this initial reframing occurs, new and partially separate processes can emerge—for example, supporting the perpetrator in ways that reduce future risk. Such approaches can indirectly contribute to safer overall outcomes.

It is equally important to note that such complexity is always present in reductionist systems as well, though often obscured by their structures and therefore less visible to practitioners. Thus, reductionist systems must make similar ethical judgments, but typically more indirectly—for example, through diagnostic labels—rather than focusing on the overall situation and its reorganization. This can increase the risk of human rights violations, because problems may be more easily reduced to an individual and their diagnosis, shaping interventions accordingly. Holistic framework instead brings ethically complex situations into view so they can be worked through and, ideally, resolved.

7.5 Medical Responsibility without Disease Reification or Disciplinary Dominance

Beyond these practical and ethical issues, operationalization raises a foundational question: what is the core mandate of mental health services? If this mandate is defined solely as resolving unfavorable situations, the boundaries between mental health care, social services, and other societal sectors may appear to blur. Yet this blurring brings an underlying tension into sharper focus: the current system already channels a wide range of psychosocial difficulties into mental health services through diagnostic categories—mainly in cases where no latent disease entity can be meaningfully assumed, and where mental health care may not represent the most appropriate or sufficient context for addressing the difficulties at hand.

A related concern is whether psychiatry ceases to be a medical specialty if it no longer treats discrete "diseases" but rather complex situations. This question points to a deeper issue: how medical illness, or more precisely, how situations that warrant medical responsibility, should be defined.

Critics have long argued that psychiatric problems cannot be regarded as diseases in the same sense as many somatic illnesses, as they cannot be reduced to identifiable cellular or physiological abnormalities (e.g., Szasz, 1961). However, it is argued that this critique overlooks the fact that numerous conditions routinely addressed within medicine—such as chronic pain, functional somatic syndromes, or headaches—are medically defined despite lacking a singular biological lesion (e.g., Benning, 2016). In these cases, medical responsibility does not arise from the presence of a discrete disease entity but from the existence of a burdened whole that requires risk assessment, protection of the service user's situation, and coordinated management of physiological, psychological, and social factors.

From this perspective, there is no logical barrier to understanding as matters of medical responsibility those complex situations and forms of distress that, within existing institutional arrangements, are assigned to psychiatry or to the mental health system as a whole. In practice, society already entrusts the mental health system, through psychiatry, with responsibility for situations characterized by etiological uncertainty and intertwined psychological, physiological, and social burdens that cannot be adequately addressed by any single sector alone. The holistic framework does not expand this mandate but rather renders it more explicit. By making this reality transparent, it allows psychiatry to articulate a clearer identity as an integrative medical field.

At the same time, understanding unfavorable situations as psychiatry's object of concern should not be confused with an expansion of psychiatric authority. Situations are not owned by psychiatry; rather, they disclose the necessity of coordinated, pluralistic responses in which medical expertise constitutes only one contribution among others. Holism thus limits disciplinary dominance rather than extending it. In this sense, holistic psychiatry is best understood as a transitional framework: it enables the reorganization of existing resources, institutional responsibilities, and system-level coordination within structures that are already in place, without requiring the dismantling of psychiatry as a medical institution or its replacement by an entirely different one. By working through psychiatry rather than around it, change becomes possible within the legal mandates, funding mechanisms, and clinical infrastructures that currently shape mental health system.

Understanding situations as the primary object of concern does not mean treating them as an additional ontological "layer" alongside the physical, psychological, and social dimensions of human existence—a move that has been critically questioned in some philosophical debates (e.g., Niemelä, 2022). Rather than ontological structures in their own right, situations are understood here in terms of contextual emergence. Instead of answering the ontological question of what it means to be human, this perspective addresses the ontological question of what situations come to be defined as mental health disorders or problems in the first place. Situations thus refer to concrete, time-bound configurations in which physical, psychological, and social processes become dynamically intertwined and become relevant for organized forms of help. They are neither mere descriptive backdrops nor reified entities; they mark the level at which human distress becomes real and consequential, insofar as individual agency and available communal resources are no longer sufficient without external support and need-based coordination. From this perspective, the object of the mental health system is not a situation as such, but a burdened whole in which physiological stress, emotional regulation, interpersonal dynamics, and environmental pressures co-constitute patterns of vulnerability that cannot be meaningfully addressed by isolating any single dimension.

The "medical" relevance of such wholes does not arise from the presence of a latent disease entity but from the risk of deterioration, harm, or collapse inherent in their configuration. Framing psychiatry's mandate in situational terms therefore does not dissolve its medical identity; on the contrary, it clarifies why psychiatry has long been entrusted with responsibility for precisely those cases marked by etiological uncertainty and multidimensional strain. At the same time, this clarification places a principled limit on psychiatric authority: situations are not appropriated by psychiatry but call for coordinated responses in which psychiatry functions as an integrative contribution rather than as a dominant explanatory framework.

More precisely, certain situations fall within the remit of psychiatry and the mental health system because they constitute wholes in which functioning, safety, physiological stress, emotion regulation, interpersonal dynamics, and environmental pressures are interlinked in ways that may lead to psychological, somatic, or social collapse unless addressed coherently. Such situations cannot be resolved solely through social services, criminal justice, or education, as each of these sectors addresses only a limited dimension of the overall configuration. Psychiatry's and mental health service's distinctive societal role lies in its mandate to take responsibility for these complex situations and to help restore the whole to a level at which the individual and their network can again function—either independently or with appropriate support from other societal sectors.

Crucially, reframing psychiatry's mandate in this way also creates more favorable conditions for interdisciplinary collaboration. When situations are approached as complex wholes rather than as expressions of discipline-specific problems, no single form of expertise can claim explanatory or practical primacy. This opens space for closer integration of psychological, social, experiential, and medical forms of knowledge, and for dialogue to function as a central coordinating process rather than as an auxiliary to predefined disciplinary solutions.

The holistic framework thus offers psychiatry a clearer and more coherent identity, one that aligns more closely with its actual societal mission and everyday practice. At the same time, it preserves and clarifies those areas of psychiatry that legitimately require more sharply defined expertise—such as forensic psychiatry or urgent symptom relief—without grounding the mental health system as a whole in the assumption that problems originate primarily from internal biological disorders.

Nevertheless, it is important to acknowledge a potential risk inherent in this reframing. If the situational mandate of psychiatry is articulated too broadly or implemented without clear limits, there is a danger that mental health services may come to assume responsibility for an ever-widening range of life difficulties. In such cases, the rearticulation of psychiatry's role—despite its holistic intent—could unintentionally expand psychiatric authority, drawing everyday adversities, social conflicts, and structural problems more firmly under medical jurisdiction. Rather than reducing medicalization, this could increase the tendency for psychiatry to take charge of situations that might be more appropriately addressed through social, educational, community-based, or political responses. This risk should be explicitly recognized and actively counterbalanced by clear boundary-setting, strong intersectoral collaboration, and a continued emphasis on shared responsibility rather than disciplinary dominance.

7.6 Common Concerns about Holistic Systems

In addition to the above challenges, holistic service systems are often associated with a set of stereotypical concerns. One of the most common is the fear that actively involving networks is inherently risky, because the family or immediate social environment may, in some cases, be a central source of the person's distress. This concern is justified, particularly in the more serious but less common situations described earlier, such as those involving domestic violence, sexual abuse, or other severely harmful relational dynamics.

At the same time, it is important to recognize that precisely in such situations, what is needed is *immediate, flexible, and multilevel network intervention*. In this context, involving the "network" does not simply mean inviting family members into meetings but comprehensively mapping the situation and bringing together those actors—professionals, authorities, and protective resources—who are capable of intervening in harmful dynamics at the right time and helping to phase the process. This kind of work primarily requires competence in network-oriented practice, which a holistic system systematically develops.

In a holistic system, the involvement of networks is not a value in itself, nor is it implemented mechanically. Meetings may be organized one-to-one, in small groups, or as broader network meetings, depending on the situation. In line with the basic premise of the holistic framework, the helping process is flexibly adapted to changing circumstances, and the role of the network is always evaluated case by case, with safety, human rights–based practice, and overall appropriateness at the center. In this sense, a holistic system does not merely *permit* active network involvement; it is better equipped to *manage* the risks associated with it than systems where encounters take place more rigidly, in segregated settings, or detached from everyday life, and where many problems therefore remain more easily out of sight.

A second common concern is the fear that people will discontinue their psychotropic medication if they are no longer told they "have" a mental disorder. This worry is understandable, because abruptly stopping medication can be associated with significant withdrawal and relapse effects. It is important to note, however, that even in the current reductionist system, adherence to psychotropic treatment is frequently problematic. People may not experience themselves as having a mental disorder, and psychotropic drugs often entail adverse effects. Withdrawal symptoms may then be interpreted as a relapse of the "underlying illness," leading to re-initiation of treatment. The person is once again encouraged or pressured to adhere to medication—sometimes via psychoeducation aimed at "improving insight"—but if they disagree with the explanatory model, the situation can easily escalate into renewed conflict, which in turn may be interpreted as further evidence of mental disorder. In practice, such cycles undermine adherence in their own right, regardless of how the person initially understands their difficulties.

As discussed above, people are more likely to engage with and adhere to medication when its effects are described as openly, honestly, and intelligibly as possible. There is, for example, no clear evidence that psychotropic drugs correct underlying brain abnormalities, or that long-term use is always necessary once certain diagnostic criteria are met. Most people, however, can readily understand that medication may be sedating, calming, or cognitively slowing, and that such effects may be useful in some circumstances. Many also understand that suddenly stopping medication can lead to increased agitation, anxiety, sleep disturbance, and thus a greater risk of rehospitalization or relapse into crisis. Such open discussion minimizes conflict and fosters collaborative relationships, which in turn improves adherence regardless of the explanatory framework. Over time, this can stabilize the overall situation and make it more feasible to optimize psychotropic treatment—for example, by identifying the lowest effective dose. This further supports adherence for many, because adverse effects tend to be less pronounced.

A third typical concern is closely related to a question already discussed: whether it makes sense for psychiatry to be involved at all if problems are not defined as medical disorders—and whether such an approach might *increase* medicalization. However, given the diagnostic inflation observed in recent decades, at the moment almost any human difficulty can, under certain conditions, be described as a psychiatric disorder—and often is. For example, when the cumulative demands of single motherhood lead to exhaustion, access to income support or temporary sick leave may require a psychiatric diagnosis, even when the primary difficulties are clearly related to caregiving responsibilities, economic strain, and insufficient social support.

It is also worth recalling that the psychiatric classification system was never intended to describe "natural kind" disease entities. Thus, it does not tell us which problems are "genuinely" psychiatric and which are not. Nor can psychiatric diagnoses be verified or falsified in the same sense as many biological diseases: if, in the clinician's judgment, the symptom criteria are met, the diagnosis is technically always "correct", because it is based on that particular situational assessment. In practice, almost any psychosocial problem can be classified as psychiatric if its etiology is unclear and it is judged to cause harm to the person or their surroundings; thus, they are already referring certain kind of situations and outcomes.

Refraining from labeling a problem as a mental disorder does *not* imply that people do not need help, or that certain experiences, behaviors, or situations cannot have severe consequences. Nor does it mean psychiatry is redundant. On the contrary, as argued above, a more holistic framework may help psychiatry to reposition itself explicitly as a field specializing in complex situations—capable of responding flexibly using both medical and non-medical means. By doing so, it simultaneously creates space for multiple forms of knowledge to inform practice, enables participation from different professional and experiential perspectives, and, over time, allows for a more precise and context-sensitive delineation of roles and responsibilities across disciplines. This kind of competence would also be valuable in other areas of medicine, particularly where the overall situation remains unclear or where establishing a working alliance with the service user is challenging.

A fourth central concern is that treatment might be delayed, or not provided at all, if it does not begin with a diagnosis or medication. This worry is often linked to the holistic system's more selective use of medication and, at times, to fears that longer term psychotherapeutic or other forms of support might decrease. In a well-functioning holistic system, however, the principle of rapid response actually allows care to begin considerably *earlier* than in typical models: the process contains no waiting lists, assessment pipelines, or gatekeeping stages that delay help. Treatment is organized around a context and an alliance that is considered one of the most important determinants of therapeutic effectiveness. When longer term psychotherapy or other ongoing support is deemed necessary, it can be arranged flexibly—either within the same service system or with the support of private- or third-sector providers.

It is nonetheless likely that, within a holistic system, not all treatments will be required as often or for as long as is typically assumed in reductionist framework. When problems are understood as situational and embedded in everyday life, some will be resolved through early dialogical encounters, mobilization of networks, and support for everyday structures—without the need for highly specialized, long-term interventions.

7.7 Summary of the Challenges in Transitioning to a Holistic System

Transitioning to a holistic framework is not merely a matter of updating individual methods or organizational structures; it represents a fundamental shift in the conceptual foundation and architecture of mental health system. Although such a shift can simultaneously address many of the challenges currently facing psychiatry and mental health care, it inevitably involves substantial risks and system-level obstacles.

Contemporary service systems are deeply embedded in a reductionist framework—one that shapes professional training, research paradigms, funding structures, and the day-to-day organization of services. Moving away from this paradigm requires professionals, policymakers, and service users to revise established ways of thinking and acting, which can be experienced as threatening. The coexistence of reductionist and holistic logics can produce friction and confusion in everyday practice, leading to uncertainty among staff and service users about how the system is intended to function. For this reason, reorganizing services toward a holistic framework must be undertaken coherently and comprehensively—yet such system-level shifts are rarely attempted without compelling arguments or evidence demonstrating that the transition is worthwhile.

There is also a risk that some groups may be left behind during structural reforms. Individuals with more severe and prolonged difficulties, or those who struggle to articulate their needs, may be particularly vulnerable to disengagement or insufficient support unless their situations receive specific and sustained attention.

A further challenge concerns operationalization, measurement, and the demonstration of effectiveness. The outcomes of a holistic system are primarily reflected in people's lived experiences and in long-term improvements in subjective well-being—dimensions that are difficult to capture with the indicators used in current funding and governance frameworks. There is a significant risk that the system will continue to be evaluated using reductionist criteria, making the holistic system appear inefficient, and leading to underinvestment or premature discontinuation of promising initiatives.

Political decision-making introduces an additional tension. Policymakers tend to prioritize short-term, highly visible results and to minimize risk, whereas holistic systems generate their most meaningful benefits only over longer timescales and require experimentation as well as temporary disruption to existing service structures. These features can make holistic reforms appear politically unattractive or overly uncertain, even if at first glance they seem to address many of the failings of current systems. This often leads to two familiar objections: that the model sounds "too good to be true," or that if such an approach were genuinely effective, it would already be widely implemented.

The holistic system also raises foundational questions about the purpose of mental health system: if difficulties are conceptualized as unfavorable situations rather than internal disorders, what then becomes the core mandate of psychiatry as a medical specialty? The holistic framework nevertheless offers a clear answer: psychiatry's role—and, through it, the role of the mental health system—can be understood as the coordinated management of complex, multidimensional situations in which psychological, physical, and social stressors interact in ways that no single sector can address alone.

From this perspective, psychiatry's medical mandate lies in safeguarding the overall situation, managing risk, and enabling coherent and comprehensive forms of help in contexts of uncertainty. At the same time, this expanded situational focus entails a risk of mandate drift and intensified medicalization if the broader paradigm shift is not realized in practice. When institutional structures, funding mechanisms, and governance models remain reductionist, situational responsibility may default to psychiatric framing and intervention, even in cases where non-medical or community-based responses would be more appropriate. Recognizing this risk is therefore essential to ensure that a holistic framework limits, rather than extends, psychiatric authority.

Meeting future challenges will require an approach that combines gradual implementation with sustained commitment. Reform can begin with small-scale pilots evaluated using new, contextually appropriate indicators, while political governance and funding models are progressively redesigned to recognize both experiential and long-term benefits. Modern digital tools and updated training structures can help reduce institutional inertia, and the risk of widening inequalities can be mitigated by proactively focusing on the needs of the most vulnerable groups. When the holistic framework is adopted as a long-term strategic direction, linked to both practical experimentation and carefully orchestrated structural reforms, it can evolve into a self-reinforcing system capable of overcoming the risks inherent to any transformative change. Scientific research plays a central role in supporting this transition and in consolidating the evidence base for holistic system development.

References

Benning, T. B. (2016). No such thing as mental illness? Critical reflections on the major ideas and legacy of Thomas Szasz. *BJPsych Bulletin, 40*(6), 292–295. https://doi.org/10.1192/pb.bp.115.053249

Iyer, S. N., Boksa, P., Joober, R., Shah, J., Fuhrer, R., Andersson, N., Lal, S., D'Andrea, G., Morrison, N., Noel, V., Rabouin, D., Cowan, T., MacDonald, K., Levasseur, M. A., Poukhovski-Sheremetyev, F., Abdel-Baki, A., Augustine, L., Friese, K., Godin, I., Hay, K., ... & Malla, A. (2025). An Approach to Providing Timely Mental Health Services to Diverse Youth Populations. *JAMA Psychiatry, 82*(5), 470–480. Advance online publication. https://doi.org/10.1001/jamapsychiatry.2024.4880

Niemelä, P. (2022). Keskustelua situationaalisuuden käsitteestä ja ilmiöstä. *Janus, 30*(3), 309–311.

Read, J., Haslam, N., Sayce, L., & Davies, E. (2006). Prejudice and schizophrenia: a review of the 'mental illness is an illness like any other' approach. *Acta Psychiatrica Scandinavica, 114*(5), 303–318. https://doi.org/10.1111/j.1600-0447.2006.00824.x

Szasz, T. S. (1961). *The myth of mental illness: Foundations of a theory of personal conduct.* Harper & Row.

World Health Organization. (2021). *Guidance on community mental health services: Promoting person-centred and rights-based approaches.* World Health Organization. https://creativecommons.org/licenses/by-nc-sa/3.0/igo/

World Health Organization (2023). *Mental health, human rights and legislation: Guidance and practice.* World Health Organization. https://www.who.int/publications/i/item/9789240080737

Part III

Research and the Future of Holistic Mental Health Care

The final part examines how a holistic framework for mental health care can be studied, evaluated, and empirically justified. It addresses a recurring concern: whether holism can be supported by scientific evidence, and what kinds of research designs are appropriate when the object of study consists of complex, context-dependent situations rather than isolated variables. The part explores how concepts such as probabilistic causality, network models, and systems theory enable psychiatric phenomena to be studied without reducing them to latent disease entities.

The part further considers how unfavorable situations can serve as a meaningful unit of analysis for psychiatric research, even when their specific content is unique. By focusing on structural and dynamic features—such as burden, relational patterns, temporal change, and the emergence of dialogical space—it demonstrates how holistic research can maintain scientific rigor without fragmenting the phenomenon under investigation. This reorientation opens the possibility of evaluating mental health care not only in terms of symptom reduction but also in terms of situational transformation, agency, and long-term trajectories.

The part begins by examining the limitations of reductionist research traditions in psychiatry and the challenges they pose for studying wholes and service systems. It then outlines alternative research strategies compatible with holistic thinking, ranging from naturalistic action research to register-based studies and cluster-randomized trials. The chapter concludes by reviewing both indirect and direct evidence for holistic care, drawing on system-level implementations such as Trieste, Open Dialogue, and Soteria. Taken together, the chapters argue that although research on fully holistic systems is still developing, there already exists a convergent and methodologically diverse body of evidence supporting a holistic reorientation of mental health care.

DOI: 10.4324/9781003777939-11

Chapter 8

Recap of Reductionist Research in Psychiatry, Its Challenges, and Ways Forward

8.1 The Point of Departure for Reductionist Research

As stated at the beginning of this book, the aim of a reductionist approach and of reductionist research is to identify cause–effect relationships that allow phenomena to be understood and modeled through their constituent parts. For instance, if the causes of the symptom constellation referred to as depression or schizophrenia were known, treatment could be directed specifically at these causal factors.

For the reductionist mode of knowledge production to be possible, phenomena must be operationalized—that is, translated into measurable form as precisely as possible. In the case of mental disorders, however, operationalization has proven to be a central challenge, because psychological and social phenomena are inherently interpretive, multifactorial in origin, and dimensional in nature. As a result, they are difficult to delimit into clear, measurable, and mutually distinct clusters of symptoms (van Os et al., 2019).

The challenges of operationalizing mental disorders help explain why existing diagnostic categories have not been successfully reduced to specific biological, psychological, or social mechanisms (Bergström, 2023). For this reason, psychiatric diagnosis remains largely descriptive and refrains from making claims about causation: if a person reports a certain number of particular "symptoms"—or these can be inferred from their behavior and background information—the "symptoms" can be operationalized as a psychiatric disorder. Because causal factors are not addressed, research on psychiatric treatment has likewise focused on identifying the factors that alleviate the reported or observed "symptoms."

Yet psychiatric "symptoms" are largely subjective and context-dependent experiences, and the alleviation of such experiences can reasonably be assumed to occur via a wide range of mechanisms—even within the same individual. For this reason, for example, the active placebo effect—an experimental design in which the control group unknowingly receives a substance

DOI: 10.4324/9781003777939-12

that produces some noticeable physical sensations—often proves so substantial that clinical trials of psychiatric medications may fail to detect clear differences between the group receiving the actual drug and the control group receiving the active placebo (Moncrieff et al., 2004). In fact, in psychiatry, the term *placebo effect* is partly misleading, because experience and its interpretation are themselves the targets of treatment and measurement, regardless of the mechanisms through which change is causally produced.

In practice, applying reductionist research ideals to psychological and social phenomena encounters constraints that do not arise in the same way in most areas of somatic medicine. In somatic disease, the primary object of study is not itself an intentional, meaning-generating subject. An inflamed pancreas does not modify its biological processes in response to how it is interpreted or investigated. By contrast, the object of study in psychiatry is a reflexive subject whose experiences, meanings, and responses are constitutive of the phenomenon under investigation; the object of study in psychiatry is often qualitatively different.

8.2 Reductionist Research Designs

Despite the unique nature of the research object and the challenges associated with operationalization, the effectiveness of psychiatric treatment is often investigated using methods similar to those employed to assess the effectiveness of other medical treatments. In practice, establishing unidirectional cause–effect relationships require a method that minimizes the influence of confounding factors—that is, factors other than the treatment itself that might account for the treatment outcome. Such factors may include, for example, the service user's expectations, background characteristics, or treatment selection bias, in which service users with more severe symptoms are more likely to receive a particular form of treatment, meaning that symptom severity may explain the treatment outcome more than the treatment per se.

In medicine, the primary method used to control for such known and unknown confounders is the randomized controlled trial (RCT). In an RCT, patients are randomly assigned either to a treatment group that receives the intervention under investigation or to a comparison group that receives a placebo, another treatment, or no treatment at all. Studies are ideally conducted in a blinded manner, meaning that patients—and often the researchers as well—do not know which group each participant is in. Randomization and blinding enable the treatment effect to be distinguished more reliably from other factors.

Treatment effects are assessed using predefined, validated measures, which in psychiatry most commonly take the form of symptom questionnaires. Repeating the research design across studies and using the same measurement instruments ensures comparability, enabling the synthesis of findings into systematic reviews and meta-analyses. These are regarded as the highest level of evidence for the efficacy of a given treatment and often form the basis for incorporating treatments into national clinical guidelines or into the range of interventions eligible for insurance reimbursement or public funding. In accordance with the logic of reductionist service provision, when a person meets a set of diagnostic criteria, efforts are made to treat them using an intervention supported by such research evidence.

However, the suitability of the traditional RCT design for psychiatric treatment research is questionable from the outset, because it presupposes the fulfillment of certain preconditions. In practice, the object of treatment, the desired treatment outcome, and the treatment modality itself must all be clearly operationalizable. In psychiatry, none of these conditions are adequately met (e.g., Thomas et al., 2012; van Os et al., 2019): diagnoses are interpretive, overlapping, and change over time, and they lack sufficient discriminative validity. Treatment outcomes are typically based on symptom questionnaires assessing subjective experience, which can be influenced by numerous factors. Moreover, the operationalization of psychosocial treatments is particularly challenging.

In practice, attempts have been made to advance the operationalization of psychosocial treatments through detailed treatment guidelines or manuals. Their purpose is to distinguish a particular treatment modality from others, ensure its replicability, and reduce dependence on the individual practitioner. In reality, however, this aim is difficult to achieve: the effectiveness of psychosocial treatments always depends, in some way, on reciprocal and therefore inherently unpredictable interaction, which is itself dependent on the participants in that interaction. Paradoxically, overly rigid guidelines may undermine the effectiveness of psychosocial treatments if the clinician fails to adapt their practice sufficiently to the specific interactional context (Leiman, 2004). Yet if a clinician adapts their practice too much, operationalization no longer holds, and the research design is no longer measuring the phenomenon it purports to measure—namely, the effect of following a specified set of instructions as faithfully as possible on a particular symptom profile.

8.3 Applying Reductionist Knowledge

Although, as noted several times earlier in this book, strict adherence to predetermined instructions in psychosocial treatments is difficult—and often unnecessary from the perspective of treatment effectiveness—the reductionist ideal of knowledge production leads to a situation in which only those treatment methods that can be studied using the experimental design described above are regarded as evidence-based (Bergström, 2023).

According to this logic, once a disorder operationalized in a particular way is identified, efforts are made to treat it with methods that meet the standards of evidence.

In practice, this most often means cognitive and behavioral therapies, which—due to their theoretical foundations—are more easily manualized for RCTs than many other therapeutic approaches (Leiman, 2004). Services are then organized so that people are directed to units and professionals specializing in specific disorders, on the basis of how their condition has been assessed. The service portfolio of these units consists of evidence-based methods for the treatment of the respective disorders, which are offered in a relatively standardized manner according to predefined criteria—regardless of the individual's particular situations.

In addition to predefined psychosocial treatments, this logic of knowledge production also favors discrete interventions such as pharmacotherapy, for which randomized controlled evidence is relatively easy to produce and which, following reductionist service-production logic, are used when the criteria for a given disorder are met. In practice, this has led to highly specialized units and practitioners who aim to offer evidence-based solutions aligned with their specific area of expertise—at the extreme, to the extent that only predefined treatments and procedures considered evidence-based within this reductionist framework are permitted in principle.

The end result is a reductionist service system in which substantial resources are devoted to assessment and categorization in order to determine which treatment is considered appropriate for each situation, while the interventions used may fail to account for people's individual life circumstances, needs, or agency. The system becomes congested, queues lengthen, and by the time people finally receive help, they may be dissatisfied with it.

Although there is extensive evidence for the efficacy and effectiveness of various psychiatric treatments—particularly regarding short-term changes in symptoms—it is important to note that, even from a reductionist perspective, there is no research evidence demonstrating the effectiveness of current mental health services or of the underlying service-production logic in the way that is often assumed. This is because RCTs measure only a very narrowly defined phenomenon and typically rely on comparisons of group averages (Greenhalgh, 2014). Consequently, for many service users, a given evidence-based method may not produce the desired outcome, and for some, it may even lead to worse results. For this reason, it is impossible to know in advance whether a particular treatment will work for an individual, even if the categorization process has been carried out as thoroughly as possible and the diagnostic criteria are met.

Moreover, evidence produced through RCTs does not transfer into practice in a straightforward way because RCTs do not measure the reductionist service-production logic itself, in which resources are allocated to defining a particular disorder and treating it with the standardized, evidence-based methods available in the service catalogue. In other words, we lack adequate research evidence on whether our way of organizing mental health services according to the reductionistic logic described above actually works. This issue is examined in greater detail in Chapter 10.

8.4 The Difference in Emphasis between Reductionist and Holistic Research in Psychiatry

The central difference between holistic and reductionist frameworks concerns the way causality is conceptualized. Reductionism typically emphasizes explanations that seek to identify unidirectional cause–effect chains, whereas holism focuses on multidirectional interactions, contextuality, and feedback loops. For example, unemployment may influence mood and self-concept, which in turn can impair functioning and further increase the risk of unemployment. As noted above, such dynamic interactional chains can generate wholes and states that cannot be understood by examining individual components in isolation, even if those components are necessary preconditions for the whole.

Modeling such multidirectional interaction networks has traditionally been difficult, though no longer as impossible as it once was. Reductionist verification of cause–effect relationships has long been the pragmatic option in situations where insufficient data or inadequate analytical methods prevented the study of large and complex datasets. Consequently, research has tended to focus on unidirectional explanations rather than on capturing the complex interaction networks that characterize real life.

However, the situation has changed. Today, abundant data are available, and methods such as machine learning, artificial intelligence, and advanced network analytics enable increasingly sophisticated examination of complex and open systems. Although these methods do not automatically reveal multidirectional causal relations, they provide powerful tools for identifying probabilities, dependencies, and structural patterns underlying phenomena.

In this context, it is essential to distinguish between deterministic and probabilistic causality (Yuan et al., 2024). Deterministic causality assumes that the same cause always leads to the same effect. Probabilistic causality, by contrast, refers to situations in which a factor increases the likelihood of a given outcome without making it inevitable. While probabilistic causality is not exclusive to holistic approaches, it is within holistic frameworks that such probabilities are treated as constitutive of the phenomenon rather than as statistical noise: a particular way of organizing services increases the probability of a dialogical space emerging; a dialogical space increases the probability that shared factors of effectiveness will be optimized; and shared understanding increases the probability of effective care.

Probabilities can rise or fall at each stage, depending on the outcomes achieved. The key is to create conditions in which the probability of success is as high as possible. From this perspective, reciprocal cause–effect relations and their probabilities can, at least in principle, also be modeled using new methods, provided there is sufficient data.

In psychiatry, modeling of this kind has already been pursued through, for example, the so-called network model (Borsboom, 2017). In network models, symptoms are assumed to influence one another reciprocally and to form emergent wholes, without the need to posit an underlying "disease" to which they all reduce. Depression provides a useful example: from a reductionist perspective, insomnia, fatigue, and difficulties concentrating are signs of a latent depressive disorder. In the network model, these symptoms are viewed as mutually reinforcing interactional relations: insomnia leads to fatigue and concentration problems, which increase stress, which worsens insomnia (Wijsen et al., 2025). A state labeled "depression" can thus be understood without assuming an underlying disorder.

In Chapter 3, the basic unit of analysis in holistic psychiatry has been defined, drawing on contextual emergence and critical realism, specifically as an unfavorable situation. This refers to a whole in which biological dispositions, psychological processes, social relationships, and environmental factors combine to create a configuration that burdens everyday life and leads a person to seek help. The logic mirrors that of network models: various factors form detrimental wholes without requiring the assumption of a single "disorder," and thus the focus of both research and treatment is the whole itself.

The principles of network models can in this way be extended from relations among individual symptoms to the dynamics of entire life situations. With greater data availability, it becomes possible to model how certain experiences, personal characteristics, and environmental factors intertwine to form adverse situations. For example, genetic sensitivity may increase social anxiety in certain environments. This may lead to negative reactions from others, which in turn reinforce withdrawal and increase the risk of stressful life events, such as bullying. This increases sleep difficulties and stress, which may further elevate the probability of psychotic experiences—ultimately increasing the risk of adverse situations regardless of context.

Because the process involves probabilistic causality, none of these outcomes is inevitable. The chain can shift at any level. A single supportive relationship may enhance feelings of safety; a positive service encounter may interrupt a negative cycle; and a small change in one component may initiate a positive developmental trajectory. The goal is not to eliminate a "cause" but to increase the probability of factors that shift the process toward improvement. For this reason, within a holistic framework, it is crucial to respond swiftly to help-seeking: the probability of favorable change is higher early on, as help-seeking itself signals an unfavorable situation. Prolonged waiting may lead individuals to adapt to unfavorable situations, strengthening negative interactional loops and increasing the difficulty of interrupting them, as the risk of the most adverse outcomes grows.

Because, from a holistic perspective, each unfavorable situation is in some way unique, this raises a central question of operationalization: if each situation is different, how can it be studied or measured without fragmenting the whole into parts?

The answer lies in a shift in how situations are examined. A holistic framework does not aim to classify situations categorically based on content, as diagnoses do, but rather to examine their structure, context, and dynamics. Although the concrete content of situations—what is happening in a person's life—is always individual, their structures share many common features. These include relationships among stressors and protective factors, shifts in interpersonal relationships, affordances and constraints in daily life, surrounding social structures, and the formation of meanings and interpretations in interaction. Situations also evolve over time: they may escalate, stabilize, or transform into new configurations. These structural and processual elements can be measured and analyzed regardless of the specific content of a situation.

In this respect, studying situations can be compared to meteorology. Each storm and their consequences are unique, but weather phenomena are not reduced to their consequences—such as observable damage. Instead, the structure of the storm is examined: air pressure, wind, humidity, patterns of flow. These variables can be measured, compared, and predicted, even though no two storms are identical in content. Psychiatric situations can be studied similarly. When the focus is on the structure of the situation—such as degree of burden, level of social support, everyday functioning, or the development of a dialogical space—the situation becomes a measurable unit of analysis without losing its unique character.

In a holistic system, situations are thus operationalized as processes rather than categories. A situation can be described by its rate of change, the interactional loops that sustain it, the involvement of close others, levels of perceived safety or uncertainty, and whether a dialogical space emerges. When measurement tools target such structural and dynamic elements, they can be applied across diverse situations, because they capture recurrent patterns underlying phenomena regardless of their specific content.

In this way, the holistic framework avoids two traditional pitfalls: it neither reduces experiences to predefined content categories nor lapses into vagueness or overgeneralization. Situations are unique in content but share structures that can be systematically studied, measured, and compared. This enables the development of services and research in a way that better reflects real life—the very complex situations that lead people to seek help.

In this sense, whether a phenomenon becomes defined as a psychiatric situation does not depend solely on what the phenomenon is but on the degree to which the whole becomes overwhelming and burdensome. Everyday concerns and stress may accumulate over time into a multilayered crisis in which emotions, thoughts, relationships, routines, and biological sensitivities begin to reinforce one another. The whole resembles a storm: rain, wind, and waves may each be harmless on their own but together form a dangerous situation. Likewise, a psychiatric situation is a storm in which usual coping mechanisms and social resources are no longer sufficient, and specialized support, safety, and coordination are needed.

It is important to note that psychiatry already functions, in practice, according to this logic. Etiology in psychiatry is often by definition unknown, and help-seeking is driven precisely by increased concern, burden, and diminished functioning. In practice, most psychiatric work begins when an unfavorable situation can no longer be resolved by the individual, family, or immediate network nor by other professionals.

Operationalizing the situation for research and service systems, however, requires substantial further development. The main challenge is to operationalize situations in a way that makes their dynamism, multidimensionality, risks, resources, and potential for change visible without reducing the whole back to isolated symptoms or diagnoses. New measurement tools and research designs are needed—ones capable of capturing situations as wholes, much as weather forecasts model the dynamics of an entire storm rather than a single variable.

Holistic psychiatry therefore does not offer a ready-made model but opens a new research program described in summary box 1: how situations can be described, monitored, and supported so that the uniqueness of the whole is preserved and people can be helped in the best possible way.

Summary Box: A Research Program for Holistic Psychiatry

Basic Idea

Holistic psychiatry treats situations—dynamic, multilevel constellations of people, contexts, meanings, and interactions—as the primary unit of analysis, rather than isolated symptoms or hypothetical disease entities. While each situation is unique in content, situations share recurring structural and dynamic patterns. Research therefore focuses on modeling these structures and the probabilistic dynamics through which situations deteriorate, stabilize, or improve.

The research program proceeds in stages: defining and measuring situational structures, accumulating longitudinal data, modeling situational dynamics, and testing system-level interventions.

Stage 1—Conceptualization and Core Measures

Develop theory-based instruments that describe situations as dynamic, relational structures, rather than as categories or person-bound attributes.

Measures focus, for example, on:

- Structural configurations, load, and safety
- Protective and buffering resources
- Interactional feedback patterns and escalation loops
- Meaning-making and narrative coherence
- Dialogical capacity and shared understanding
- Volatility and potential for change

Purpose:

To make situations empirically describable and comparable without reducing them to symptoms, diagnoses, or isolated components.

Stage 2—Large-Scale Data Collection

Implement situational measures across services.

- Repeated assessments embedded in routine encounters (e.g., first contact, network meetings, follow-up)
- Inclusion of multiple perspectives where possible
- Linkage with registries, ecological momentary assessments, and contextual indicators

Purpose:

To generate sufficiently rich, longitudinal datasets capable of capturing how situations evolve over time.

Stage 3—Modeling Dynamics

Use machine learning, network modeling, and probabilistic causal inference to explore:

- How situational factors interact across time
- Which configurations increase or decrease the probability of worsening or improvement
- Which early signals precede tipping points or rapid change
- Which conditions reliably precede the emergence of a dialogical space
- How component-level features (e.g., basic dispositional or contextual factors) can be used in more reductionist models to predict the likelihood of specific situational trajectories under given context

Purpose:

To identify recurring dynamic patterns and leverage points within complex, multilevel situations, while allowing component-level predictive models where these improve situational understanding without replacing the situation as the primary unit of analysis.

Stage 4—Designing Interventions

Translate model insights into practical, situation-sensitive tools:

- Rapid-response triggers for escalating situations
- Situation profiles supporting case-by-case decision-making
- Indicators for intensifying network involvement or reducing medicalization
- Early-warning signals for escalating situations

Purpose:

To improve the precision and timing of holistic care while maintaining a non-reductionist framework.

Stage 5—System-Level Trials

Test holistic service models using natural experiments, registry-based follow-ups, and cluster-randomized trials. Evaluate effects on:

- Continuity and responsiveness of care
- Severity, duration, and recurrence of adverse situations

- Use of coercion and restrictive interventions
- Medication use and adverse effects
- Long-term functioning (work, education, social participation)
- User-defined recovery and meaning-making

Purpose:
To establish robust evidence for situational and dialogical systems in real-world practice.

Stage 6—Implementation and Continuous Learning

Use real-time feedback loops to refine services. Mental health services function as a learning system in which:

- Every encounter contributes to situational knowledge
- Teams are supported by situational analytics rather than diagnostic algorithms
- Practice evolves iteratively based on lived experience and empirical findings

Purpose:
To integrate theory, research, and care into a single adaptive system.

References

Bergström, T. (2023). From treatment of mental disorders to the treatment of difficult life situations: A hypothesis and rationale. *Medical Hypotheses, 176*, 111099. https://doi.org/10.1016/j.mehy.2023.111099

Borsboom D. (2017). A network theory of mental disorders. *World Psychiatry: Official Journal of the World Psychiatric Association (WPA)*, *16*(1), 5–13. https://doi.org/10.1002/wps.20375

Greenhalgh, T., Howick, J., Maskrey, N., & Evidence Based Medicine Renaissance Group (2014). Evidence based medicine: A movement in crisis?. *BMJ (Clinical Research ed.)*, *348*, g3725. https://doi.org/10.1136/bmj.g3725

Leiman, M. (2004). Vaikuttavuustutkimuksen pulmallisuus psykoterapiassa. *Duodecim, 120*(22), 2645–2653.

Moncrieff, J., Wessely, S., & Hardy, R. (2004). Active placebos versus antidepressants for depression. *The Cochrane Database of Systematic Reviews, 2004*(1), CD003012. https://doi.org/10.1002/14651858.CD003012.pub2

Thomas, P., Bracken, P., & Timini, S. (2012). The limits of evidence-based medicine in psychiatry. *Philosophy, Psychiatry, & Psychology, 19*(4), 295–308.

van Os, J., Guloksuz, S., Vijn, T. W., Hafkenscheid, A., & Delespaul, P. (2019). The evidence-based group-level symptom-reduction model as the organizing principle for mental health care: Time for change? *World Psychiatry, 18*(1), 88–96. https://doi.org/10.1002/wps.20609

Wijsen, L., Van Bork, R., Haig, B., & Borsboom, D. (2025). Reflective, formative, and network models: Causal interpretations of three different psychometric models. In *The SAGE handbook of theoretical psychology* (p. 212). SAGE Publications, Henderikus J. Stam & Huib Looren de Jong.

Yuan, B., Zhang, J., Lyu, A., Wu, J., Wang, Z., Yang, M., Liu, K., Mou, M., & Cui, P. (2024). Emergence and causality in complex systems: A survey of causal emergence and related quantitative studies. *Entropy, 26*(2), 108. https://doi.org/10.3390/e26020108

Chapter 9

Holistic Research on Mental Health Care and Services

This chapter examines how a holistic framework reshapes psychiatric research and modeling on mental health care and service systems. Rather than focusing on isolated interventions, diagnoses, or narrowly defined outcomes, this chapter treats services themselves as complex, open systems whose effects emerge through interaction, context, and time. The aim is to clarify how causal reasoning, hypothesis formation, and research design must adapt when the object of study is not a discrete treatment or disorder but a living service ecology embedded in everyday life.

This chapter proceeds by outlining key methodological premises of holistic research, including exploratory, bottom-up knowledge production and methodological pluralism. It then presents three complementary research designs—naturalistic action research, register- and cohort-based studies, and cluster-randomized trials—that together allow increasingly specific causal claims while preserving ecological validity. This chapter concludes by synthesizing these approaches into a coherent model of holistic service research that complements, rather than replaces, reductionist research traditions.

9.1 Premise

For analytical clarity, it is useful to distinguish between different temporal and functional levels within a holistic research framework. *Basic disposition,* as described in Chapter 3, refers to the slowly changing, developmentally shaped constellation of embodied, psychological, and relational capacities through which individuals encounter and respond to their environments. *Situations*, by contrast, function as an analytic unit capturing rapidly evolving configurations in which these capacities interact with relationships, meanings, and contextual constraints, sometimes in ways that become adverse. *Services and interventions* can then be understood as external perturbations introduced into these configurations, altering interactional patterns and shifting probabilities of change.

DOI: 10.4324/9781003777939-13

This distinction does not imply separate causal layers or independent entities. Rather, it clarifies why holistic psychiatry focuses analytically on situations: it is at the level of situational dynamics that both dispositional influences and intervention effects become empirically visible, manifesting as changes in structure, feedback loops, and developmental trajectories. At the same time, the framework permits more reductionist modeling strategies when these are methodologically appropriate. In particular, basic disposition can be used to construct probabilistic models that examine how specific dispositional features—such as heightened emotional/embodied reactivity, cognitive style, or social skills—interact with historically and culturally specific environments to increase the likelihood of certain types of situations.

For example, traits that may have been neutral or adaptive in earlier historical contexts can, under contemporary conditions characterized by constant social comparison, accelerated information flows, and high-performance demands, increase the probability of situations marked by chronic stress, withdrawal, or loss of agency. Such models do not treat basic disposition as a direct cause of such difficulties, but rather as a contextualized susceptibility that shapes which situational trajectories become more likely in a given cultural and historical moment.

Holism, in this sense, does not replace reductionist inquiry but situates it within a broader framework that specifies when and how component-level predictions are informative. It also clarifies the division of labor among different disciplines. For example, mental functions associated with basic disposition can be investigated within the general psychological sciences without requiring psychiatric terminology or medical models when artificial symptom thresholds are reached. Similarly, social and cultural phenomena can be more precisely studied and applied within their respective fields, rather than being subsumed under psychiatric categories.

This perspective contributes to a more accurate understanding of human experience, behavior, and interpretation, while also enabling more generalizable models. Psychiatry, within this framework, narrows its ontological focus to specific situational configurations, thereby facilitating the appropriate application of findings from other disciplines. In doing so, the framework helps address a persistent problem in current practice, namely, the tendency to approach a wide range of human phenomena primarily through psychiatric and medical frameworks, even when these phenomena are not qualitatively distinct from non-clinical variations of human-life phenomena. Approaching them instead through broader theories and disciplinary perspectives allows for deeper understanding and more proportionate forms of explanation and response.

Beyond this first premise concerning the appropriate ontological scope of psychiatric inquiry, adopting a holistic framework also reshapes how causal relationships and hypotheses are examined. The dominant approach based on null hypothesis testing and p-values works best when the phenomenon under investigation is relatively simple—for example, when a cause–effect relationship can be reasonably assumed—and when the data meet the relevant methodological assumptions. The null hypothesis refers to the assumption that there is no true effect or difference between conditions or groups. A p-value indicates the probability of obtaining a result at least as extreme as the observed one if the null hypothesis is true.

If, for instance, the goal is to determine whether a new medication reduces patients' pain more effectively than a placebo, the null hypothesis might be that the medication has no true effect on pain experience. If the resulting *p*-value is 0.03, this means that if the medication truly had no effect, an observed difference of that magnitude between groups would occur by chance in about 3% of studies. In other words, the difference between the treatment and control groups would be considered statistically significant at the 0.05 significance level.

Although *p*-value-based tests do not strictly require linearity or normal distribution, many commonly used statistical procedures assume independence of observations, normally distributed errors, homoscedasticity, and an appropriately specified model. When the phenomenon under investigation is hierarchical, multilevel, dynamic, or nonlinear, these assumptions are easily violated. In complex and open systems such as psychiatric situations and mental health services, variables are often strongly interdependent, and the structure of the phenomenon may therefore differ markedly from the assumptions underlying traditional tests. In such cases, conventional null hypothesis significance testing may readily lead to incomplete or misleading interpretations.

To account for the complexity emphasized in a holistic framework, more flexible methods can be employed—such as Bayesian modeling, multilevel models, nonlinear and nonparametric approaches, and simulation-based models (e.g., McElreath, 2020). These methods can represent complex dependency networks and the dynamics of phenomena more comprehensively, without the constraints of traditional hypothesis testing, because they allow the integration of prior knowledge with new observations and provide direct insight into how probable different explanations are.

When studying wholes and complex systems, it is also often useful to employ an exploratory approach. The aim is not to test a single precise hypothesis but to identify new phenomena, interactions, and possible mechanisms from which more specific and testable hypotheses can later be developed. In research on complex psychological and social phenomena, the progression should typically move from broader, hypothesis-generating studies toward more specific, hypothesis-testing ones (Scheel et al., 2021)—in much the same way that holistic care moves from general dialogue toward more specific interventions, if these are needed at all.

In psychiatry and psychology, however, the order of operations has often been reversed. This can partly be understood as a consequence of efforts to strengthen their status as "hard sciences" by adopting a research logic inherited from the natural sciences and the ideal of methodological monism. This ideal emphasizes a reductionist perspective and thus privileges traditional null hypothesis testing at the expense of other research designs.

In psychology, this approach has been linked to the so-called replication crisis: imprecisely defined concepts, poorly articulated theories, and the vague hypotheses derived from them make research findings difficult to reproduce reliably across studies (Scheel et al., 2021). The phenomenon has also been reinforced by biased research practices and selective reporting. When hypotheses are not derived from clearly structured concepts and theories, researchers—often consciously or unconsciously—may adjust analyses, variable selections, the number and type of statistical tests conducted, or reporting practices so that results become statistically significant even when they do not reflect true effects (Tackett et al., 2019).

Similar patterns can be observed in the history of psychiatric research, in which complex phenomena have often been simplified into supposed regularities that fail to capture their multidimensional nature. Combined with publication bias—where journals tend to favor statistically significant findings—this helps explain why scientific research often fails to replicate specific results.

In other words, understanding phenomena would require first articulating them more clearly and identifying the right questions—only then can robust, testable hypotheses be constructed. Thus, in service system research grounded in a holistic framework, the order of operations is reversed: first, exploratory mapping of phenomena using big data and multimethod observations; then, the development of hypotheses and theories; and only thereafter, more conventional hypothesis testing. Whereas reductionist research proceeds "top-down," holistic research proceeds more "bottom-up."

A third key principle of the holistic framework is methodological pluralism. Whereas reductionism easily leads to methodological monism—the attempt to study phenomena using one and the same method—methodological pluralism recognizes that different kinds of phenomena can and should be studied using different kinds of methods. For example, biological processes can be examined using neuroimaging, genetics, or physiological measures; psychological experiences can be studied through qualitative methods, interviews, or experience sampling; social relationships and networks can be analyzed using social network analysis or ethnography; the functioning of service systems can be studied through participant observation or service design; and lived experience can be approached through phenomenological methods that aim to describe phenomena as they appear to the person experiencing them.

A fourth principle is that mental health services and their effects can themselves be examined as wholes. The questions of interest concern what actually happens in services, how they appear to different participants, and what real-world effects they produce from multiple perspectives. In practice, this requires diverse research designs and the integration of different methodologies. The following section outlines three example research designs that progress from more holistic to more reductionist—each providing a basis for assessing causal relationships in increasingly specific ways.

9.2 Naturalistic Action Research

In naturalistic action research, research and practical activity are tightly interwoven (Holter & Schwartz-Barcott, 1993). Its point of departure is that complex social and psychological phenomena cannot be understood apart from the contexts in which they occur. Research is conducted in real-world environments, often in close collaboration with various stakeholders such as mental health professionals and service users. The aim is not only to generate knowledge but also to develop and transform practices during the research process. This approach is well suited to the study of holistic systems, as it accounts for both people's experiences and the structural features of their environments—elements that cannot be separated without narrowing the overall picture.

Naturalistic action research can integrate a wide range of research methods. Registry data can be used to examine service use and temporal trends. Interviews and surveys can capture information about service functioning and care experiences from both staff and service users. Observation—including participant observation in consultations or team meetings—may reveal everyday practices that do not surface through self-report. Ethnographic methods help illuminate service culture and interactional dynamics. Experience sampling methods can follow service users' daily emotions and activities in real time, revealing how services shape their everyday lives. In addition, action-oriented workshops, service design methodologies, and prototype testing can be used to develop solutions jointly with service users and professionals. These insights can be directly applied to service development, and the same methods can be used to assess whether improvements become visible, for example, in registry data or in users' experiences.

Naturalistic action research enables the immediate development of services through research-based means. Instead of implementing predefined interventions, attention is directed to the challenges and strengths that actually emerge in services and to how these can be addressed within the specific service system in question. At the same time, this approach generates knowledge about what works and what does not—information that can guide further development.

However, naturalistic action research has limitations in terms of strict scientific hypothesis testing, particularly when compared with randomized controlled trials (RCTs). First, the research design and research questions may evolve during the study, which makes this approach less suitable for answering narrowly defined questions or producing generalizable knowledge. Second, naturalistic studies do not offer tight control over confounding factors, making it difficult to demonstrate that an observed outcome is caused by a particular mechanism under investigation. Findings may show that a presumed effect does not manifest in practice, but the reasons for this may be manifold—such as contextual variation or differences in how services are implemented. In practice, naturalistic research is therefore more oriented toward generating and refining hypotheses than rigorously testing them.

9.3 Register- and Cohort-Based Follow-Up Studies

Register- and cohort-based follow-up studies rely on large, often longitudinal datasets that can be used to describe, for example, long-term service use and patterns of functioning. Unlike tightly controlled experimental designs, they allow phenomena to be examined in naturalistic settings, since the data largely originate from real-life situations. Such studies can therefore reveal differences across large populations, long-term outcomes, and the diversity of trajectories that do not emerge in controlled or short-term experimental settings. Register and cohort studies thus offer insight into how treatments and services function in practice and under what conditions people tend to do well.

In register-based research, for example, lifetime information on service use and other life domains can be collected from all individuals entering treatment at a particular time. These data allow a wide range of research questions to be addressed through different study designs. Descriptive studies can provide information about who uses services and whether there are temporal trends in service use. Such information is useful, for instance, in supporting naturalistic action research. In addition, background factors that predict particular patterns of service use can be examined, enabling these factors to be considered in service planning and resource allocation.

Register studies can also be used for comparative research that evaluates the functioning of services in real-world conditions. Long follow-up periods allow the examination of broader and more ecologically valid outcome measures than symptom questionnaires alone, such as work ability, mortality, family circumstances, and long-term need for services. If a service has previously been developed through naturalistic action research, register data can be used to collect information on everyone who has used that service, enabling a before–after comparison. This makes it possible to assess whether the development work has influenced outcomes, while accounting analytically for differences in service user characteristics across time periods.

In addition to before–after designs, registry research can compare the effectiveness of different services. For example, data can be collected from mental health services that have been developed in a particular way and compared with regions where services have been developed differently. This can be implemented quasi-experimentally by selecting certain regions as development sites and comparing them with regions where no corresponding development has taken place. As in before–after designs, various confounding factors can be statistically controlled, and long follow-up periods can be used. This approach yields a more realistic understanding of overall service functioning, people's real-world outcomes, and the factors that shape them.

A limitation of register studies, however, is that they also make it difficult to draw strong causal conclusions (Thygesen & Ersbøll, 2014). For example, if a before–after comparison or a quasi-experimental design shows that mortality has decreased and service user experiences have improved in a unit undergoing development, it still cannot be stated with certainty that these changes result from the development work. The findings may be explained by confounding factors that are not captured in the data—such as local characteristics, simultaneous changes in the service system, broader societal trends, or demographic shifts.

Nonetheless, various advanced statistical methods can now be used in register research to strengthen causal inference. Machine learning models can support the analysis of large datasets and the identification of risk profiles. Counterfactual models (Voter et al., 2025) can be constructed to estimate what an individual's situation would have been had they received a particular treatment—or had they not received it. One concrete method is inverse probability of treatment weighting, in which individuals with a low probability of receiving the treatment are given more weight, and those with a high probability are given less weight (Chesnaye et al., 2021). This reduces selection bias and approximates a randomized situation in which the background characteristics of study groups are as similar as possible. While such methods do not eliminate all limitations of register studies, they provide a stronger basis for causal reasoning in naturalistic conditions.

9.4 Cluster-Randomized Trials

A cluster-randomized trial (cluster RCT) is a research design in which randomization occurs at the level of groups or units rather than individuals

(Hemming & Taljaard, 2023). Such units may include, for example, healthcare units, outpatient clinics, or entire areas. Compared with a traditional RCT, a cluster RCT brings research closer to real-world practice and thereby increases ecological validity, as it provides a more accurate picture of how service development actually influences outcomes. By randomizing units into intervention and control groups, systematic differences can be minimized, allowing causal conclusions to be drawn even in practical settings.

For example, if naturalistic action research has led to the development of certain practices that qualitative studies and registry-based analyses suggest are associated with improved outcomes, one may hypothesize that similar development work could enhance the functioning of mental health services. This hypothesis can be tested using a cluster experimental design in which mental health units within a given region are randomized into two groups: some operate as intervention clinics where the development work is implemented, and others as control clinics where usual care continues. If the intervention clinics achieve better outcomes, it is more plausible to conclude that the observed changes result from the implemented measures, since randomization balances both known and unknown confounding factors.

Cluster RCTs could also be used to study the holistic service system described in this book. One could hypothesize that reorganizing services according to a holistic framework would improve the efficiency and effectiveness of mental health care in a resource-sustainable way. By randomizing units so that some are reorganized according to the holistic framework and others continue with the current model of service provision, it becomes possible to test whether the holistic framework has an impact on service outcomes.

A key advantage of the cluster RCT is that it enables the evaluation of interventions that cannot be implemented at the individual level, such as organizational programs or entire service models. Its challenge, however, is that differences between units—such as staff expertise, resources, or regional characteristics—may influence results and introduce confounding factors that may not be fully controllable. From a strict scientific perspective, a cluster RCT can nevertheless falsify or support hypotheses in much the same way as an individual-level RCT, even if the level of control is not as clean.

The greatest challenge of cluster RCTs is their complexity and cost. Implementation typically requires substantial preliminary information and a large number of clusters or participants to ensure adequate statistical power (Hemming & Taljaard, 2023). Moreover, they require strong organizational commitment and often affect a large number of staff and service users. For this reason, cluster RCTs are not well suited for flexible hypothesis generation in the way naturalistic action research or register studies are. Instead, they are appropriate for more rigorous hypothesis testing when prior research has already produced promising findings and experimental evidence of effects is needed.

9.5 Summary of Holistic Service Research

Within a holistic framework, the aim of research is to understand psychological and social phenomena as comprehensively as possible and in the context of real life. For this reason, holistic research proceeds in a different order than reductionist research. Rather than beginning with narrowly defined hypotheses and tightly controlled experimental designs to test them, the holistic framework first seeks to capture the complexity of phenomena and to build an understanding of how they function in practice. Scientific research is therefore needed not only to test hypotheses but also to generate the concepts, theories, hypotheses, and research questions themselves.

By combining different sources of information and using an exploratory approach, a more detailed overall picture can be constructed and new hypotheses that can later be tested confirmatory in more controlled settings. In this sense, holistic research does not exclude reductionist designs; rather, it shifts their role in the research process: validity is prioritized over repeatability, and complex real-world wholes form the starting point for inquiry.

In mental health services research, this means that naturalistic action research and other exploratory designs constitute the first phase of investigation. Conducted in real service environments and directly connected to everyday practice, they make it possible to understand how people, situations, and services function in daily life and what kinds of needs for change emerge within services. Such designs produce context-sensitive knowledge that helps identify phenomena and structural patterns that cannot be accessed through controlled designs. At the same time, they provide the foundation for theories and hypotheses that arise from lived reality rather than from preconceived assumptions.

Service research can then be complemented by register and cohort studies, which examine large populations and long-term trajectories. Register data make it possible to assess how services function in real-world conditions and what consequences they have for, for example, work ability, functioning, mortality, or overall service use. These studies provide a broad overview of phenomena—something essential for holistic thinking and hypothesis formation.

When naturalistic and register-based studies together generate promising signals regarding the benefits of a given approach, more rigorous hypothesis testing can be undertaken, for example, through cluster-randomized trials. A cluster RCT—in which units are randomized to development conditions or to continue as usual—brings the experimental design closer to real-world service contexts and allows entire work communities or service models to be evaluated experimentally. Because cluster randomization balances both observed and unobserved confounders, it provides stronger causal evidence about whether service development works in practice, though it also requires substantial resources and organizational commitment. In a holistic framework, this phase comes only after a sufficiently broad understanding of the phenomenon has been achieved: first, wide exploration and theory building, then—if needed—testing.

The central challenge of the holistic framework concerns how complex, context-dependent phenomena can be operationalized in measurable form without losing their essential features. Phenomena that unfold across multiple levels and in relation to their environment do not easily translate into narrow or commensurable variables without being reduced in some way. Yet recent advances in multilevel modeling, network analysis, machine learning, and continuous monitoring of everyday experiences have provided new ways to measure and describe such phenomena without compressing them into a single dimension. With these methods, it becomes possible to examine dynamic interactional chains, person–environment fit, and the formation of overall situations.

It is important to note, however, that the challenge of operationalization also applies to reductionist psychiatry. In practice, psychiatric diagnoses already describe heterogeneous symptom networks, accumulated life events, and interactions between psychological, social, and biological factors—in other words, complex situations that ultimately lead people to seek help or enter services. In this sense, the reductionist system too must work with situations, even if it attempts to reduce them as categories and characteristics of the individual.

In the holistic framework, the challenge of operationalization is taken as a starting point of research, and the situation itself becomes the basic unit of analysis. Situations are not reduced in advance to predefined categories; instead, they are examined as structures and processes: as constellations of stressors and protective factors, as interactional loops, as unfolding meanings, and as potentials for change. This requires theory-based measures that can capture the essential structures of situations without flattening their unique content. When such measures are used widely and repeatedly, they produce sufficiently rich data to allow the later modeling of dynamic developmental trajectories—through methods such as machine learning, network models, and probabilistic causality.

For precisely this reason, the holistic framework may offer a stronger starting point for addressing the operationalization challenge. When a phenomenon is recognized from the outset as multidimensional and context-dependent, its components can later be refined and structured using more reductionist approaches. This opens new long-term opportunities: if sufficiently large datasets reveal recurring structural patterns or mechanisms underlying certain types of situations, more targeted treatments or interventions may be developed. The holistic framework does not therefore exclude reductionism; rather, it creates better conditions for it. Research can move from the whole situation toward its component mechanisms when the data justify such movement. In this way, the holistic framework forms a research program in which the whole is not lost, yet the parts can gradually be clarified—without detaching them from the context in which they originally emerge.

References

Chesnaye, N. C., Stel, V. S., Tripepi, G., Dekker, F. W., Fu, E. L., Zoccali, C., & Jager, K. J. (2021). An introduction to inverse probability of treatment weighting in observational research. *Clinical Kidney Journal*, *15*(1), 14–20. https://doi.org/10.1093/ckj/sfab158

Hemming, K., & Taljaard, M. (2023). Key considerations for designing, conducting and analysing a cluster randomized trial. *International Journal of Epidemiology*, *52*(5), 1648–1658. https://doi.org/10.1093/ije/dyad064

Holter, I. M., & Schwartz-Barcott, D. (1993). Action research: What is it? How has it been used and how can it be used in nursing? *Journal of Advanced Nursing*, *18*(2), 298–304. https://doi.org/10.1046/j.1365-2648.1993.18020298.x

McElreath, R. (2020). *Statistical rethinking: A Bayesian course with examples in r and stan*. Chapman & Hall/CRC.

Scheel, A. M., Tiokhin, L., Isager, P. M., & Lakens, D. (2021). Why hypothesis testers should spend less time testing hypotheses. *Perspectives on Psychological Science*, *16*(4), 744–755. https://doi.org/10.1177/1745691620966795

Tackett, J. L., Brandes, C. M., King, K. M., & Markon, K. E. (2019). Psychology's replication crisis and clinical psychological science. *Annual Review of Clinical Psychology*, *15*, 579–604. https://doi.org/10.1146/annurev-clinpsy-050718-095710

Thygesen, L. C., & Ersbøll, A. K. (2014). When the entire population is the sample: Strengths and limitations in register-based epidemiology. *European Journal of Epidemiology*, *29*(8), 551–558. https://doi.org/10.1007/s10654-013-9873-0

Voter, S. C., Dahabreh, I. J., Boyer, C. B., Rahbar, H., Kontos, D., & Steingrimsson, J. A. (2025). Counterfactual prediction from machine learning models: transportability and joint analysis for model development and evaluation using multi-source data. *Diagnostic and Prognostic Research*, *9*(1), 22. https://doi.org/10.1186/s41512-025-00201-y

Chapter 10

Evidence for Holistic Care

This chapter brings together the empirical implications of the holistic framework developed throughout this book. While earlier chapters have examined the conceptual foundations of holism and the methodological issues involved in studying complex service systems, the focus here is on the available research evidence. This chapter addresses a central and often-repeated concern: whether holistic mental health care can be supported by empirical data and, if so, what kind of evidence is methodologically appropriate given the nature of the phenomena under investigation.

Although a holistic framework and the mental health service system built upon it can be theoretically justified, empirical research on its effectiveness remains limited. This is primarily due to the dominant modes of knowledge production and organization, which rely heavily on reductionist logic. As a result, even research designs intended to be holistic are often forced to conform reductionistic thinking.

For example, phenomenological research could illuminate what life and treatment actually feel like for a person who, at a given moment, meets the diagnostic criteria for schizophrenia. In practice, however, research is typically tied to the reductionist definition of schizophrenia—as if the person's lived experience were the outcome of some internal, stable disorder. Similarly, register studies show that most individuals diagnosed with schizophrenia become occupationally disabled or repeatedly hospitalized—a pattern frequently interpreted as evidence of the assumed chronicity of the disorder. A more holistic interpretation would note that diagnostic criteria themselves, in effect, define a form of chronicity that registers then confirms, and that the ways people are met and supported may also shape the overall situation that becomes visible in registers.

A second reason for the scarcity of holistic research is the lack of a suitable unit of analysis. When mental health problems are assumed to be internal characteristics of the individual, research inevitably focuses on isolated symptoms, mechanisms, or biomarkers—elements compatible with the reductionist paradigm but unable to capture the dynamic, multilevel

DOI: 10.4324/9781003777939-14

configurations through which a phenomenon comes to be defined as a mental disorder in the first place. Holistic research, by contrast, targets wholes and situations, which do not fit easily into traditional research designs and measurement tools. This structural incompatibility has made holistic approaches appear difficult to operationalize and measure, even when they may describe clinical reality more accurately.

A third and perhaps most significant reason is that psychiatry has not previously had a systematically formulated theory or conceptual framework that would render holistic thinking scientifically coherent and empirically researchable. Without a shared ontology, a clear articulation of the object of study, and an account of how it should be measured, the concept of holism has remained vague. The practices to which it refers have appeared as separate therapeutic traditions or service models without a common theoretical core that would allow for a cumulative research and development program. As a consequence, holistic phenomena have been evaluated using reductionist measures that cannot capture their actual logic of impact—perpetuating the impression that holism cannot be studied, when in fact the problem has been the absence of an adequate theoretical foundation.

Despite these limitations, there is already a considerable amount of indirect evidence supporting a holistic framework.

10.1 Indirect Evidence

10.1.1 First Source of Indirect Evidence

Reductionist research has produced a great deal of indirect evidence that is difficult to explain from a reductionist standpoint but fully coherent from a holistic framework. One of the most central observations relates to the phenomenon described at the beginning of this book: despite decades of work and substantial resources, no psychiatric disorder has been shown to have a clear, singular biological etiology that would allow mental disorders to be reduced to well-defined neurobiological mechanisms (Cuthbert & Insel, 2013).

Although individual biomarkers have been proposed to explain certain disorders, the findings do not replicate across studies, and psychiatric diagnoses still cannot be verified through neuroimaging or laboratory tests. In practice, biological findings serve mainly exclusionary purposes: only after neurological, endocrinological, or somatic causes have been ruled out is the situation considered psychiatric.

In this respect, psychiatry is facing a replication crisis similar to that of psychology. The crisis is understandable: both fields study complex, interactive processes using methods originally designed for far simpler phenomena.

This situation is difficult to account for within a reductionist framework. Diagnostic categories have been carefully operationalized, diagnostic systems are updated regularly according to established standards, and a large, well-funded etiological research program would suggest that at least some subtypes of psychiatric disorders should be verifiable through biological markers. From a holistic standpoint, however, the situation is unsurprising: what is operationalized as a mental disorder encompasses an extremely broad range of phenomena tied to subjective experiences, life situations, and social contexts. It is unrealistic to expect universal, consistently recurring mechanisms that can be systematically traced back to the individual.

This improbability is reinforced by the plasticity of the brain and body and by the experiential nature of psychological and social phenomena. Moreover, in psychiatric situations, favorability or unfavorability is always determined in relation to context—not solely by internal characteristics. From a holistic perspective, human experience does not reduce to bodily components alone, even if bodily structures are necessary conditions for it. Thus, identifying a precise, generalizable, individual-level etiology for a single experience is neither meaningful nor useful when the primary focus is on the situation as a whole and its dynamic formation.

10.1.2 Second Source of Indirect Evidence

A second body of indirect evidence concerns research on psychiatric treatments, which repeatedly shows that therapeutic effectiveness does not derive from specific methods and differs little from active placebo effects. For example, psychotherapy research has long shown that there are no substantial differences in effectiveness between different therapeutic schools (Wampold, 2015). Rather, outcomes are explained primarily by common factors independent of modality—such as the quality of the therapeutic relationship, expectations, and the personal characteristics of both therapist and service user. In fact, from a contextual perspective, these phenomena are not unique to mental health care or psychotherapy but reflect more generally human healing and helping traditions that emerge from relational processes (Wampold & Imel, 2015). This finding is problematic for a reductionist framework, which assumes that effectiveness should be method-specific and directed precisely at the disorder in question.

A similar issue of nonspecificity applies to psychiatric medications. Their symptom-relieving effects do not appear to stem from correcting mechanisms that are specifically tied to particular disorders or medication effects (e.g., Aftab & Stein, 2022; Moncrieff, 2018). Still, reductionist thinking has long assumed that mental disorders arise from disruptions in certain neurotransmitter systems that medication "restores." Yet this neurotransmitter hypothesis has not been substantiated (Pierre, 2019); it was originally derived more from examining how medications act than from genuine etiological evidence.

It is undeniable that psychiatric medications have effects that cut across diagnostic categories. Many different drugs can alleviate similar symptoms even when their mechanisms of action are entirely distinct. From a reductionist standpoint, such nonspecificity is difficult to reconcile with the idea that a drug's mechanism reveals the causal basis of a disorder.

From a holistic perspective, these findings are expected: while psychiatric medications influence specific neurotransmitter systems, such mechanisms do not reveal the origins of symptoms nor fully explain changes in psychological experience. Alcohol, for instance, can reduce shyness, yet shyness is not understood to result from a deficiency in the gamma-aminobutyric acid neurotransmitter system, even if alcohol affects that system.

Whether a chemical is classified as a "medication" or a "psychoactive substance" is largely conventional and culturally dependent, conditioned by how the chemical is used. From this viewpoint, the symptom-relieving effects of psychotropics can be understood similarly to the way psychoactive substances alter experience or painkillers reduce pain: they change experience without eliminating or correcting the underlying cause.

For example, anti-inflammatory drugs and some other painkillers inhibit the formation of prostaglandins, weakening pain signaling and reducing the sensation of pain, although the underlying cause of the inflammation or pain (such as infection, injury, or autoimmune disease) may still remain. Analogously, psychiatric medications affect key neurotransmitters such as serotonin or dopamine, relieving anxiety, low mood, or agitation even though the underlying sources of distress persist. This is not unexpected, given that these neurotransmitter systems play a central role in shaping human experience and affect regulation, while the origins of distress are typically embedded in complex relational, social, and existential contexts that cannot be reduced to neurochemical processes alone.

10.1.3 Third Source of Indirect Evidence

A third source of indirect evidence is the observation that the effectiveness of mental health care and the functioning of service systems have not markedly improved, even though treatment methods have diversified, evidence-based interventions are more widely available than ever, and the number of mental health professionals relative to the population is at its highest in history (Timimi, 2014; WHO, 2021). According to reductionist logic, this should be reflected in greater treatment effectiveness, decreasing service needs over time, and improved population mental health.

In practice, the opposite has occurred. The expansion of evidence-based treatments and the growing number of professionals appear in many countries to have increased service use, and in long-term follow-ups, neither prolonged treatment episodes nor the risk of mental health–related disability has decreased as methods have become more available (Bergström et al., 2025a; WHO, 2021). Internationally, outcomes for severe mental health problems appear to have remained largely unchanged and, in some respects, may even have worsened (Jääskeläinen et al., 2013; WHO, 2021), and premature mortality relative to the general population has increased (Lee et al., 2018).

From a holistic framework, these findings are likewise expected: the reductionist logic of service production easily overlooks people's actual and changing needs, and reducing diverse psychological and social problems to individual disorders increases service demand. When services are built around predefined disorder-specific treatments, people may feel they are not genuinely met, leading to frustration and repeated help-seeking. This, in turn, increases resource needs—especially for assessment—because at every encounter the individual is again fitted into predefined categories that often do not align with their real-life situation. As demand grows, more resources are allocated to services, which paradoxically further increases demand.

When general indicators are considered, the strongest argument usually presented in support of the reductionist framework and service logic is the linear decline in suicide mortality over recent decades in many Western countries. This trend is often attributed particularly to the increased use of newer antidepressants (Isacsson et al., 2010). However, there is evidence that the decline in suicide mortality began before newer antidepressants entered the market (Isacsson et al., 2010; Safer & Zito, 2007) and more likely reflects broader cultural, economic, and societal changes—such as rising living standards, strengthened social welfare systems, and greater general health awareness—rather than the linear effects of psychiatric treatment.

Suicide is inherently a multifactorial phenomenon influenced by individual, communal, and societal factors alike (Bergström et al., 2026). Its decline cannot therefore be taken as straightforward evidence of the success of a reductionist psychiatric service logic, but rather as an example of how complex human phenomena are embedded in context and require a similarly holistic framework in research. In some countries, and particularly within certain sociodemographic groups, suicide rates have also remained the same and begun to rise (GBD 2021; Suicide Collaborators, 2025).

10.2 Direct Evidence

Direct research evidence on holistic mental healthcare systems is still limited, for the reasons outlined above. Internationally, the best known examples that can be regarded as holistic in the sense defined above, that are included in WHO (2021) guidelines, and for which comparative research data are available, are the community-based system in Trieste Italy, the Open Dialogue approach from Finnish Western Lapland and Soteria model originated in the United States.

10.2.1 The Trieste Community Care Model

The community care model in Trieste offers a concrete example of how a holistic framework can be implemented in practice at the level of an entire service system. Beginning in the 1970s, the city moved away from institutional psychiatry toward a "whole system, whole community" model in which mental health care is closely linked to everyday life and the local social environment (Mezzina, 2014). This transformation was not merely a clinical or systemic reform but a profound ethical, political, and anti-institutional shift that redefined mental health care as a matter of community citizenship, subjectivity, human rights, and social inclusion rather than the pathologization of distress and its control (Saraceno & Sashidharan, 2020).

In Trieste, services were organized through community-based mental health centers that were open around the clock, without waiting lists and without diagnostic requirements (WHO, 2021). In line with the original principles articulated by Franco Basaglia, the Trieste system sought to dismantle the power asymmetries embedded in traditional psychiatry and to replace institutional containment with negotiated, person-centered forms of care that are delivered seamlessly within the community and embedded in the context of everyday life (Saraceno & Sashidharan, 2020).

Each center in Trieste functions as a low-threshold outpatient unit and is responsible for coordinating all mental health services in its catchment area. The centers also have a small number of beds (typically six to eight), which can be used on a voluntary basis and without referral. There is one six-bed psychiatric acute ward in the general hospital, but in practice, most crises can be managed in the community centers or in the person's own living environment.

The Trieste model has demonstrated that a comprehensive, community-integrated approach can improve both psychological and social outcomes (WHO, 2021). Early follow-up studies showed better functioning and overall outcomes among people diagnosed with schizophrenia compared with traditional treatment systems (Kemali et al., 1989). Later longitudinal analyses have also documented low rates of compulsory treatment and significant improvements in social participation, housing stability, and engagement in work (WHO, 2021). In the Trieste system, crises are treated primarily in the community, in open units and in people's own environments, which has generally reduced the need for hospital care to a fraction of previous levels (Mezzina, 2014).

Cost and follow-up data indicate that the strength of the Trieste model lies precisely in its integrated system, in which treatment, social support, housing, and work are brought together within a single service structure (WHO, 2021). This system-level transformation has yielded not only better outcomes but also cost savings, as long hospital stays and recurrent crises have been reduced (WHO, 2021). Trieste now serves as a WHO collaborating center and an international example of how a holistic, community-based mental health system can be implemented consistently and comprehensively.

10.2.2 *The Open Dialogue*

A second example of a holistic service model is the Open Dialogue approach (Bergström et al., 2025a; Seikkula, 2025), discussed in detail earlier in this book. This model emerged through long-term naturalistic and action research in Finnish Western Lapland, initiated in the 1980s to address poor outcomes in the treatment of situations diagnosed as psychosis. Rather than applying predefined therapeutic methods, the focus shifted to studying everyday treatment practices (Seikkula & Olson, 2003; Seikkula et al., 2011). Influenced by the need-adapted approach (Alanen, 2009), social constructionist and dialogical theories, particularly Bakhtin's notion of polyphony, the dialogue itself became the central therapeutic action associating with favorable outcomes (Seikkula & Olson, 2003). Key elements to support dialogism included an immediate response to crises, the early involvement of the person's social network, flexibility in time and place, shared professional responsibility, psychological continuity, and a tolerance of uncertainty. Over time, these practices crystallized into Open Dialogue as a whole-service approach in which recovery is supported by sustained, inclusive dialogue embedded in the organization of care.

In Western Lapland, the entire psychiatric and mental healthcare system was reorganized around a 24/7 crisis line and a low-threshold walk-in outpatient clinic. Instead of prior assessments and referrals, the person seeking help and their network are invited directly to a meeting where the aim is to build a shared understanding of the situation through dialogical encounters. Care is then adapted to the situation on the basis of this understanding, and the same staff members are responsible for continuity throughout the process by organizing further network meetings whenever needed.

The effectiveness of Open Dialogue has been evaluated using regional historical comparisons and later register-based cohort studies. In five-year follow-ups of first-episode psychosis, about 80% of service users were symptom-free and 73% were working or studying at the end of follow-up; days in hospital and use of neuroleptic medication were substantially lower than in the rest of Finland (Seikkula et al., 2003; 2006; 2011). A later 19-year follow-up with national register comparisons of psychosis cohorts confirmed these findings: among Open Dialogue service users, the risks of disability and long-term care were clearly lower than elsewhere, even after controlling statistically for confounding factors (Bergström et al., 2018). Independent national register studies (e.g., Karolaakso et al., 2021; Karvonen et al., 2008; Kiviniemi, 2014) have likewise found that in Western Lapland, people treated for psychosis have the fewest hospital days, the lowest use of psychiatric medication, lower rates of disability, and the lowest overall treatment costs in the country.

In adolescent psychiatry, register studies have shown that young people treated within Open Dialogue had, over ten years of follow-up, lower risks of out-of-home interventions (Bergström et al., 2023), disability, long-term service use, and cumulative total costs than other young Finnish users of adolescent psychiatric services (Bergström et al., 2022).

Similar findings have been reported internationally from regions where services have been reorganized according to the Open Dialogue model. In Denmark, youth psychiatric services organized along Open Dialogue principles were associated with reduced disability and less use of acute psychiatric services (Buus et al., 2019). In the United States, an acute psychiatric unit reorganized in line with Open Dialogue showed substantially lower rates of hospitalization and lower costs than typical care (Bouchery et al., 2018). Comparable quantitative results have been reported from other settings as well (Granö et al., 2016; Pocobello et al., 2024), and service users' experiences have been positive (Gidugu et al., 2021; Hendy & Pearson, 2020; Sunthararajah et al., 2022; Wusinich et al., 2020).

Currently, Open Dialogue is being studied in a multisite cluster randomized trial (the ODDESSI trial) within the National Health Service in the United Kingdom, in which mental health crisis services have been randomized to either Open Dialogue clinics or treatment-as-usual clinics (Pilling et al., 2025). Preliminary results from the United Kingdom have been favorable, indicating both improved outcomes (Kinane et al., 2022) and the feasibility of the trial (Pilling et al., 2025).

Despite promising results, there are also indication on significant challenges in the implementation and transferability of Open Dialogue (Bergström et al., 2026; Buus et al., 2021; Heumann et al., 2023; Lennon et al., 2023; Pocobello et al., 2023; Waters et al., 2021), which stem at least partially from tensions between its holistic ontology and the reductionistic structures of healthcare service organizations (Bergström et al., 2025a; 2026), including prevailing models of implementation, service reform and development, and leadership practices.

10.2.3 Soteria

The Soteria model was developed in the United States in the 1970s as a response to hospital-centered psychiatric care (Mosher, 1999). Its aim was to offer people experiencing acute psychosis a homelike, calm, and humane environment in which support was based primarily on interpersonal interaction and ordinary daily life (Bola & Mosher, 2003). Staff were mostly nonmedically trained, present around the clock, and their role was to "be with" the person rather than to administer technical treatments. The use of neuroleptic medication and coercive measures was minimized, and central importance was placed on understanding the meanings people themselves gave to their experiences (Mosher, 1999).

In the original randomized trials, functional recovery and social outcomes in the Soteria group were at least as good as, and in many respects better than, those in standard hospital care at one- to two-year follow-up (Calton et al., 2008; Mosher, 1999). In Soteria, neuroleptics were used with only about one-third of residents, whereas in the comparison groups, nearly all received neuroleptic medication—yet many outcomes were better in Soteria, and the model was more cost-effective than standard hospitalization (Mosher, 1999).

Later studies and international adaptations of Soteria have reinforced these findings. In the Soteria Bern model in Switzerland, the need for hospital care was low, coercive measures were rare, and at two-year follow-up, rates of work and study participation were higher than in conventional treatment (Ciompi & Hoffman, 2004). The results demonstrated that acute psychosis can be treated safely and effectively without extensive pharmacotherapy and institutional structures, and that a relational, homelike environment can itself function as a therapeutic factor.

From a holistic perspective, the core contribution of the Soteria model is the finding that when environment, interaction, and meaningful presence are placed at the center of care, recovery from situations diagnosable as psychosis can proceed as well as—or better than—in conventional, medication- and hospital-based treatment. This challenges the reductionist assumption that the essence of acute psychosis treatment lies primarily in biological intervention and highlights the powerful role of social context and human support in shaping the course of recovery. Historically, similar observations have been made in relation to so-called milieu therapy, where a central idea has been that the most important elements of effective psychiatric care are compassion and understanding (Hoffman, 1982).

10.2.4 Other Direct Evidence

Although direct evidence on entire mental healthcare systems operating within a holistic framework is still limited, there is robust evidence for several specific approaches that are compatible with a holistic perspective. These include personalized pharmacological treatment (Bousman et al., 2023; Maj et al., 2020, 2021); integrative and common factors–based psychotherapies (Ardito & Rabellino, 2011; Flückiger et al., 2018; Goldman et al., 2018; Norcross & Goldfried, 2019; Wampold, 2015; Zarbo et al., 2016); family therapies (Carr, 2009; Sexton & Lebow, 2016) and group therapies (Burlingame et al., 2020; Janis et al., 2021); peer support (Smit et al., 2023); and integrative low-threshold service models such as assertive community treatment, which emphasize early intervention, outreach support in everyday environments, and flexible use of different treatment methods (Kane et al., 2016; Marshall & Creed, 2000; Stanley et al., 2025; Ziguras & Stuart, 2000). In reductionistic service systems, however, these positive effects do not necessarily persist over the longer term (Secher et al., 2015).

In addition, there is substantial evidence that many so-called complementary approaches—such as physical exercise, lifestyle changes (Teasdale et al., 2025), and attending to spiritual or existential dimensions in treatment (de Diego-Cordero et al., 2022; Gonçalves et al., 2015)—have beneficial effects. Self-directed care and personal budget models, in which individuals can choose from a menu of available services, have also shown both clinical and cost-effectiveness (Cook et al., 2023; Webber et al., 2014).

10.3 Summary of the Research Evidence

Research evidence on fully holistic systems is still limited, but three internationally significant examples—Trieste, Open Dialogue, and Soteria—have accumulated independent, comparable, and convergent findings. What unites these models is not a single method but a comprehensive system logic: low-threshold access, rapid response, work anchored in everyday life, community orientation, involvement of networks, and continuity of care with the same staff.

From the standpoint of research evidence, it is crucial that these models have emerged independently of one another in different cultural contexts yet have consistently yielded very similar results: reduced need for hospitalization, improved long-term functioning and social participation, fewer coercive measures, and lower costs. WHO's (2021) international reviews support the same conclusion: when services are organized close to people's everyday lives and practice is grounded in collaboration, predictability, attention to wholes, and egalitarian dialogue, the functioning of mental health systems improves.

Taken together, the available evidence converges in support of a holistic system of care. The Trieste model illustrates how shifting services away from institutions and into communities can support active participation and address difficulties within people's lived situations. Open Dialogue demonstrates how rapid, network-oriented responses can effectively address acute crises in which agency is threatened and existing resources are insufficient, and how entire care processes can be coordinated in holistic manner. Soteria, in turn, provides an example of longer term, non-coercive support for people with enduring or recurrent difficulties.

There is also substantial direct—and in many cases randomized—evidence for individual treatments and approaches that align with a holistic system. A holistic system is built by integrating such approaches, and this can reasonably be expected to enhance overall service effectiveness. Although research on entire service structures is still scarce, the existing evidence consistently suggests that this kind of approach has beneficial effects.

It is also important to note that there is no comparable body of research directly evaluating the reductionist logic of service production as a system-level approach in contrast to alternative service logics. Randomized controlled trials typically assess the efficacy of specific methods for specific symptoms under controlled conditions, but they rarely examine how the broader logic of implementing these methods functions within real-world service systems, or how such systems perform relative to alternative organizational models. In this sense, the evidence base for reductionist service organization is more limited than is often assumed. By contrast, there is a growing and cumulative body of research on holistic and system-oriented service models. The approaches described above, for example, have been studied using diverse longitudinal and naturalistic data across different regions and time periods, providing a substantial empirical foundation at the level of service systems. Importantly, these studies often rely on outcome measures that are, in many respects, more valid and societally relevant than short-term changes in symptom questionnaires, such as long-term functioning, service use, social participation, continuity of care, and outcomes defined by service users themselves.

There is still a need for a more systematic research program on holistic service systems in order to produce comparable and measurable evidence. At the same time, the research history of psychiatry can be viewed as a form of indirect support for a holistic ontology: the field has repeatedly encountered dead ends when relying on reductionist explanatory models, while many of these "unexplained" phenomena become more coherent and intelligible within a holistic framework. From this perspective, the central problem is less a lack of research than the absence of a shared conceptual framework.

References

Aftab, A., & Stein, D. J. (2022). Psychopharmacology and explanatory pluralism. *JAMA Psychiatry*, *79*(6), 522–523. https://doi.org/10.1001/jamapsychiatry.2022.0470

Alanen, Y. O. (2009). Towards a more humanistic psychiatry: Development of need-adapted treatment of schizophrenia group psychoses. *Psychosis, 1*(2), 156–166. https://doi.org/10.1080/17522430902795667

Ardito, R. B., & Rabellino, D. (2011). Therapeutic alliance and outcome of psychotherapy: Historical excursus, measurements, and prospects for research. *Frontiers in Psychology*, *2*, 270. https://doi.org/10.3389/fpsyg.2011.00270

Bergström, T., Gaily-Luoma, S., Kurtti, M., Miettunen, J., Partonen, T., Suvisaari, J., Taskila, J. J., & Alaräisänen, A. (2026). Characteristics of people who died by suicide in a hospital district providing open dialogue-based psychiatric services: a nationwide cluster analysis. *Nordic journal of psychiatry*, *80*(1), 2–9. https://doi.org/10.1080/08039488.2025.2548235

Bergström, T., Kurtti, M., Duthie, A., Valtanen, K., & Seikkula, J. (2025b). Open dialogue. In O. Smoliak, E. Tseliou, T. Strong, S. Bava, & P. Muntigl (Eds.), *The Routledge international handbook of postmodern therapies* (pp. 174–185). Routledge. https://doi.org/10.4324/9781003376231-14

Bergström, T., Kurtti, M., Miettunen, J., Yliruka, L., & Valtanen, K. (2023). Out-of-home interventions for adolescents who were treated according to the Open Dialogue model for mental health care. *Child Abuse & Neglect, 145,* 106408. https://doi.org/10.1016/j.chiabu.2023.106408

Bergström, T., Miettunen, J., Partanen, K., Yrjänheikki, V., Rantamaa, K., Hietasaari, T., Öfverberg, E., Gauffin, T., & Petäjäniemi, J. (2026). After the open dialogue: A within-area comparison of treatment, experiences, and outcomes in western lapland 20 years after service fragmentation. *Community Mental Health Journal*, Early online. https://doi.org/10.1007/s10597-026-01591-z

Bergström, T., Seikkula, J., Alakare, B., Kurtti, M., Köngäs-Saviaro, P., Löhönen, E., ... & Valtanen, K. (2022). The 10-year treatment outcome of Open Dialogue-based psychiatric services for adolescents: A nationwide longitudinal register-based study. *Early Intervention in Psychiatry, 16*(12), 1368–1375. https://doi.org/10.1111/eip.13286

Bergström, T., Seikkula, J., Alakare, B., Mäki, P., Köngäs-Saviaro, P., Taskila, J. J., Tolvanen, A., & Aaltonen, J. (2018). The family-oriented Open Dialogue approach in the treatment of first-episode psychosis: Nineteen-year outcomes. *Psychiatry Research, 270,* 168–175. https://doi.org/10.1016/j.psychres.2018.09.039

Bergström, T., Valtanen, K., Miettunen, J., Gauffin, T., & Kurtti, M. (2025a). Temporal patterns in adolescent psychiatric treatment and outcomes: a nationwide register-based cohort follow-up. *European Child & Adolescent Psychiatry, 34*(3), 1171–1181. https://doi.org/10.1007/s00787-024-02554-z

Bola, J. R., & Mosher, L. (2003). Treatment of acute psychosis without neuroleptics: Two-year outcomes from the Soteria project. *Journal of Nervous and Mental Disease, 191*(4), 219–229.

Bouchery, E. E., Barna, M., Babalola, E., Friend, D., Brown, J. D., Blyler, C., & Ireys, H. T. (2018). The effectiveness of a peer-staffed crisis respite program as an alternative to hospitalization. *Psychiatric Services, 69*(10), 1069–1074. https://doi.org/10.1176/appi.ps.201700451

Bousman, C. A., Maruf, A. A., Marques, D. F., Brown, L. C., & Müller, D. J. (2023). The emergence, implementation, and future growth of pharmacogenomics in psychiatry: a narrative review. *Psychological Medicine, 53*(16), 7983–7993. https://doi.org/10.1017/S0033291723002817

Burlingame, G. M., Svien, H., Hoppe, L., Hunt, I., & Rosendahl, J. (2020). Group therapy for schizophrenia: A meta-analysis. *Psychotherapy (Chicago, Ill.), 57*(2), 219–236. https://doi.org/10.1037/pst0000293

Buus, N., Kragh Jacobsen, E., Bojesen, A. B., Bikic, A., Müller-Nielsen, K., Aagaard, J. & Erlangsen, A. (2019). The association between Open Dialogue to young Danes in acute psychiatric crisis and their use of health care and social services: A retrospective register-based cohort study. *International Journal of Nursing Studies, 91*, 119–127. https://doi.org/10.1016/j.ijnurstu.2018.12.015

Buus, N., Ong, B., Einboden, R., Lennon, E., Mikes-Liu, K., Mayers, S., & McCloughen, A. (2021). Implementing open dialogue approaches: A scoping review. *Family Process, 60*(4), 1117–1133. https://doi.org/10.1111/famp.12695

Calton, T., Ferriter, M., Huband, N., & Spandler, H. (2008). A systematic review of the Soteria paradigm for the treatment of people diagnosed with schizophrenia. *Schizophrenia Bulletin, 34*(1), 181–192. https://doi.org/10.1093/schbul/sbm047

Carr, A. (2009). *The effectiveness of family therapy and systemic interventions for child-focused problems. Journal of Family Therapy, 31*(1), 3–45.

Ciompi, L., & Hoffmann, H. (2004). Soteria Berne: An innovative milieu therapeutic approach to acute schizophrenia based on the concept of affect-logic. *World Psychiatry, 3*(3), 140–146.

Cook, J. A., Jonikas, J. A., Burke-Miller, J. K., Hamilton, M., Falconer, C., Blessing, M., Aranda, F., Johns, G., & Cauffield, C. (2023). Randomized controlled trial of self-directed care for medically uninsured adults with serious mental illness. *Psychiatric Services (Washington, D.C.), 74*(10), 1027–1036. https://doi.org/10.1176/appi.ps.20220508

Cuthbert, B. N., & Insel, T. R. (2013). Toward the future of psychiatric diagnosis: The seven pillars of RDoC. *BMC Medicine, 11,* Article 126. https://doi.org/10.1186/1741-7015-11-126

de Diego-Cordero, R., Suárez-Reina, P., Badanta, B., Lucchetti, G., & Vega-Escaño, J. (2022). The efficacy of religious and spiritual interventions in nursing care to promote mental, physical and spiritual health: A systematic review and meta-analysis. *Applied Nursing Research: ANR, 67*, 151618. https://doi.org/10.1016/j.apnr.2022.151618

Flückiger, C., Del Re, A. C., Wampold, B. E., & Horvath, A. O. (2018). The alliance in adult psychotherapy: A meta-analytic synthesis. *Psychotherapy, 55*(4), 316–340. https://doi.org/10.1037/pst0000172

GBD 2021 Suicide Collaborators (2025). Global, regional, and national burden of suicide, 1990–2021: A systematic analysis for the Global Burden of Disease Study 2021. *The Lancet. Public Health, 10*(3), e189–e202. https://doi.org/10.1016/S2468-2667(25)00006-4

Gidugu, V., Rogers, E. S., Gordon, C., Elwy, A. R. & Drainoni, M. L. (2021). Client, family, and clinician experiences of Open Dialogue-based services. *Psychological Services*, *18*(2), 154–163. https://doi.org/10.1037/ser0000404

Goldman, R. E., Hilsenroth, M. J., Gold, J. R., Owen, J. J., & Levy, S. R. (2018). *Psychotherapy integration and alliance: An examination across treatment outcomes. Journal of Psychotherapy Integration, 28*(1), 14–30.

Gonçalves, J. P., Lucchetti, G., Menezes, P. R., & Vallada, H. (2015). Religious and spiritual interventions in mental health care: a systematic review and meta-analysis of randomized controlled clinical trials. *Psychological Medicine*, *45*(14), 2937–2949. https://doi.org/10.1017/S0033291715001166

Granö, N., Karjalainen, M., Ranta, K., Lindgren, M., Roine, M. & Therman, S. (2016). Community-oriented family-based intervention superior to standard treatment in improving depression, hopelessness and functioning among adolescents with any psychosis-risk symptoms. *Psychiatry Research*, *237*, 9–16. https://doi.org/10.1016/j.psychres.2016.01.037

Hendy, C., & Pearson, M. (2020). Peer supported open dialogue in a UK NHS trust – a qualitative exploration of cliens' and network members' experiences. *The Journal of Mental Health Training, Education and Practice*, *15*(2), 95–103. https://doi.org/10.1108/JMHTEP-10-2019-0052

Heumann, K., Kuhlmann, M., Böning, M., Tülsner, H., Pocobello, R., Ignatyev, Y., Aderhold, V., & von Peter, S. (2023). Implementation of open dialogue in Germany: Efforts, challenges, and obstacles. *Frontiers in Psychology*, *13*, Article 1072719. https://doi.org /10.3389/fpsyg.2022.1072719

Hoffman, L. (1982). An historical overview of milieu therapy. In L. Hoffman (Ed.), *The evaluation and care of severely disturbed children and their families* (pp. 1–8). Springer. https://doi.org/10.1007/978-94-011-6299-9_1

Isacsson, G., Rich, C. L., Jureidini, J., & Raven, M. (2010). The increased use of antidepressants has contributed to the worldwide reduction in suicide rates. *The British Journal of Psychiatry: The Journal of Mental Science*, *196*(6), 429–433. https://doi.org/10.1192/bjp.bp.109.076166

Jääskeläinen, E., Juola, P., Hirvonen, N., McGrath, J. J., Saha, S., Isohanni, M., & Miettunen, J. (2013). A systematic review and meta-analysis of recovery in schizophrenia. *Schizophrenia Bulletin, 39*(6), 1296–1306.

Janis, R. A., Burlingame, G. M., Svien, H., Jensen, J., & Lundgreen, R. (2021). Group therapy for mood disorders: A meta-analysis. *Psychotherapy Research : Journal of the Society for Psychotherapy Research*, *31*(3), 342–358. https://doi.org/10.1080/10503307.2020.1817603

Kane, J. M., Robinson, D. G., Schooler, N. R., Mueser, K. T., Penn, D. L., Rosenheck, R. A., Addington, J., Brunette, M. F., Correll, C. U., Estroff, S. E., Marcy, P., Robinson, J., Meyer-Kalos, P. S., Gottlieb, J. D., Glynn, S. M., Lynde, D. W., Pipes, R., Kurian, B. T., Miller, A. L., Azrin, S. T., … & Heinssen, R. K. (2016). Comprehensive versus usual community care for first-episode psychosis: 2-year outcomes from the NIMH RAISE early treatment program. *The American Journal of Psychiatry*, *173*(4), 362–372. https://doi.org/10.1176/appi.ajp.2015.15050632

Karolaakso, T., Autio, R., Näppilä, T., Leppänen, H., Rissanen, P., Tuomisto, M. T., Karvonen, S., & Pirkola, S. (2021). Contextual and mental health service factors in mental disorder-based disability pensioning in Finland - a regional comparison. *BMC HealthSservices Research*, *21*(1), 1081. https://doi.org/10.1186/s12913-021-07099-4

Karvonen, M., Peltola, M., Isohanni, M., Pirkola, S., Suvisaari, J., Lehtinen, K., Hella, P., & Häkkinen, U. (2008). PERFECT-Skitsofrenia. Stakesin työpapereita 8/2008. https://urn.fi/URN:NBN:fi–fe201204193950

Kemali, D., Maj, M., Carpiniello, B., Giurazza, R. D., Impagnatiello, M., & Lojacono, D., et al. (1989). Patterns of care in Italian psychiatric services and psycho-social outcome of schizophrenic patients: A three-year prospective study. *Psychiatry and Psychobiology, 4*(1), 23–31.

Kinane, C., Osborne, J., Ishaq, Y., Colman, M., & MacInnes, D. (2022). Peer supported Open Dialogue in the National Health Service: Implementing and evaluating a new approach to Mental Health Care. *BMC Psychiatry*, *22*(1), 138. https://doi.org/10.1186/s12888-022-03731-7

Kiviniemi, M. (2014). Mortality, disability, psychiatric treatment and medication in first-onset schizophrenia in Finland: The register linkage study. *Acta Universitatis Ouluensis D Medica, 1267.* https://urn.fi/URN:ISBN:9789526206325

Lee, E. E., Liu, J., Tu, X., Palmer, B. W., Eyler, L. T., & Jeste, D. V. (2018). A widening longevity gap between people with schizophrenia and general population: A literature review and call for action. *Schizophrenia Research, 196,* 9–13.

Lennon, E., Hopkins, L., Einboden, R., McCloughen, A., Dawson, L., & Buus, N. (2023). Organizational change in complex systems: Organizational and leadership factors in the introduction of open dialogue to mental health care services. *Community Mental Health Journal*, *59*(1), 95–104. https://doi.org/10.1007/s10597-022-00984-0

Maj, M., Stein, D. J., Parker, G., Zimmerman, M., Fava, G. A., De Hert, M., Demyttenaere, K., McIntyre, R. S., Widiger, T., & Wittchen, H. U. (2020). The clinical characterization of the adult patient with depression aimed at personalization of management. *World Psychiatry: Official Journal of the World Psychiatric Association (WPA)*, *19*(3), 269–293. https://doi.org/10.1002/wps.20771

Maj, M., van Os, J., De Hert, M., Gaebel, W., Galderisi, S., Green, M. F., Guloksuz, S., Harvey, P. D., Jones, P. B., Malaspina, D., McGorry, P., Miettunen, J., Murray, R. M., Nuechterlein, K. H., Peralta, V., Thornicroft, G., van Winkel, R., & Ventura, J. (2021). The clinical characterization of the patient with primary psychosis aimed at personalization of management. *World Psychiatry: Official Journal of the World Psychiatric Association (WPA)*, *20*(1), 4–33. https://doi.org/10.1002/wps.20809

Marshall, M., & Creed, F. (2000). Assertive community treatment – is it the future of community care in the UK? *International Review of Psychiatry, 12*(3), 137–148.

Mezzina, R. (2014). Community mental health care in Trieste and beyond: An "Open Door-No Restraint" system of care for recovery and citizenship. *Journal of Nervous and Mental Disease, 202,* 440–445. https://doi.org/10.1097/nmd.0000000000000142

Moncrieff, J. (2018). Research on a "drug-centred" approach to psychiatric drug treatment: Assessing the impact of mental and behavioural alterations produced by psychiatric drugs. *Epidemiology and Psychiatric Sciences, 27*(2), 133–140. https://doi.org/10.1017/S2045796017000555

Mosher, L. R. (1999). Soteria and other alternatives to acute psychiatric hospitalization: A personal and professional review. *The Journal of Nervous and Mental Disease, 187*(3), 142–149. https://doi.org/10.1097/00005053-199903000-00003

Norcross, J. C., & Goldfried, M. R. (2019). *Handbook of psychotherapy integration* (3rd ed.). Oxford University Press. https://doi.org/10.1093/med-psych/9780190690465.001.0001

Pierre, J. M. (2019). Debunking the two chemical imbalance myths, again. *Psychiatric Times, 36*(11). https://www.psychiatrictimes.com/view/debunking-two-chemical-imbalance-myths-again

Pilling, S., James, K., Clarke, K., Craig, T., Hassan, S., Ishaq, Y., Kinane, C., Osborne, J., Parker, G., Razzaque, R., & Landau, S. (2025). *Open Dialogue compared to usual care for adults experiencing a mental health crisis: A feasibility study for the ODDESSI trial* [Preprint]. medRxiv. https://doi.org/10.1101/2025.10.28.25332665

Pocobello, R., Camilli, F., Alvarez-Monjaras, M., Bergström, T., von Peter, S., Hopfenbeck, M., ... & el Sehity, T. J. (2023). Open Dialogue services around the world: A scoping survey exploring organizational characteristics in the implementation of the Open Dialogue approach in mental health services. *Frontiers in Psychology, 14,* Article 1241936. https://doi.org/10.3389/fpsyg.2023.1241936

Pocobello, R., Camilli, F., Ridente, P., Caloro, G., Balice, M. G., Tibaldi, G., Macario, M., d'Alema, M., Gulino, E., & El Sehity, T. (2024). Evaluating Open Dialogue in Italian mental health services: Evidence from a multisite prospective cohort study. *Frontiers in Psychology, 15,* 1428689. https://doi.org/10.3389/fpsyg.2024.1428689

Safer, D. J., & Zito, J. M. (2007). Do antidepressants reduce suicide rates? *Public Health, 121*(4), 274–277. https://doi.org/10.1016/j.puhe.2006.09.024

Saraceno, B., & Sashidharan, S. P. (2020). Basaglia's international influence. In T. Burns & J. Foot (Eds.), *Basaglia's international legacy: From asylum to community* (pp. 79-94). Oxford University Press.

Secher, R. G., Hjorthøj, C. R., Austin, S. F., Thorup, A., Jeppesen, P., Mors, O., & Nordentoft, M. (2015). Ten-year follow-up of the OPUS specialized early intervention trial for patients with a first episode of psychosis. *Schizophrenia Bulletin, 41*(3), 617–626. https://doi.org/10.1093/schbul/sbu155

Seikkula, J. (2025). *Why dialogue does cure: Explaining what makes dialogue unprecedentedly effective in difficult crises.* Springer Nature Switzerland AG. https://doi.org/10.1007/978-3-031-91294-8

Seikkula, J., Aaltonen, J., Alakare, B., Haarakangas, K., Keränen, J., & Lehtinen, K. (2006). Five-year experience of first-episode nonaffective psychosis in Open Dialogue approach: Treatment principles, follow-up outcomes, and two case studies. *Psychotherapy Research, 16*(2), 214–218. https://doi.org/10.1080/10503300500268490

Seikkula, J., Alakare, B., & Aaltonen, J. (2011). The comprehensive Open Dialogue approach in Western Lapland: II. Long-term stability of acute psychosis outcomes in advanced community care. *Psychosis, 3*(3), 192–204. https://doi.org/10.1080/17522439.2011.595819

Seikkula, J., Alakare, B., Aaltonen, J., Holma, J. M., Rasikangas, A., & Lehtinen, V. (2003). Open Dialogue approach: Treatment principles and preliminary results of a two-year follow-up on first episode schizophrenia. *Ethical Human Psychology and Psychiatry, 5*(3), 163–182.

Seikkula, J., & Olson, M. E. (2003). The Open Dialogue approach to acute psychosis: Its poetics and micropolitics. *Family Process, 42*(3), 403–418. https://doi.org/10.1111/j.1545-5300.2003.00403.x

Sexton, T. L., & Lebow, J. (Eds.). (2016). *Handbook of family therapy: The science and practice of working with families and couples*. Routledge.

Smit, D., Miguel, C., Vrijsen, J. N., Groeneweg, B., Spijker, J., & Cuijpers, P. (2023). The effectiveness of peer support for individuals with mental illness: Systematic review and meta-analysis. *Psychological Medicine, 53*(11), 5332–5341.

Stanley, S., Velayudhan, A., Hellewell, A., Bhatt, M., & Isaac, M. (2025). Longitudinal record linked analysis of an assertive community treatment programme in a suburban mental health hospital: Emergency department presentations, hospital admissions and bed days. *Social Psychiatry and Psychiatric Epidemiology, 60*(9), 2099–2106.

Sunthararajah, S., Clarke, K., Razzaque, R., Chmielowska, M., Brandrett, B. & Pilling, S. (2022). Exploring patients' experience of peer-supported open dialogue and standard care following a mental health crisis: Qualitative 3-month follow-up study. *Bjpsych Open, 8*(4), e139. https://doi.org/10.1192/bjo.2022.542

Teasdale, S. B., Machaczek, K. K., Marx, W., Eaton, M., Chapman, J., Milton, A., Oyeyemi, A. L., Pelupessy, D. C., Schuch, F. B., Gatera, G., Ahmed, H. U., Diatri, H., Jidda, I. M., Gutiérrez-Peláez, M., Elshazly, M., Fugu, M. A., Grinko, N., Indu, P. S., Oo, S. S., Balasubramanian, S., ... Rosenbaum, S. (2025). Implementing lifestyle interventions in mental health care: third report of the Lancet Psychiatry Physical Health Commission. *The Lancet. Psychiatry, 12*(9), 700–722. https://doi.org/10.1016/S2215-0366(25)00170-1

Timimi, S. (2014). No more psychiatric labels: Why formal psychiatric diagnostic systems should be abolished. *International Journal of Clinical and Health Psychology, 14*(3), 208–215. https://doi.org/10.1016/j.ijchp.2014.03.004

Wampold B. E. (2015). How important are the common factors in psychotherapy? An update. *World Psychiatry: Official Journal of the World Psychiatric Association (WPA), 14*(3), 270–277. https://doi.org/10.1002/wps.20238

Wampold, B. E., & Imel, Z. E. (2015). *The great psychotherapy debate: The evidence for what makes psychotherapy work* (2nd ed.). Routledge.

Waters, E., Ong, B., Mikes-Liu, K., McCloughen, A., Rosen, A., Mayers, S., Sidis, A., Dawson, L., & Buus, N. (2021). Open dialogue, need-adapted mental health care, and implementation fidelity: A discussion paper. *International Journal of Mental Health Nursing, 30*(3), 811–816. https://doi.org/10.1111/inm.12866

Webber, M., Treacy, S., Carr, S., Clark, M., & Parker, G. (2014). The effectiveness of personal budgets for people with mental health problems: A systematic review. *Journal of Mental Health (Abingdon, England), 23*(3), 146–155. https://doi.org/10.3109/09638237.2014.910642

World Health Organization. (2021). *Guidance on community mental health services: Promoting person-centred and rights-based approaches*. World Health Organization. https://creativecommons.org/licenses/by-nc-sa/3.0/igo/

Wusinich, C., Lindy, D. C., Russell, D., Pessin, N. & Friesen, P. (2020). Experiences of Parachute NYC: An integration of open dialogue and intentional peer support. *Community Mental Health Journal*, *56*(6), 1033–1043. https://doi.org/10.1007/s10597-020-00556-0

Zarbo, C., Tasca, G. A., Cattafi, F., & Compare, A. (2016). Integrative Psychotherapy Works. *Frontiers in Psychology*, 6, 2021. https://doi.org/10.3389/fpsyg.2015.02021

Ziguras, S. J., & Stuart, G. W. (2000). A meta-analysis of the effectiveness of mental health case management over 20 years. *Psychiatric Services (Washington, D.C.)*, *51*(11), 1410–1421. https://doi.org/10.1176/appi.ps.51.11.1410

Chapter 11

Conclusion and Future Directions

Mental health services are undergoing a period of transition. For decades, the reductionist system provided a clear and manageable framework, yet its limits have become increasingly apparent: services are overwhelmed, diagnostic categories expand without clear benefit, and many people feel they are not genuinely helped. At the same time, theoretical developments in psychopathology have generated a range of promising models—from network theories (Borsboom, 2017) and 4E/5E mental health (Rose, 2025) to complexity science (Olthof et al., 2023) and common factors in psychotherapy (Wampold, 2015)—but these approaches tend to evolve in isolation, lacking a shared language or clear clinical applicability. What psychiatry—and, through it, the wider mental health service system—has been missing is an ontological foundation capable of bringing together embodiment, lived experience, and the social world into a coherent whole.

The holistic, contextual framework aims to address that gap. It does not overturn existing theories; instead, it situates them within a shared structure in which they can complement one another. Within this framework, contextual emergentism and critical realism form the conceptual foundation, allowing network models, dimensionality, 4E/5E cognition, phenomenology, common factors, systemic perspectives, and experiential knowledge to be integrated into a unified architecture. This architecture clarifies why psychiatric phenomena resist simple reduction—and why treatment outcomes across modalities appear to be driven largely by generic mechanisms related to the quality of human interaction.

In practical terms, the holistic framework shifts the focus of mental health care from individuals to situations. A disorder is not a latent entity or a property of the person, but a dynamic configuration that develops over time and through interaction, in which biological sensitivities, personal meanings, relational patterns, and social contexts together form a burdensome constellation—an unfavorable situation that pushes someone, or their network, to seek help.

DOI: 10.4324/9781003777939-15

When the target of treatment becomes an unfavorable situation rather than an internal disorder, the foundational event of care becomes the dialogical space. A dialogical space is not an add-on technique, but a way of organizing encounters so that the unfavorable situation can acquire new, shared meanings. It is a space in which no voice is privileged, curiosity replaces certainty, and the goal is not to provide the correct interpretation but to co-create an understanding of what is happening in a person's life and what might genuinely change. This allows the helping process to develop from the bottom up: first a shared understanding of the situation is formed, common factors are optimized, and then actions are taken where change is immediately possible. More reductionist interventions—medication, individual therapy, hospitalization—remain part of the toolkit, but they become situationally embedded, applied case-by-case, and reserved for moments when they are really needed.

When this logic is extended to the level of the service system, a different, lighter, and more functional structure emerges: people enter services based on expressed concern rather than diagnosis; the first step is not assessment but a meeting; and a single team holds responsibility for the entire process. Hospitals and specialist services function as internal supports rather than parallel, competing systems. Care can be brought into people's everyday environments—homes, schools, workplaces, communities—because it is there that unfavorable situations form and change. Psychiatry's central task becomes helping the person and their network identify the specific points of change that can ease the situation or reduce the likelihood of deterioration of situations.

A holistic framework does not exclude reductionism. There are many situations in which more precise problem definition and targeted, modality-specific interventions are appropriate and effective. Yet such situations are most readily identified when the initial engagement is holistic and dialogical, allowing the problem and its solutions to be reduced more precisely only when necessary. The reason is pragmatic: it is far easier to move from a holistic understanding toward reductionist targeting than to attempt to open a complex situation from within a narrow reductionistic frame. For this reason, the holistic framework should serve as the primary starting point for mental health services—not as an exception or a special practice, as it often is today.

11.1 From Theory to Practice: Implementing the Holistic Framework

While any individual practitioner can already begin shifting their work toward a more holistic orientation, a broader implementation requires reorganization at the system level: continuity and responsibility must remain within one team, teams must be able to respond rapidly, and assessment must be dialogical rather than a mechanical inventory of symptoms. In many settings, such a reorganization does not require additional resources but a different distribution of work and priorities—shifting capacity from specialized units and gatekeeping to immediate engagement with people seeking help.

The measurement tools presented in the appendices of this book are designed as practical supports for initiating the development of holistic practice and research. All of these tools are derived directly from the theory of holistic psychiatry presented in this book and are explicitly illustrative in nature. They have not yet undergone empirical instrument development or validation, and they should therefore not be treated as standardized measures, fidelity scales, or outcome indicators. Their function is to serve as starting points by illustrating what holistic instruments might look like and how they might operate, while making key concerns visible and discussable—such as continuity and responsibility at the system level, dialogical conditions in meetings, and the multidimensional lived "shape" of a situation as experienced by different participants.

Appendix A presents a phased roadmap for developing a holistic mental health system over time. It offers an implementation-oriented sequence—from preparation and piloting to scaling and long-term integration. The roadmap is a planning aid rather than a prescriptive model; it provides one way to think about structural reform while leaving room for local adaptation.

Appendix B introduces the Holistic System Readiness Assessment (HSRA), a structural scoring framework for estimating how well a service system is architecturally prepared to implement holistic, dialogically oriented care. HSRA focuses on system design features—such as overall responsibility, degree of internal specialization, and worker scope of influence—rather than individual competence or treatment techniques. The proposed scoring bands and interpretive "zones" are proportional examples intended to stimulate evaluation and comparison; they require empirical validation and may later need different weighting, thresholds, or item structure.

Appendix C provides the Dialogical Meeting Checklist, a practice-oriented reflection and fidelity aid for network meetings. It summarizes core process elements that tend to support polyphony, shared understanding, continuity, and a not-knowing stance across the phases of a meeting. The checklist is not meant to evaluate clinicians as individuals, nor to function as a standardized observational measure. It is a situational guide for teams to reflect on whether dialogical conditions are being actively created and maintained, and it too is theory-derived and in need of validation.

Appendix D presents the Situational Map, a brief non-diagnostic questionnaire that describes a situation as a whole using experience-near dimensions such as burden, manageability, predictability, relational connectedness, shared sense-making, hope, and safety. It is intended to produce a multidimensional profile rather than a single total score, and it can be completed either from one's own perspective or by describing another person's likely experience. The tool is designed to make perspectives comparable without reducing complex situations to symptom checklists or diagnostic categories, and its psychometric properties, interpretive use, and sensitivity to change require empirical study. If this kind of instrument proves feasible and relevant for people seeking help, it could be used as an outcome measure prioritized over symptom checklists, thereby immediately shifting what services and professional work aim to achieve.

In line with critical realism, the claims implied by this toolkit remain open to empirical testing and, in principle, to refutation. Future work should therefore evaluate their reliability, usability, sensitivity to change, and relationship to observable practices and outcomes, and refine them accordingly.

Note also that validated adherence (Lotmore et al., 2023) and fidelity measures (Alvarez-Monjaras et al., 2023) for dialogical practice already exist and can serve as a concrete starting point for the evaluation and further development of holistic, dialogically oriented services. In addition, the World Health Organization (WHO) (2019, 2021, 2023) provides free training materials, online courses, and guidance for both practitioners and policymakers to support person-centered and rights-based mental health service systems aligned with a holistic framework.

Finally, it is important to remember that the major advances in the history of psychiatry have emerged precisely when the field has moved toward holism: when people have been treated more comprehensively and equitably, when their experiences have been taken seriously, when their rights have been strengthened, and when care has been brought closer to everyday life. Conversely, psychiatry's darkest moments have arisen when complex problems have been forced into single, narrow explanations and treatment has lost contact with lived reality. In this sense, the holistic framework is not a radical departure but a way of articulating what psychiatry, at its best, has long attempted to do.

Despite this, maintaining holistic practices and systems has proven challenging. Services and clinical work frequently revert to approaches that emphasize reductionism: these may offer clinicians and policymakers a sense of control, but at the same time, they narrow the interpretation of situations and heighten uncertainty. In my view, the greatest challenge has been the absence of a shared theoretical foundation.

Because the holistic practices have been developed in isolation from one another, the evidence for their effectiveness has remained fragmented and difficult to integrate.

I personally grappled with these questions for years while working as a clinical and supervising psychologist at Keropudas Hospital, known internationally for the Open Dialogue approach discussed in this book. Although the Open Dialogue always felt both humane and remarkably effective in practice, its original constructionist explanation did not seem sufficient to account for the complex phenomena I encountered within the services. The approach also shared much with other traditions, but these traditions rarely spoke to each other, as they rested on different philosophical assumptions. As a result, methods were taught and researched separately—and sometimes competitively—mainly to fit into a reductionist scientific paradigm.

Keropudas Hospital closed in 2022. The building had reached the end of its lifespan. Moreover, national reforms were steering local services back toward top-down, diagnosis-centered structures. The gradual erosion of a once-functional system made many of the phenomena described in this book clearly visible, even though I lacked the vocabulary at the time to articulate them.

While clearing out my office during the move, I found an old handwritten letter. It was from Lauri Rauhala—in Finland, a well-known psychologist and philosopher who has developed an existential-phenomenological, or in his terms, a holistic conception of the human being, drawing on Husserl and Heidegger. Rauhala was also one of Finland's first psychologists to work clinically in a Nikkilä psychiatric hospital in the 1950s, and his writings since the 1960s developed a new way of understanding psychological suffering within its phenomenological context. Throughout his life he also engaged in active debate with Finnish psychiatrists, defending views that often clashed with the dominant ontology—or more precisely, with psychiatry's lack of a coherent ontology.

In the letter, Lauri wrote that he had read in the newspaper about the Open Dialogue approach at Keropudas and felt that it was the practical realization of what he had been theorizing for decades. Inspired by his letter, I revisited his work and gradually recognized a convergence: Rauhala's holistic conception of the human being provided the missing theoretical foundation capable of uniting the practical observations and theoretical directions I had been trying to bring together.

This is the picture that has emerged from those pieces. Since Lauri Rauhala is no longer here to comment on it, it is now our turn to continue the dialogue and carry the development of holistic helping practices forward.

References

Alvarez-Monjaras, M., Lotmore, M., Razzaque, R., Hopfenbeck, M. S., & Pilling, S. (2023). The community mental health team fidelity scale: A measure of program fidelity of social networks interventions for severe mental illness. *Frontiers in Psychology, 14,* Article 1076791. https://doi.org/10.3389/fpsyg.2023.1076791

Borsboom D. (2017). A network theory of mental disorders. *World Psychiatry: Official Journal of the World Psychiatric Association (WPA), 16*(1), 5–13. https://doi.org/10.1002/wps.20375

Lotmore, M., Ziedonis, D., Alvarez Monjaras, M., Hopfenbeck, M., Razzaque, R., Wilson, E., & Pilling, S. (2023). Development and refinement of the open dialog adherence protocol in complex mental health care. *Frontiers in Psychology, 13,* 1041375. https://doi.org/10.3389/fpsyg.2022.1041375

Olthof, M., Hasselman, F., Oude Maatman, F., Bosman, A. M. T., & Lichtwarck-Aschoff, A. (2023). Complexity theory of psychopathology. *Journal of Psychopathology and Clinical Science, 132*(3), 314–323. https://doi.org/10.1037/abn0000740

Rose N. (2025). 5E Mental Health? Notes on an emerging style of thought. *Transcultural Psychiatry, 62*(3), 325–340. https://doi.org/10.1177/13634615251327862

Wampold, B. E. (2015). How important are the common factors in psychotherapy? An update. *World Psychiatry: Official Journal of the World Psychiatric Association (WPA), 14*(3), 270–277. https://doi.org/10.1002/wps.20238

World Health Organization. (2019). *Human rights: WHO QualityRights core training – For all services and all people. Course guide.* World Health Organization. https://apps.who.int/iris

World Health Organization. (2021). *Guidance on community mental health services: Promoting person-centred and rights-based approaches.* World Health Organization. https://creativecommons.org/licenses/by-nc-sa/3.0/igo/

World Health Organization. (2023). *Mental health, human rights and legislation: Guidance and practice.* World Health Organization. https://www.who.int/publications/i/item/9789240080737

Appendix A

A Roadmap for Developing a Holistic System

This appendix presents an illustrative roadmap for the gradual development of a holistic mental health system. Rather than prescribing a fixed implementation model, it outlines a structured yet adaptive process through which holistic principles can be translated into everyday practice, organizational arrangements, governance, and learning. The roadmap moves from establishing shared principles and protected spaces for research and learning, through participatory inquiry and small-scale pilots, toward formalization, gradual expansion, and long-term cultural grounding. At each stage, attention is given to responsibilities, safety and accountability, research/learning processes, and the integration of research into routine work. The framework is intended to support real-world service systems in navigating complexity and uncertainty while sustaining continuity, dialogue, and shared responsibility over time.

Although presented sequentially for clarity, the phases overlap in practice and often develop recursively.

A roadmap for developing a holistic system

Phase	*Purpose*	*What is concretely done*	*What shows progress*
1 Shared principles and protected research space	Create conditions for research and learning before solutions	• Define core principles of the holistic framework • Appoint a responsible system-level development lead/team • Establish collaboration with universities/research partners	Principles explicitly named (rapid access; continuity; situation-centered support; dialogism; shared responsibility; minimal use of coercion); responsibility clear; research collaboration active

(Continued)

SUPPORT MATERIAL

A roadmap for developing a holistic system

Phase	*Purpose*	*What is concretely done*	*What shows progress*
		• Agree on safety and responsibility boundaries • Allow limited deviation from routine for research and learning purposes	
2 Participatory observation and current-state understanding	Understand where the system actually is	• Engage staff and service users in participatory, observational inquiry • Study everyday work practices as they are • Identify existing dialogical capacities and bottlenecks • Integrate reflection and documentation into daily work	Shared, realistic understanding of current practice and readiness
3 Small-scale area pilots (structural experimentation)	Test holistic principles in practice	• Launch limited, safe area pilots and training • Combine or strengthen team-based responsibility • Simplify intake and reduce unnecessary handovers • Centralize overall responsibility from start to finish • Facilitate dialogical spaces as core practice • Continue naturalistic research as part of work	Improved access and continuity; dialogical work sustained; safety maintained
4 Refinement, risk clarification, and regulatory development	Turn learning into system understanding	• Analyze findings from naturalistic research • Refine principles, roles, and structures • Identify real (not assumed) risks • Develop legal and administrative guidance based on practice	Risks explicitly addressed; guidance aligned with real practice

(Continued)

A roadmap for developing a holistic system

Phase	*Purpose*	*What is concretely done*	*What shows progress*
5 Formalizing shared direction (mandate)	Confirm and protect what has proven meaningful	• Articulate shared understanding of what works and why • Secure formal leadership and/ or political commitment • Embed principles and responsibilities into strategy	Mandate grounded in lived evidence; clear system ownership
6 Gradual expansion with learning intact	Extend without mechanical replication	• Introduce principles to new areas based on readiness • Support local adaptation rather than copying • Maintain research and reflection during expansion • Cluster-RCT if feasible	Principles adopted across contexts with local variation
7 Ongoing monitoring as shared sense-making	Keep the system learning	• Follow indicators meaningful to people (continuity, safety, experience, coercion) • Use research data for adaptive and context-specific system adjustment • Treat monitoring as dialogue, not control	Learning continuously informs practice and decisions
8 Cultural grounding and sustainability	Make the new way of working normal	• Maintain shared language and narrative • Integrate principles into leadership and onboarding • Address drift back to old practices	Holistic framework sustained over time

Appendix B

Holistic System Readiness Assessment

The Holistic System Readiness Assessment (HSRA) is an evaluation tool designed to assess the extent to which a mental health service system is prepared to implement a holistic, dialogically oriented model of care. The assessment focuses on structural conditions rather than individual competencies or treatment methods, recognizing that dialogical practice is an emergent property of the service system as a whole.

A core prerequisite for holistic, dialogical work is that service structures support continuity, shared responsibility, and low levels of internal specialization. Systems that are structurally fragmented—such as those divided into multiple hierarchical layers, parallel service lines, or narrowly specialized teams—tend to disrupt relational continuity and limit the possibility of sustained dialogical processes.

HSRA is explicitly normative in orientation: it is grounded in the assumption that holistic and dialogical models require integrated service structures with clear overall responsibility. The tool does not aim to evaluate clinical quality, professional skill, or adherence to specific therapeutic techniques. Instead, it examines whether the organizational architecture enables or constrains a holistic system.

The assessment proceeds from the highest structural level of the service system to the level of individual workers. This reflects the assumption that readiness for holistic practice cannot be reduced to team- or individual-level factors, but is shaped primarily by system-level design choices.

HSRA is based only on theory rather than empirical validation. The framework presented here should thus be understood as an illustrative example of a structurally oriented readiness assessment, rather than as a finalized or validated measurement instrument. The scoring structure, assessment levels, and point distributions are provisional and based on theoretical assumptions regarding the structural prerequisites of a holistic system.

SUPPORT MATERIAL

A subsequent validation phase is required to evaluate the functioning of HSRA in real-world service contexts. This phase should examine, among other factors:

- how different assessment levels and scores relate to actual clinical and organizational practices.
- whether all levels contribute equally to system readiness or whether differential weighting of levels or items is warranted.
- the extent to which HSRA scores correspond with observable indicators of continuity, shared responsibility, and dialogical working practices.
- the sensitivity of the tool to change over time during structural reforms.

Empirical validation should be conducted across diverse service settings and organizational contexts to assess the robustness, relevance, and practical utility of the framework. Findings from such studies may lead to revisions of the assessment structure, scoring logic, or interpretive thresholds.

Holistic System Readiness Assessment

Level 1—Organization of the Entire Service Area (0–3 points)

Assesses whether the area has a single entity that carries full responsibility for the overall process.

Structural Option	*Description*	*Points*
A Single fully responsible service	One organization coordinates the entire mental health care process (intake, assessment, treatment, and follow-up). No division between basic and specialized care.	3
B Two parallel systems	For example, basic level + specialized level. Responsibility is divided.	2
C Multiple separate service lines	More than one differentiated entity with no clear overall responsibility.	1
D No responsible entity / fragmented structure	Service users are passed between multiple care systems.	0

Level 2—Internal Service Structure of the Responsible Entity (0–3 points)

Assesses how much the system is divided into specialized units.

Structural Option	Description	Points
A One general unit	All services within one overall structure; only essential distinctions (e.g., outpatient vs. inpatient).	3
B Some specialized units	For example, the distinction between basic and specialist services.	2
C Several specialized service lines	For example, psychosis, mood, and anxiety pathways.	1
D Deeply siloed structure	Multiple parallel units operating independently.	0

Level 3—Unit-Level Structure (0–3 points)

Assesses whether units contain further internal subdivision.

Structural Option	Description	Points
A One team per unit	Teams cover the entire unit's service user base.	3
B 2–3 teams for different phases	Light specialization (e.g., division according to treatment phase).	2
C Multiple specialized teams	Teams organized by diagnosis or predefined care pathway.	1
D Extensive micro-siloing	Clearly demarcated teams operating in "pockets."	0

Level 4—Individual-Level Scope of Influence (0–3 points)

Assesses workers' ability to influence the process across structural boundaries.

Structural Option	Description	Points
A Broad autonomous flexibility	Workers can make decisions, shift flexibly according to need, and take responsibility for the process	3
B Light role division	Some task division and transfer of responsibility	2
C Limited influence	Work is strictly governed by unit-level instructions and/or professional roles.	1
D No influence	Workers operate only within a narrow, predefined role.	0

Proportional example of scoring and interpretation (validation required)

Total Score	*Readiness Level*	*Interpretation*
10–12	Green zone—High readiness	The structure supports a single-responsibility model; holistic systems are structurally enabled.
7–9	Yellow zone—Moderate readiness	The system has some specialization, but a holistic framework is feasible with improved interfaces.
4–6	Orange zone—Low readiness	Fragmentation is significant; substantial structural reorganization is required.
0–3	Red zone—Not ready	The system is deeply fragmented; major structural reform is needed before implementation.

Appendix C

Dialogical Meeting Checklist

Dialogical Meeting Checklist describes the core process elements of a dialogically oriented encounter and meeting. It functions as a practice-oriented reflection and fidelity aid, supporting professionals in creating conditions for dialogical space: shared understanding, continuity, and polyphony throughout the meeting process.

The checklist is not an evaluation of individual competence or clinical skill, nor is it intended as a standardized fidelity or outcome measure. Instead, it serves as a situational guide to help teams reflect on whether key dialogical conditions are being *actively supported* before, during, and after a meeting.

The checklist is derived from theoretical and practice-based descriptions of dialogical and network-oriented work rather than from empirical measurement development. As such, it should be understood as an illustrative and normative framework rather than a validated instrument. Empirical validation is required to examine its reliability, practical usability, and its relationship to observable interactional features, continuity of care, and participant experiences. Future research may lead to refinement of items, clarification of thresholds for use, or the development of complementary observational or outcome-based measures.

Dialogical Meeting Checklist

Before the Meeting

- ☐ Contact answered by a trained professional
- ☐ Meeting arranged within 24–72 hours, or at a time preferred by the people seeking help
- ☐ Service user asked whom they want to invite
- ☐ Location chosen to support comfort or preferred by the service user
- ☐ Minimum of two professionals included (pair/team)

- ☐ Not-knowing stance adopted; background information reviewed only to the extent necessary for safety, continuity, and practical coordination.
- ☐ Safety considerations confirmed (sleep, substances, self-harm, aggression, subjective sense of safety)

Opening of the Meeting

- ☐ Context and background of the meeting explained
- ☐ A gentle space and pace established; multiple viewpoints normalized

Dialogue Phase

- ☐ Open and clarifying questions used
- ☐ Active listening demonstrated (e.g., repeating, paraphrasing, summarizing)
- ☐ Own contributions connected to what the previous speaker has said or done
- ☐ Polyphony encouraged; attention paid to emotion and context; all participants included
- ☐ Professionals reflected aloud to each other in the first person
- ☐ Premature interpretations, problem definitions, pathological language, and the introduction of themes not related to the ongoing dialogue avoided
- ☐ Silence allowed; the conversation slowed

Shared Understanding

- ☐ Summaries and reflections offered by professionals
- ☐ Agreement with the plan confirmed by all participants
- ☐ Emotional tone checked: participants are asked whether they feel okay after the meeting

  If these conditions are not met, consider scheduling the next meeting as soon as possible.

  If the conditions continue to be unmet, consider involving an external reflector or adjusting the team composition.

Planning

- ☐ Concrete next steps agreed upon (small, reversible)
- ☐ Roles of staff and network members confirmed
- ☐ If needed, symptomatic support or crisis measures are planned together, and potential benefits and harms are discussed openly.
- ☐ Next meeting date is set, or care is concluded by mutual agreement; team continuity and availability are ensured (contact information provided).

Documentation

- ☐ Documentation completed collaboratively (summary and shared plan)
- ☐ Contextual factors, resources, risks, and next steps noted
- ☐ The plan and documentation ensured to be simple, descriptive, readable, and transparent to all participants

Appendix D

The Situational Map

The Situational Map is a brief, non-diagnostic questionnaire designed to describe a current situation as a whole. It does not focus on symptoms, diagnoses, or predefined problem categories. Instead, it captures key structural, relational, and experiential features of a situation, such as ease, manageability, calmness, sense of safety, relational connectedness, shared understanding, predictability, agency, and perceived possibility of change. The items are formulated in plain, experience-near language and do not require the disclosure of detailed personal or medical information. The aim is to make complex situations comparable and discussable without reducing them to isolated components or narrowly defined clinical concerns.

The underlying assumption of the instrument is that situations are dynamic and relational rather than static states. Situations may stabilize, escalate, or transform over time through feedback loops between lived experience, relationships, available support, and surrounding conditions. Accordingly, items are presented as opposing experiential anchors on visual analog scales (VASs), allowing respondents to indicate where the situation currently lies along each dimension. As the dimensions describe interrelated aspects of the same situation rather than independent traits, a correlation between items is expected and conceptually meaningful.

The questionnaire can be used to examine different situations from multiple perspectives. In order for responses to be understandable and comparable, it is essential to agree in advance on which situation is being examined and from whose perspective the responses are given. The situation and perspective can be defined jointly depending on the purpose of use. The situation may, for example, be one that has led to the use of services, a life situation to which services are currently directed, a specific treatment encounter, the treatment process as a whole, or a particular everyday situation under examination.

In practice, the instrument can be used to describe either one's own situation or another person's situation. In Form A, the respondent describes their own situation or experience; the respondent may be anyone, including a person using services, a professional, or a family member describing their own experience. In Form B, the respondent describes another person's situation from that person's perspective, assessing how the situation is likely experienced by the person concerned. The arrangement can also be reversed, resulting in parallel descriptions of the same situation from different perspectives. Such parallel profiles help identify areas of shared understanding as well as points of divergence, which are treated as situational information rather than errors.

Although the questions in both forms are identical, responses have different meanings depending on whether one's own experience or another person's situation is being described. For this reason, it is crucial that the unit of analysis—who is responding and whose situation is being described—is kept explicit and consistent throughout the assessment. When this is ensured, responses can be interpreted correctly and situations can be meaningfully operationalized to support research, treatment, and shared understanding.

Responses are interpreted as multidimensional situational profiles rather than as a single summary score. Profiles can be visualized using, for example, radar (spider) charts, making similarities and differences between perspectives visible and supporting reflection, dialogue, and shared sense-making. The instrument is intended for flexible use across settings and formats, including paper-based and digital administration. Because it focuses on general situational features rather than sensitive clinical content, it is suitable for low-threshold and repeated use.

As the instrument continues to be developed, the number of items, instructional wording, and operationalization of the unit of analysis may be refined based on empirical research and accumulated use. Such refinements aim to improve clarity, validity, and applicability while preserving the core situational and experiential focus of the scale.

Form A—Instructions

This questionnaire concerns your situation.

Before responding, please take a moment to specify which situation you are describing (for example, your current life situation, the situation that brought you to services, your current treatment situation, or another specific situation from your everyday life).

Please consider the time period indicated above (for example, right now or over the past week).

For each scale, mark the point that best describes how your situation has felt overall during this period.

The Situation Feels:

Extremely burdensome ———————————— Not burdensome at all
Completely unmanageable ———————————— Manageable
Uncertain and unpredictable ———————————— Clear and predictable
Getting more difficult ———————————— Getting easier

I Feel That:

I am completely alone ———————————— I am not alone
I am not understood ———————————— I am understood
I cannot talk openly about things ———————————— I can talk openly and make sense of things together
Support is not available or does not help ———————————— Support is available and helpful
Things cannot improve ———————————— Things can improve
I am unsafe ———————————— I am safe

Form B—Instructions

This questionnaire concerns another person's situation.

Before responding, please take a moment to clearly define the situation being described. (for example, person's current life situation, the situation that brought person to services, person's current treatment situation, or another specific situation from person's everyday life).

When responding, please try to describe the situation from that person's perspective rather than from your own experience.

Please consider the time period indicated above (e.g., *right now* or *over the past week*).

For each scale, mark the point that best reflects how the situation is likely experienced by that person overall during this period.

The Situation Feels (from the Person's Perspective):

Extremely burdensome ———————————— Not burdensome at all
Completely unmanageable ———————————— Manageable
Uncertain and unpredictable ———————————— Clear and predictable
Getting more difficult ———————————— Getting easier

The Person Feels That:

They are completely alone ———————————— They are not alone

They are not understood ———————— They are understood
They cannot talk openly about things ————————
They can talk openly and make sense of things together
Support is not available or does not help ————————
Support is available and helpful
Things cannot improve ———————— Things can improve
They are unsafe ———————— They are safe

Scoring and Interpretation

Rating Format

Each item is rated on a VAS between two opposing experiential descriptions.

- The left anchor represents a more constrained, burdensome, or vulnerable situational state.
- The right anchor represents a more stable, manageable, or enabling situational state.

Responses are recorded as a continuous value from 0 to 100, where:

- 0 indicates very low ease, manageability, connectedness, safety, or perceived change potential
- 100 indicates very high ease, manageability, connectedness, safety, or perceived change potential

All items are scored in the same direction. Higher scores consistently reflect a more enabling situational configuration.

During the validation phase, reverse items can be used to assess potential acquiescence and response-style bias.

Use of Scores

The instrument is designed to produce a multidimensional situational map, not a diagnostic classification or symptom severity index.

- Each item represents a distinct situational dimension.
- Scores should be interpreted dimension by dimension and as a pattern or configuration across dimensions, rather than as isolated values.
- A single total score is not required and should be used only with caution (e.g., for descriptive monitoring or aggregated reporting).

Conceptual Clusters (Interpretive Aid)

For interpretive purposes, the dimensions can be understood as forming three conceptually related clusters.

These clusters are heuristic guides, not latent scales or mandatory sub-scores.

1 **Situational Structure**
Includes:

- Situational ease
- Manageability and agency
- Predictability
- Direction of change

This cluster describes how the situation is currently organized and functioning:

how heavy it feels, whether it is manageable, how foreseeable it is, and whether it appears to be improving or worsening.

2 **Relational Field**
Includes:

- Connectedness to others
- Feeling understood
- Shared sense-making
- Availability of support

This cluster reflects the relational and dialogical space of the situation:

whether one is alone or connected, understood or misunderstood, able to talk openly and make sense of things together, and whether support is present and helpful.

3 **Hope and Safety**
Includes:

- Possibility of change
- Sense of safety

This cluster captures the existential ground of the situation:

whether improvement is conceivable and whether the situation feels safe enough to remain in and work with.

Interpretation: Implications for Support and Helping

Low scores in specific dimensions or clusters should not be interpreted as deficits in the person but as signals about where the situation may currently lack supportive conditions.

- Low scores in Situational Structure may indicate that the situation is experienced as overwhelming, chaotic, or rapidly deteriorating.
    - → Helpful responses may focus on *reducing load, clarifying next steps, and stabilizing the situation before pursuing change.*
- Low scores in the Relational Field suggest relational isolation, lack of understanding, or limited dialogical space.
    - → Support may need to prioritize *presence*, *listening*, *shared understanding*, and *coordination between people involved*, rather than problem-solving alone.
- Low scores in Hope and Safety indicate that the situation may not yet feel safe or changeable enough to engage in active intervention.
    - → Initial efforts may need to focus on *restoring basic safety*, *predictability*, and *containment*, before expecting progress or commitment to change.

Patterns across clusters may be more informative than any single score. For example, a situation may be structurally manageable but relationally fragmented, or relationally supportive but experienced as unsafe or hopeless. Such configurations can guide discussion about *what kind of support is needed next*, rather than *what is wrong*.

Multiple Respondents

The questionnaire may be completed by:

- the person directly concerned,
- family members or other close or network participants,
- professionals involved in the situation.

Differences between respondents' profiles are treated as meaningful information about perspectival variation, shared understanding, and available dialogical space, rather than as measurement error.

Longitudinal Use

When administered repeatedly over time:

- each dimension can be examined as a time series,

- attention should be paid to:
  - direction of change,
  - speed of change,
  - convergence or divergence between dimensions or clusters.

Changes in the overall configuration are interpreted as changes in how the situation is organized and experienced, not as improvement or deterioration of a fixed condition.

Visualization

Scores can be visualized using a radar (spider) chart with a 0–100 scale on each axis.

- Adjacent dimensions reflect conceptual proximity.
- The overall shape of the profile is intended to support reflection, dialogue, and shared sense-making.

Profiles from different respondents may be overlaid in the same chart, making visible:

- areas of overlap (shared understanding), and
- areas of divergence (differences in experience, interpretation, or access to information).

Such differences are interpreted as situational information, not as disagreement or inconsistency.

Index

Note: **Bold** page numbers refer to tables and *italic* page numbers refer to figures.

For Product Safety Concerns and Information please contact our EU representative GPSR@taylorandfrancis.com
Taylor & Francis Verlag GmbH, Kaufingerstraße 24, 80331 München, Germany

www.ingramcontent.com/pod-product-compliance
Ingram Content Group UK Ltd.
Pitfield, Milton Keynes, MK11 3LW, UK
UKHW022351190926
475702UK00015B/2220
* 9 7 8 1 0 4 1 3 0 0 9 7 7 *